Losers, Loners, and Rebels

LOSERS, LONERS, AND REBELS

The Spiritual Struggles of Boys

Robert C. Dykstra
Allan Hugh Cole Jr.
Donald Capps

Westminster John Knox Press
LOUISVILLE • LONDON

Scripture quotations from the New Revised Standard Version of the Bible are copyright © 1989 by the Division of Christian Education of the National Council of the Churches of Christ in the U.S.A. and are used by permission.

"Adults Only," copyright 1962, 1998 by the Estate of William Stafford. Reprinted from *The Way It Is: New & Selected Poems* with the permission of Graywolf Press, Saint Paul, Minnesota.

"Halley's Comet," from *The Collected Poems*, by Stanley Kunitz. Copyright © 2000 by Stanley Kunitz. Used by permission of W. W. Norton & Company, Inc.

"Mother's Day," copyright 1987, 1998 by the Estate of William Stafford. Reprinted from *The Way It Is: New & Selected Poems* with the permission of Graywolf Press, Saint Paul, Minnesota.

"On Turning Ten," from *The Art of Drowning*, by Billy Collins, © 1995. Reprinted by permission of the University of Pittsburgh Press.

"Sure You Do," copyright 1998 by the Estate of William Stafford. Reprinted from *The Way It Is: New & Selected Poems* with the permission of Graywolf Press, Saint Paul, Minnesota.

Book design by Sharon Adams
Cover design by Eric Walljasper, Minneapolis, MN

First edition
Published by Westminster John Knox Press
Louisville, Kentucky

This book is printed on acid-free paper that meets the American National Standards Institute Z39.48 standard. ♾

PRINTED IN THE UNITED STATES OF AMERICA

07 08 09 10 11 12 13 14 15 16 — 10 9 8 7 6 5 4 3 2

Library of Congress Cataloging-in-Publication Data

Dykstra, Robert C.
    Losers, loners, and rebels : the spiritual struggles of boys / by Robert C. Dykstra, Allan Hugh Cole, Jr., Donald Capps.
        p. cm.
    Includes bibliographical references and index.
    ISBN 978-0-664-22961-0 (alk. paper)
    1. Church work with children. 2. Boys—Religious life. 3. Teenage boys—Religious life. I. Cole, Allan Hugh. II. Capps, Donald. III. Title.

    BV4450.D95 2007
    259' .23—dc22

                                                          2007003349

Sure You Do

Remember the person you thought you were? That summer
sleepwalking into your teens? And your body ambushing
the self that skipped from school? And you wandered into
this carnival where all the animals in the ark began
to pace and howl? The swing they strapped you in?
The descent through air that came alive, till
the pause at the top? The door on the way down
that opened on joy? And then, and then, it was
a trap. You would get used to it: like the others
you could shoulder your way through the years, take on
what came and stare without flinching, but you knew at the time
it was goodby to everything else in your life.
The great door that opened on terror swung open.

William Stafford (1998)

Contents

Acknowledgments

We especially want to thank Jon Berquist, our editor, for encouraging us to write a book on young boys. The four of us had an unforgettable lunch meeting at Winberries, a restaurant in Princeton, New Jersey, during which Jon set forth his vision for the book. During lunch, Jon alluded to the fact that he is the stepfather of an early adolescent boy, and as he told us about him, it was evident to us how much he loves and cares for him. For two of us, this conversation brought back memories of our attendance at Jon's wedding, in which this stepson was the groom's best man. The groom and his best man were dressed exactly the same, and as they walked down the aisle together it occurred to us at the time that the two of them were illustrative of the fact, reflected in the Gospel of Matthew and in the Epistles of Paul, that God is represented as an adoptive Father, a spiritual Father who responds to a boy's hidden desire to be another man's son.

We would also like to express appreciation to Aaron Findley, a student at Austin Presbyterian Theological Seminary, who worked with such grace and competence in preparing this book's index. Finally, we would like to thank our male students who have, in various ways, shared with us their stories of what they experienced as boys in early adolescence.

Introduction

This is a book that focuses on early adolescent boys. By *early adolescent* we mean boys who are eleven through fourteen years old. Although such a boy may be said to be a child until he becomes an adult, he is really too old to be considered a "child," and teachers in grades six, seven, and eight know better than to refer to him as such. Usually he does not, though, object to being called a "kid," which has playful ("kid around") and affectionate ("kid brother") connotations. The older boys in this group of early adolescents are teenagers, but they have only recently become so, and experts in the field of developmental psychology note how different they are from later adolescents, or boys of high school age. The paradigmatic boy that we have in mind here is a twelve-year-old; a boy as young as ten would not necessarily be excluded from this cohort group, and a fourteen-year-old is on the verge of passing out of this group portrait altogether.

To put it another way, these are the boys that a listener thinks is implied when an adult says, "When I was a boy . . ." or sighs, "If only I could be a boy again." Men tend to idealize or glorify these early adolescent years, to think of them as a time when they were happy and carefree. After all, late adolescence, with all of its confusions, tensions, and conflicts, had not happened yet. But the early adolescent years are not all fun and games either. For some boys, it was a truly miserable time. For others, these were years of anxiety, worry, bewilderment, uncertainty, doubt, and yes—pain.

BOYS' HUNGER FOR CONNECTEDNESS

The early adolescent boy is now receiving the focused attention from clinical psychologists, psychotherapists, and counselors that they have devoted to the

1

troubled teenager, and many books have been written recently for parents who are troubled, and justifiably so, about their own early adolescent boys.

William Pollack's *Real Boys: Rescuing Our Sons from the Myths of Boyhood* (1998) begins this way:

> Boys today are in serious trouble, including many who seem "normal" and to be doing just fine. Confused by society's mixed messages about what's expected of them as boys, and later as men, many feel a sadness and disconnection they cannot even name. New research shows that boys are faring less well in school than they did in the past and in comparison to girls, that many boys have remarkably fragile self-esteem, and that the rates of both depression and suicide in boys are frighteningly on the rise. Many of our own sons are currently in a desperate crisis. . . . Over the last several years, I and other professionals who work with boys have become increasingly aware that even boys who seem OK on the surface are suffering silently inside—from confusion, a sense of isolation, and despair. They feel detached from their own selves, and often feel alienated from parents, siblings, and peers. Many boys feel a loneliness that may last throughout boyhood and continue into adult life. (xix)

Pollack focuses especially on boys' experiences of loneliness, shame, and disconnection, and raises the question whether the "attention deficit disorder" to which boys are especially susceptible may be better understood as the "loss of connection" (36–37).

Lack or loss of connection is, for Pollack, the basic, underlying problem, for loneliness and shame result from weak or nonexistent connections. He emphasizes that a boy's desire to remain within his mother's realm is normal, and he also emphasizes the boy's need for connectedness to his father. A recurring theme throughout the book, however, is that fathers experience difficulty in connecting with their boys, in large part because they did not experience such connectedness with their fathers when they were boys. In his discussion of the emotionally absent father, he points out that

> father absence has been correctly linked to a host of ills for boys: diminished self-esteem, depression, delinquency, violence, crime, gang membership, academic failure, and difficulties with emotional commitment. But what this absence also does is provide boys with a warped model of parenting—one that teaches them that it's acceptable not to have a father who "stays in the picture." Boys who are raised with this model, not surprisingly, may find it difficult, when they become fathers, to feel confident about being a parent. (124–25)

Pollack suggests that men whose fathers "were not there for them" can take a few important steps so that they may be better parents than their own fathers were. One important step is to spend time with other dads in the neighborhood or to join a father's group at church, school, or social center. Fathers "benefit enormously from sharing stories, ideas, and concerns with other fathers." Fathers can also take cues from their wives. By observing how mom handles various situations with a boy and "translating" her approach into his own "dad version," a father "can often find the confidence and know-how necessary to deal with situations when it's his turn to take the lead with his son." By watching and modeling himself after her approach, he will not only feel less anxious but will also provide her with a healthy dose of his loving affirmation and bring the two of them closer in the process (125).

CONNECTING WITH OUR OWN BOYHOOD

As we thought about William Pollack's view that the underlying cause of early adolescent boys' struggles and difficulties is the lack or deficiency in connectedness, and especially the fact that the most self-evident form of such disconnectedness is the distance they experience from their fathers, it occurred to us that there is a third step that fathers of boys can take to enable them to be more emotionally accessible to their sons: becoming better connected to their own boyhood. Much of the disconnectedness that today's fathers feel from their own sons is due to the fact that their fathers were not there for them when they were boys, but we also think that another reason is their disconnectedness from their own boyhoods. In other words, there is a disconnectedness *within* themselves, a disconnectedness of the man from the boy. When this disconnectedness is recognized as a contributing factor in the father's disconnectedness from his son, he can take steps to deal with it, and very significant benefits to himself, his son, and his wife or partner will result.

But how does a man connect with his own boyhood? Some men try to do this by attempting to live their sons' lives for them. For example, they become overly invested in their boys' success in sports, or they try to relate to their sons' friends as though they were themselves "one of the boys." We do not recommend this way of connecting with one's own boyhood, for it denies the fact that one is, after all, an adult and no longer a boy. In addition, it usurps one's son's own life, and, in a perverse sort of way, deprives *him* of important elements of his own boyhood. Put simply, it is an act of thievery.

The better approach is for a man to reclaim his own boyhood through an intentional process of remembering it. This is not as easy as it sounds. In fact, in comparison with the two steps that Pollack recommends for connecting with one's son, it is likely to be more difficult. One of the difficulties lies in the fact that so much of our boyhood is permanently lost because we simply cannot remember everything that happened. Another difficulty is that what does come back to us is not entirely welcome. The first difficulty can be partially overcome by making use of "relics" from the past: photos, letters, or memorabilia that have survived (perhaps because our parents were reluctant to dispose of them). The second difficulty may be addressed by sharing one's discoveries with others, perhaps in company with other fathers in the group that Pollack recommends.

The three of us are seminary teachers, and most of our students are in their early and mid-twenties. More than half of them are male. We teach the kinds of courses that, directly or indirectly, invite these young men to share their own lives with us, and, on occasion, with their classmates. They share with us through the papers that they write, or by asking us if they may come and talk with us about a personal matter or concern. One of the recurrent themes in the stories they tell us is that their relationships with their fathers were not what they had hoped and longed for. Another recurrent theme is that they were attracted to the ministry when they were boys. We think that these two themes are interrelated, so we encourage our male students to explore their own boyhoods in order to gain a better understanding of why they are pursuing a career in ministry and what they hope, perhaps unconsciously, that it will do for them. We ask them to consider whether this profession can fulfill the expectations that they have placed upon it, especially the connectedness that they wanted so badly when they were boys. Our object is not to dissuade them from entering the ministry but to help them gain greater insight into the emotional burdens they have placed upon their career choice and into some of the dangers that may lurk therein in the likely event that it cannot bear up under the weight of it all.

Because we invite and encourage our male students in particular to reflect on their own boyhoods, we have felt that it is only appropriate that we do the same. We have gone about this in different ways, and we believe that the validity of these different approaches needs to be affirmed. This is not, therefore, a book that recommends a single approach to reconnecting with one's boyhood. But there is no mystery about the ways that we have done this: We have shared our early life experiences with therapists and counselors, with pastors and teachers, with other men, either older or the same age as ourselves, and with male students (within appropriate boundaries). We have also engaged in various forms of personal reflection, including autobiographical writing, the writing of "letters" to our fathers who are no longer living, and reflection and writing on other men (famous or not) whose lives remind us in significant ways of ourselves.

The chapters that we have written here are a reflection of our own efforts to reconnect with our own boyhoods. They are not perfect models of how to go about reconnecting with one's boyhood, but they are illustrative, and, we hope, will stimulate other men to engage in their own process of reconnecting with their boyhoods. We especially want to emphasize that this is not an act of self-indulgence or some sort of navel-gazing exercise. Instead, it is a truly moral thing to do, for the lives of our own and other men's boys depend, in part, on our ability to reconnect with our own boyhoods. If we are to help our sons and the sons of other men to experience the connectedness for which they so desperately hunger, we need to reconnect with our own boyhoods, with the boy who continues to live inside of us and who deserves to be not only heard but treated as an equal to our adult self.

The experts who work with troubled boys—and what boy is not, to some degree, troubled?—emphasize that growing up today is much more difficult than it was for boys of earlier generations. Due to new technologies—especially the Internet—they are far more influenced than boys of earlier generations by the surrounding culture, much of which is subversive of the values that good parents seek to instill in their children. They are under greater pressure to perform and compete in and out of the classroom. Much of this pressure comes from parents who are already concerned that their boy establish the kind of academic record that will enable him to be admitted to a prestigious college or university eight or ten years down the road. Some parents ask teachers to recommend that their sons be held back a year so that they will be smarter and more socially adept than the other children in their class. Because there is more divorce and remarriage among young parents, the "absent father" problem is greater than ever, for he is not only emotionally but also physically absent from the home, and usually seen, if at all, only on weekends. Blended families place enormous pressures on young boys to get along with their stepfathers (and with stepbrothers and stepsisters). Some boys bond with their stepfathers, but for many, the stepfather, especially if he is partial to his own offspring, is worse than no father at all.

We do not pretend that our proposal for men to reconnect with their own boyhoods will enable them to understand everything that their own boys are going through today. We are even prepared to admit that reconnecting with their own boyhoods may contribute to the tendency of fathers to minimize or to treat lightly what their sons are going through. On the other hand, we believe that there is greater likelihood that reconnecting with their own boyhoods will enable them to view their sons' struggles with greater empathy and greater desire to be a "real father" to their "real boys." This will occur because a father will have taken the time to listen to the boy who is inside of him and to attend to his story. Through this personal exercise, a father will make himself more available to his own son and to the sons of other men.

SPIRITUALITY: WHAT ALL BOYS SHARE IN COMMON

Those who work with troubled boys tend to emphasize how the lives of boys today are so different from the lives of boys of previous generations. It is extremely important that we recognize these differences. But is there something that all boys, extending far back in time and into the unforeseeable future, share in common? Is there something that truly connects all boys to one another, not only their own contemporaries but also their fathers, their father's fathers, and so forth? Is there an *identity* between them that persists in spite of their social and cultural differences, some continuity or sameness that exists despite all of the factors that conspire to make them strangers to one another? We believe that there is and that this identity is their *spirituality*.

We came to this important insight as we thought about the tendency of men to sentimentalize their own boyhoods, especially the early adolescent years. For many men, these were their "golden years," the years in which they were consummately happy, without a care in the world. Having engaged in an effort to reconnect with our own boyhoods, we knew that this picture of the golden years of boyhood was largely a myth. So we asked ourselves: What in the world is going on here? How could men misrepresent their boyhoods to such an egregious degree? Do they really expect us to believe them? More importantly, do they believe it themselves? Then, however, we posed a somewhat different question: Is there some element of truth in these mythical renditions of their boyhoods? And is this a truth that is so important to men that even the boys of today will, one day, create the same myths and expect others to believe them? Despite our skepticism, we came around to the view that the answer to these questions is yes. And the word *spirit* is probably the best word we have in the English language for identifying this element of truth.

However exaggerated or distorted these accounts of boyhood may be, there *is* something uniquely special about this period in our lives, and we believe, further, that it has something to do with the fact that these are the years when a boy experiences himself as having something that he did not have before. This "something" is an ineffable and somewhat mysterious but altogether real and palpable sense of *spirit*.

Some boys of this age seem to stand out in this regard. An adult may say of a boy who runs faster than all the other boys, "That boy has spirit," and may vocalize the implied prediction, "He'll go far one day." For other boys, this sense of spirit is less visible to adults. It could be expressed in a boy's reading of a book, a magazine article, or a Web site about a famous athlete, a great musician, a funny comedian, or a dedicated scientist. As he reads, a sense of spirit wells up inside of him as he imagines himself performing these skills, dedicating himself to these pursuits, and aspiring to comparable levels of achievement. For still other boys—or the same boys but in a different context—this sense of spirit is experienced in their engagement in a common enterprise, in working together as a team, as in sports, or in hiking together. We submit that boys acquire this sense of spirit and become aware of its place in their lives in the early adolescent years, and it is this sense of spirit—this ineffable sense of vigor, enthusiasm, and excitement—that we have in mind when we ourselves consider the title of this book.

The word *spirituality* has come to mean so many different things that it would be futile to try to offer a definition that everyone would find acceptable. In fact, the word points to some ineffable quality that is itself indefinable, so it should not surprise us if any attempt to define the word would fail to capture its meaning. For the purposes of this book, though, we suggest that the spirituality of early adolescent boys has everything to do with their newly discovered *sense of spirit*. We further suggest that this sense of spirit has many qualities that are involved in the shaping of a boy's spirituality, but we believe that the central ones are *self-awareness*, *self-transcendence*, and *self-sufficiency*.

The Quality of Self-Awareness

By *self-awareness* we mean that the early adolescent boy is becoming aware that he has thoughts and emotions that are uniquely his own and that they are not necessarily in tune with the thoughts and emotions of the other boys and girls with whom he associates. These thoughts and emotions may be confusing to him: Why do I think these thoughts? Why do I feel this way? They may also be pleasing to him: What a fascinating idea! I like this feeling! Whatever the effect of any given thought or emotion, they collectively produce in him a sense that there is something going on "inside" of him, and this means that there is much more to him than meets the eye. Because of this "something," he may become impatient with or even contemptuous of adults or other kids who think they know him and who treat him according to this presumed knowledge. He may feel that they do not or could not know that there is a "side" to him that is not as good or meritorious as they take him on the whole to be. Or he may feel that they do not or could not know that there is a "side" to him that, if they could perceive it, would lead them to have a much higher opinion of him than they do.

In either case, his sense of self-awareness leads him to feel that he is, to some degree, misunderstood. He wants to say, "I am not who you take me to be. I am more, less, or different from the image you have of me." But he finds it impossible to say this, as it would take too much explaining, and the explaining itself would lead to further misunderstanding and miscomprehension. In time, this sense of self-awareness may begin to feel more natural and may even be experienced as the precious gift that it is. But because it is something new to him, the early adolescent boy is likely to experience it as burdensome, and he may long for the days when he was just an "innocent" child, happy in his self-ignorance, like his lovable but stupid younger brother who hasn't a clue about himself and behaves accordingly.

The Quality of Self-Transcendence

By *self-transcendence* we mean that the early adolescent boy experiences himself as a participant in something much larger and more momentous than the ordinary world in which he finds himself. The spirit that he experiences within himself as he runs a race, reads an inspiring book, participates in an exhilarating or strenuous group activity, or feels a special intimacy with a particular friend, testifies to the Spirit that inheres in all things, and his spirit is part and parcel of it. This sense of self-transcendence is often supported by experiences of observing the sky on a clear, starry night, sensing the immensity of the world, and knowing that he belongs to everything that is and ever will be. Although such experiences may seem to confirm his insignificance in light of his awareness that the universe stretches to infinity—both spatially and temporally—they evoke the sense that he belongs to the universe, a sense that he is recognized and known by its creator or by some feature or segment of this universe to which his senses and emotions are particularly drawn. This sense of being connected to all that is has its local confirmations in the boy's connectedness to other boys, to heroes of the present and past, and especially to the spirit that he feels inside himself.

The Quality of Self-Sufficiency

The early adolescent boy knows, of course, that he is dependent on others, especially his parents, for his basic needs. In this sense, he is anything but self-sufficient. But we mean by *self-sufficient* the sense that in some situations, he is able to take care of himself. He can do things without the help or guidance of others. He can take initiative without having to be told or instructed to do so. This sense of self-sufficiency is typically expressed in the words "I can do it myself." The *it* in this case may be a project requiring manual dexterity, a task demanding physical strength and endurance, or a problem requiring mental concentration. The project, task, or problem may be one that he accomplishes alone, or it may be one in which he is part of a group or team, in which case he makes his contribution to a larger enterprise. In either case, his experience of himself is that of being able to do or to achieve what needs to be done without the guidance or interference of another, whether a parent, a teacher, an older brother or sister, or one of his own peers. In short, he is learning to count on himself and wants others to know that they can count on him. By the same token, he has his own sense of timing, and this may be frustrating or even aggravating to those who believe he is taking too long or being overly deliberate in the accomplishment of the task, or, alternatively, that his pace is too rapid, that the task requires and deserves greater care than the seemingly slapdash manner in which he has chosen to go about it. But what matters to him is that he has begun to experience *himself* as reliable and self-reliant, an experience based on the fact that his mind, his heart, and body are working together in concert toward the desired goal.

We do not claim that early adolescent boys experience these qualities of spirit on a regular, predictable basis. Nor do we believe that boys have more of these experiences than they do of experiences of a very different kind. We do not challenge the view of the experts that early adolescence is a time when boys, especially today, are in serious trouble. We merely want to affirm that this is the period in life when something very important, however fragile, is coming to life in a boy and that this "something" is best described as a sense of spirit.

We also recognize and celebrate the fact that there are other ways in which a boy's sense of spirit begins to manifest itself in the early adolescent years. But these three will serve as our working definition of *spirituality* for the purposes of this book. We recognize that the second of these—self-transcendence—is the one most commonly associated with this venerable word. But self-awareness and self-sufficiency are equally important because, together, these three qualities form a *system of spirituality* in which they are interactive and mutually supportive. We also believe that there are vital connections between these three expressions of the early adolescent boy's spirituality and the spirituality of adult men, but making this case is beyond our present concerns.[1]

NEGATIVE EXPERIENCES GIVE RISE TO SPIRITUALITY

Now that we have presented the view of spirituality that informs our undertaking here, we can state the basic thesis of this book. We do not expect our readers to endorse this thesis immediately, but we hope that you will at least

---

[1]One way to make this case would be to look for the themes of *self-awareness, self-transcendence,* and *self-sufficiency* in the essays in Culbertson 2000.

give us the benefit of the doubt. Simply put, our thesis is that *the spirituality of early adolescent boys is more likely to issue from experiences the boy considers negative than from experiences he considers positive.* That is, an early adolescent boy's spirituality is formed out of experiences that he wishes he had not had and that he as an adult may therefore forget that he had or, if he remembers them, will treat them as insignificant and unimportant.

Our purpose in advancing this thesis is not to claim that men are wrong to view their early adolescent years with affection, fondness, and good feeling. We have already indicated that we believe there is a fundamental truth in the highly mythical accounts they give of their early adolescent years. Nor is it to suggest that adults should go out of their way to make sure that the early adolescent boys in their homes, schools, churches, and communities have bad experiences so that they will enter their late adolescent years with a firmly established spirituality. The very idea that adults might construct the perfect "boot camp" for the development of the spirituality of early adolescent boys violates the fundamental assumption of this book—and of most understandings of spirituality: that spirituality has its origins inside of a person, making comparisons with the baby growing inside its mother's womb seem particularly apt.

Our point, rather, is that in the normal course of things early adolescent boys will have experiences that they consider negative, and that these very experiences are the anvil on which their sense of themselves as self-aware, self-transcendent, and self-sufficient will be forged. If the boys of today are in serious trouble, this also means that they may be having more of the experiences that evoke or promote the development of this sense of spirit. We would caution, however, that not all negative experiences are conducive to the emergence of this sense of spirit, and if there are simply too many negative experiences, or too many in a concentrated period of time, a boy's sense of spirit may be permanently and irrevocably destroyed. Even as we need to view men's romanticized versions of their own boyhood with skepticism, so we also need to be careful not to romanticize the negative experiences to which a boy may be subject on the grounds that they are conducive to the development of a sense of spirit. Rather, our point is that a boy would have no need to develop this sense of spirit if his boyhood was in fact the mythical golden age that men like to portray it as being.

In a sense, there is nothing especially odd or strange about this thesis of ours. That spirituality is formed in and through one's experience of "the dark night of the soul" is a deeply held conviction of many who are experts in spirituality and in the ways that it is cultivated and developed in the life of one who seeks to become a more spiritual person. The experiences of the early adolescent boy may be a far cry from the devastating but profoundly life-transforming experience of "the dark night of the soul," but we believe that these experiences are genuinely spiritual because they involve or precipitate a great deal of "soul-searching." What may be somewhat novel is our contention that such experiences are unlikely to be viewed as spiritual by the boy who is having them, because he doesn't think of them as positive ones. And this means that he does not necessarily want to be—or be thought to be—a spiritual person. His parents and other adults may want this for him, but the very fact that they do may be puzzling or exasperating to him: "I don't want to be spiritual. I want to be a normal kid."

For our purposes here, we suggest that there are three general types of negatively perceived experiences that contribute to an early adolescent boy's emerging spirituality and that they correspond, more or less, to the three manifestations of spirituality already noted. While these correspondences are a little contrived—after all, it is the very nature of the spiritual that it cannot be pigeonholed or forced into neat little categories—they have the merit of connecting spiritual modalities to psychological realities. In our view, the very reason certain experiences are deemed negative by a boy himself is that they are perceived as more than mere isolated experiences. Rather, they reveal something about the boy himself. They tell him, rightly or wrongly, that he is a certain type or kind of boy. Thus, they foster in him a certain negative image, an image that he thinks others ascribe to him as well.

This image can be one of three: the *loser*, the *loner*, or the *rebel*. In general, these are not positive self-images, though some boys may, over time, embrace them as though they were positive. We propose a rough correlation between the loser and self-awareness, the loner and self-transcendence, and the rebel and self-sufficiency. Like the spiritual qualities, however, we view these three self-images as a system or cluster of images, so that a boy may experience himself as predominantly a loser, or a loner, or a rebel but also have a sense of himself as being, to a lesser degree, one or both of the others. In the very course of his early adolescent years, he may shift from one to another, depending, in part, on contextual factors beyond his control. These, therefore, are types, and individual boys may relate to them in various and idiosyncratic ways. They are also, in the American context, familiar social types and are portrayed in films, books, magazines, and other media. These social types have a long tradition of their own, and this very fact contributes to our conviction that the sense of spirit that emerges in boyhood is what affords men across the generations a sense of common brotherhood. More specifically, they provide a bridge for fathers and sons to walk across and meet one another halfway. If the boys of today are losers, loners, and rebels, so their fathers have been, and so their fathers' fathers have been.

The Early Adolescent Boy as Loser

An experience that early adolescent boys perceive as overwhelmingly negative is that of losing. Especially in athletics, but in other areas of life as well, boys want to win. There is little if any satisfaction or pleasure in losing, and a contest that ends in a tie is almost as bad as a loss. Adults tend to foster an ethos of winning, and sometimes they encourage an attitude of winning at all costs. We believe, though, that a boy's experience of losing and especially his perception of himself as a *total loser* is a major factor in his capacity for self-awareness, his consciousness of the thoughts and emotions that occur inside of him. *Webster's New World College Dictionary* has many definitions of the word *lose*, but the ones that seem most relevant to the common experiences of early adolescent boys are these: (1) to fail to win or to experience defeat (as in a game); (2) to be unable to find one's way, go astray, or become bewildered; to disappear from view or notice (to get lost); and (3) to fail to keep or maintain (as in losing one's advantage, whether through negligence, the preferential treatment of others, or some other cause) (based on Agnes 2001, 848). *Loser* is defined as a person "who seems doomed to lose, especially an ineffectual person who habitually fails or is easily victimized" (848). Because there is a sense of being "doomed" or "fated" to lose, such a person may be called, or may call himself, a *born loser*. The dictionary also mentions the *poor loser*, a person who reacts to loss or defeat in what is perceived to be an ungracious or unsportsmanlike manner.

The use of terms such as *born loser* and *poor loser* reaches a kind of frenzied boiling point in the early adolescent years, either as terms of self-identification or as phrases applied to others. *Born loser* is usually used in a critical way, though it may, on occasion, be used sympathetically. An early adolescent boy does not like to think of himself as a born loser, and other boys generally don't like to associate with a born loser, unless, perhaps, they think of themselves this way and feel that losers need to stick together and provide each other company and mutual solace. Unlike the born loser, who may evoke sympathy and even a measure of affection, there is little good to be said for the poor loser. The poor loser is typically viewed by early adolescent boys as immature and as lacking an essential quality of character: the ability to accept defeat with grace and dignity. It is appropriate and commendable that a boy will use a defeat as a stimulus to greater efforts to succeed the next time, but attacking the winner or threatening revenge is unacceptable. In this book, we are more interested in the born loser than the poor loser because we believe that this self-image has greater bearing on an early adolescent boy's spirituality.

As the chapters (1 and 2) by Robert Dykstra suggest, losing can be a very demoralizing experience for an early adolescent boy, especially because this is an age when boys place high value on competing successfully with and against others, become exhilarated when they win, and feel embarrassed and even humiliated when they lose. This is also the period in life when a boy is most subject to the label of *loser.* Other boys perceive that he seems doomed to fail or, what is even worse, that he is likely to drag *them* down to defeat if they invite or allow him to become a member of their group or team. If forced to do so, they will give him the position where he will do the least damage to their collective efforts (the notorious right fielder on a baseball team or the cymbal player in the school orchestra). He may also begin to apply the label to himself if he suffers several personal defeats in a row, comes in dead last in a competition, receives the lowest grade on an exam, or fumbles a teacher's question that classmates are able to answer with ease.

As Dykstra shows, however, losing or even being perceived by oneself or others as a loser is not an unmitigated evil, despite the fact that it feels this way at the time. There are certain potential advantages to losing and some unexpected blessings that may come to an early adolescent boy by way of defeat, especially given a sufficiently attentive social environment. For example, it may require a stunning failure or defeat in one area of his life to enable him to turn his attention to some other area that will have more enduring interest and appeal. In our schema, however, the most important benefit that losing and even experiencing himself as a loser affords a boy is that it contributes to his *awareness of himself*, which also means having thoughts and feelings of which others are unaware. There are various experiences that contribute to a boy's awareness of himself, and certainly not all of them are negatively experienced or perceived, but the experiences of defeat, failure, bewilderment, and of losing ground to others are especially conducive to making a boy aware of himself, of having inner emotions and thoughts about himself that others do not know about and would almost certainly misunderstand if they did. Compare a busload of early adolescent boys who are returning home from a game that they have won with that of a boy who has received an "F" on an exam or had his effort to be friends with another boy rebuffed, and it becomes immediately evident that it is the boy who has failed or been rejected—not the busload of self-congratulatory victors—who is experiencing a new depth of self-awareness.

The Early Adolescent Boy as Loner

Another experience that an early adolescent boy and his peers perceive as overwhelmingly negative is being alone or feeling desperately lonely. One or even a few isolated experiences of being alone may be experienced as exciting, as a chance to do whatever one wants to do without being subject to the suspicions and inquisitions of parents or the annoying presence of brothers and sisters.

The experience of walking home alone after school—perhaps because the friend with whom one normally walks home is ill and didn't come to school that day—may be unexpectedly liberating, a chance to take a different path or walk at a more leisurely pace. Even the occasional experience of being alone in the classroom—daydreaming, perhaps, or lost in thought while the teacher and other kids discuss the lesson—can be an exhilarating experience. But many or frequent experiences of being alone may lead to a pervasive sense of loneliness and lead, eventually, to the preadolescent boy's experience of himself as a loner.

Webster's New World College Dictionary provides several definitions of the word *lonely:* (1) alone or solitary; (2) standing apart from others of its kind, thus isolated; and (3) being unhappy at being alone, and thus longing for friends, company, and companionship (based on Agnes 2001, 845). The dictionary defines the *loner* as a person who actually prefers to be independent of others, to live or work alone. In our use of the word *loner* here, we do not assume that the early adolescent boy prefers to be alone. In fact, we believe that he and his peers view being a loner as a negative thing. An early adolescent boy does not aspire to be a loner. If he is one, he and his peers think there is something wrong with him.

We believe, though, that a boy's experience of deep or pervasive loneliness, of being, in some true and genuine sense of the word, a loner, is what also enables him to experience a sense of self-transcendence. Through his loneliness, he becomes aware of his belongingness to that which is beyond and above what he knows and experiences in his everyday world. While experiences of belonging to a class, a team, or a group provide instances and models of his connectedness, it is his experience of loneliness—perhaps especially his loneliness when he is in a group or crowd—that inspires his sense of *self-transcendence,* of his connectedness to all that is.

As the chapters (3 and 4) by Allan Cole suggest, loneliness is likely to be a very distressing experience for an early adolescent boy because this is an age when boys tend to seek and to place high value on sharing each other's company and on being members of a class, team, musical group, or organization. On the other hand, Cole points out that to be alone or solitary is likely to enhance one's sense of being an integral part of the eternal order of life. He distinguishes between *loneliness*—in the sense of being unhappy at being alone and thus longing for friends and company—and *solitude,* in which a boy experiences himself as connected to, or in the presence of, the One who is there when no one else is present. Thus, if a boy did not experience loneliness, he would never experience solitude, for loneliness is the precondition for the experience of solitude. Far from being harmful, therefore, loneliness that evolves into solitude enriches a boy's life and promotes emotional maturity. In light of the association we are making here between loneliness, the loner, and self-transcendence, it is especially appropriate that Cole gives much attention to the boy's understanding of God and contrasts the God of loneliness with the God of solitude.

Having introduced the two images of the *loser* and the *loner*, we may note the similarity in the two words. The single letter difference—"n" and "s"—in the very middle of these two words suggests that they overlap, that the boy who experiences himself as a loser is very likely to feel alone, for who really wants to associate with or be known as a friend or comrade of a loser? Conversely, the boy who experiences himself as a loner is likely to feel that his lack of friends is sufficient reason to think of himself as a loser, no matter how competent or even gifted he may be in carrying out class assignments, playing a musical instrument, or devoting time and energy to a favorite hobby. Given these experiential connections, we should expect there to be a corresponding link between a boy's senses of self-awareness and self-transcendence, that the deeper his sense of something occurring *inside* of him, the greater his sense of being connected to a larger reality *beyond* him, one that envelopes him and affords his sense of belonging to something so much larger than himself and the social world around him. Thus, the chapters by Robert Dykstra on the loser and those by Allan Cole on the loner are themselves connected and are thus illustrative of the ways in which the boy's—and man's—spirituality is a *system* of qualities.

The Early Adolescent as Rebel

An experience most early adolescent boys feel in its initial stages to be overwhelmingly negative is that of rebellion. Boys do not normally set out to be rebels. Rather, they act in rebellious ways because they feel that they have been provoked or pressured to do so. When they have been rebellious, challenging or breaking the rules to which they are subject, they typically experience little if any satisfaction in having done so; on the contrary, they typically experience remorse. When an adult admonishes or punishes a boy for his rebellion against authority, the boy will generally make a promise to avoid such behavior in the future. This promise is not merely intended to mollify the adults. Rather, it is a promise to himself, a vow to himself that he will not do it again, that he will henceforth conform his behavior to the rules and regulations that the adults have established for the benefit and collective well-being of everyone concerned.

But if a boy fails to keep this promise to himself and persists in such rebellious actions, he will begin to identify himself as a rebel, and the other boys will also see him as one. When this occurs, they may avoid him, because they do not want to be associated with a boy who gets into trouble with the adults.

He may, in that case, seem to these kids as indistinguishable from the loser. Alternatively, a couple of boys will join forces and reinforce one another's rebellious tendencies. They, in turn, may draw a third boy into their confederacy, and these three may form the nucleus of a gang. Adults, of course, worry about the contagious quality of rebellion and do what they can to discourage the other kids from viewing the rebel as worthy of support or emulation.

Webster's New World College Dictionary defines *rebellion* as an act or expression of resistance, of opposition to the control of others. A *rebel* is a person who is actively defiant in his resistance to the authority of others (based on Agnes 2001, 1194). In *The Roget Thesaurus of the English Language, rebellion* is listed among such related words as *disobedience, insubordination, noncompliance, obstinacy, recalcitrance,* and *headstrong.*

The rebel label is unlikely to be applied to a boy who has not yet reached the years of early adolescence. This is partly because younger boys aren't thought to have developed their rebellious spirit into a settled personality or character trait. But a more important reason is that these are the years in life when a boy believes he has sufficient reason or cause to rebel against one or another form or expression of adult authority and control. He may feel that he has been the object—even the victim—of an injustice, and early adolescence is that period in life when a boy becomes conscious of the importance of justice, fairness, and fair play. Early adolescent boys are sensitive to evidence of favoritism, especially when adults are the perpetrators. They believe that virtue should be rewarded and wrongdoing should be punished, and they feel that the punishment should fit the offense (that it should be neither too lenient nor too harsh). The early adolescent boy is also aware that among his peers, there are those who have advantages they have not earned on their own, and there are those who are disadvantaged through no fault or responsibility of their own. So his belief in justice is complicated by what he perceives to be injustices for which those who are disadvantaged—himself or others—bear no personal responsibility.

In some Christian circles, rebellion is equated with sin, even as obedience is synonymous with godliness. We think, though, that rebellion is not the unmitigated evil that the boys themselves consider it to be, for a boy's experiences of rebellion and his sense of himself as being a rebel both reflect and promote his newly emerging sense of self-sufficiency. This is because he learns that there is a limit to what he can expect from adults by way of assistance and beneficence. The rebellious boy provokes the adults' impatience, ire, even hostility, and in doing so, he discovers that he cannot and should not take their support and helpfulness for granted. He is thrown back on his own resources instead. To be sure, there are other ways to learn self-sufficiency, but rebellion is certainly one of the most effective.

It is not surprising that adults view the early adolescent boy's rebellion negatively. After all, adults are generally the ones against whom the rebellion is directed. But the chapters (5 and 6) by Donald Capps suggest that this is also how the boy himself tends to view his rebellion. Most early adolescent boys are conformists, and they take pride in the fact that they conform to the rules that the adults have established, more often than not for the boys' own benefit. To rebel against adult authority and control is therefore perceived just as negatively as the experience of defeat (the loser) or the experience of loneliness (the loner). For this very reason, Capps does not advocate that early adolescent boys become rebels who are at permanent odds with adult authority. His point, rather, is that "soft" expressions of rebellion are most conducive to the development of the spirit of self-sufficiency, the perception of oneself as able to "do it" or to "make it" on his own. In fact, it is only when the experience of rebellion is balanced by a strong respect for authority and a personal habit of conformity that an empowering sense of self-sufficiency results.

As with the experiences of being a loner and a loser, we think that connections can be made between the rebel and the loner, on the one hand, and, on the other hand, between the rebel and the loser. But these connections are probably the strongest between the rebel and the loser. As we have pointed out, one of the ways that an early adolescent boy experiences himself as a loser is that he feels he is losing ground to others either through his own negligence or through the preferential treatment of others. The preferential treatment of others is especially likely to cause him to believe that an injustice has been committed. If this was an injustice committed by an adult, the boy may choose to rebel against this adult's authority. Given this link between the loser and the rebel, and our previous link between the loser and the loner, we suggest that the theme of the loser belongs exactly where we have placed it, namely, at the very beginning of our book. This also means that becoming self-aware is the impetus behind the development of an early adolescent boy's spirituality.

We realize that others may view the spirituality of boys quite differently from the way we present it here. Some readers may feel that we have given too much attention to certain aspects of early adolescent boys' spirituality and have neglected other aspects that are just as important. Other readers may feel that the experiences we have emphasized here have little to do with spirituality as such. To these responses, we can only say that we have tried to the best of our ability to view the spirituality of early adolescent boys *from the perspective of early adolescent boys.*

Thus, we have tried not to impose understandings of spirituality that derive from a later—or even an earlier—stage or period in a boy's life. One of the reasons that boys' spirituality has proven so difficult to identify and describe is that adult forms of spirituality have been read back into the early adolescent experience, and this has meant that only a few boys—those who have precociously developed some of these adult forms—have been thought to have a spirituality worthy of the name. In our view, *all* boys have spirituality, not just those that adults consider spiritually attuned. Also, because understandings of spirituality are to some extent a product or expression of gender, we have focused our attention here only on what we consider to be the spirituality of boys. So we caution against any attempt to extrapolate what we have written here to the spirituality of early adolescent girls. Nor should what may be known or assumed about the spirituality of girls be used to assess or evaluate the picture of early adolescent boys' spirituality presented here. The very fact that men typically perceive themselves to be less spiritually inclined than women may have its roots in the early adolescent period itself, and if so, this book may challenge this very self-perception by inviting men to think of the early adolescent experiences that they considered negative as having shaped and formed their spiritual natures.

EXPLORING THE SPIRITUALITY
OF EARLY ADOLESCENT BOYS

We have already indicated that our personal reflections on our own early adolescent years have been a key factor in the evolution and formulation of our understanding of the spirituality of early adolescent boys. Now, however, we want to say a few things about how the book itself has come into being.

There are essentially three ways in which we adults can go about studying the spirituality of early adolescent boys. One is to devise an empirical study of them. To ensure validity, such a study would require the use of several different kinds of research instruments and procedures, including questionnaires, inventories, interviews, and observation of boys in a variety of social situations. It might also include the request that the participants in the study write a brief essay on the subject "My Spirituality" or "What Makes Me a Spiritual Person." Unlike those who have a bias against empirical research on the grounds that it tends to turn human subjects into guinea pigs, we have considerable respect for this approach, but due to the fact that we are seminary professors who need to devote much of our time to teaching, we are not in a position to carry out an empirical study of this nature.

A second approach is to engage in counseling and other forms of rehabilitative work with early adolescent boys whose parents and/or teachers are justifiably worried about their behavior, whether at home, in the classroom, or on the playground. Many of the books written about troubled boys are written by child psychologists, therapists who specialize in working with children or with families. This approach has the advantage of enabling one to identify the ways in which boys are able to respond to empathetic adults, but, as with the first approach, we are not in a position to devote ourselves to the counseling of individual boys.

A third approach is to engage in a personal process of exploring one's own boyhood, and to do so for the basic reason we set forth at the beginning of this introduction, namely, to demonstrate that by connecting with one's boyhood one is better able to connect with one's own and other men's sons. In comparison with the other two approaches, this may seem to be the lazy man's approach, the sort of armchair theorizing of which professors are often, and justifiably, accused. By way of defense, we can only say that this can be—and for us has been—an emotionally draining enterprise, and while one derives a great deal of benefit from it, we doubt that anyone would actually engage in it if he were not concerned for the boys whom authors like Pollack so eloquently write about in their books. In fact, the very engagement in this enterprise has increased our sympathy for the men who would prefer to leave their golden myths of their own boyhoods intact, and for the men who, fully aware that their boyhoods were hellish, prefer to let the dead bury the dead, and get on with their adult lives.

As noted, each of us has engaged, in more than one way, in the broader exploration of our own personal histories. But for the purposes of this book, we assigned ourselves the more specific and concentrated task of focusing on our early adolescent years. We especially assigned ourselves the task of recalling those experiences in our own early adolescent years that tend to get slighted or even omitted from the rather idealized, if not glamorized, picture of these years that men are prone to create. We tried to recall our own early adolescent years, and to do so as accurately and honestly as possible. We also tried, as best we could, to avoid thinking of these years from the perspective of where we are now. The early adolescent boy does not yet know what the future holds, and the fact that he doesn't is an integral part of his experience. We used whatever documentary evidence that was available to us to help us in our recollections. As the reader might expect, there wasn't much to work with. It was too early in life to keep a journal or diary. But there were a few things that our parents had saved—a letter home from camp, a class writing assignment, some report cards, a scrapbook. Not much, but whatever we had available to us, we used. We also read books about early adolescent boys and informally observed boys whom we judged to be between the ages of eleven and fourteen to jog our memories and remind us of experiences long since forgotten or actively repressed.

This book was inspired by Robert Dykstra's contributions to the Princeton Lectures on Youth, Church, and Culture, sponsored by the Institute for Youth

Ministry at Princeton Theological Seminary (Dykstra 2003a; 2003b). His lectures focused on the loneliness of the adolescent boy and girl, and emphasized that adolescence is a necessarily lonely time of life, such that adults should not be too eager to herd adolescents into groups or compel them to crowd together (like the occupants of Noah's ark). Dykstra also affirmed the importance of solitude in adolescence as the perspective from which a young person may learn to love, to think, to speak, and to listen for God's call.

Encouraged by the warm response to his lectures, he invited Allan Cole and Donald Capps to join him in writing a book on the loneliness of adolescent boys. We began, therefore, with the idea of naming our book *The Long Loneliness*, the title of an autobiography by Dorothy Day (1952), and we also made the decision—based in part on the fact that most of the illustrations in his lectures involved early adolescents—that we would center this book on that particular period in a boy's life, with hopes of writing a sequel on the late adolescent boy. The title of Day's autobiography would enable us to say that despite the fact that the early adolescent boy is involved in many social activities—as was Dorothy Day, a founder of the Catholic Worker movement, herself—the early adolescent period is one of an abiding, even fierce and relentless, loneliness. As each of us also experienced himself as being inwardly religious or spiritually inclined, we felt that this evocation of a book written by a woman whose adult life was steeped in Catholic spirituality would make the point that our loneliness, too, was at the very heart and soul of our own early adolescent spirituality.

As we continued to reflect on our early adolescent years, however, it became evident to us that loneliness, however central it was to our own spiritual sense of ourselves, was not the only experience that made us feel this way. Even if this second insight had not come to us in the natural course of reviewing our own early adolescent years, it would have been more or less forced upon us when Allan Cole's chapters, "Loneliness as a Condition of Boyhood" and "Solitude and God: A Lonely Boy's Allies"—inspired, in part, by Dykstra's lectures for the Forum on Youth Ministry—were circulated among us and the others realized that there was very little that they could add to what he had already written. This realization prompted us to further reflection on our early adolescent years and to the discovery of the experiences of losing and rebelling.

We were aware, of course, that losing and rebelling are topics and themes found in contemporary literature on boys. There is a substantial literature that takes exception to the ways in which adults promote an ethos of winning among boys, and an even more sizeable literature on rebellious boys and the methods that adults may employ to turn these boys around before they become hardened criminals. But books and articles that view losing and rebelling as having positive value (despite what boys themselves think of them) are virtually nonexistent. And we found nothing that even remotely suggested that these were important forms and expressions of the spirituality of boys.

We concluded that this situation was largely due to the fact that those who write books about boys typically write from the perspective of concerned adults (parents, teachers, counselors) and not as adults who are attempting to recover and then reflect upon their own experiences of early adolescence. When we assimilated the idea that there is more to the spirituality of early adolescent boys than the experience of loneliness, we felt we had also realized the important insight that the spirituality of preadolescent boys is multifaceted, and that the three themes of loneliness, losing, and rebelling are interactive. This made for a more complex view of the spirituality of early adolescent boys than the one with which we had initially begun.

THE TOUGH THREAD THAT
CONNECTED THE THREE OF US

We have noted that the three of us made ourselves the subjects of our study, setting ourselves the task of recalling and reflecting upon our own early adolescent experiences, and doing so as accurately and as honestly as we could. We know that this approach invites a host of possible criticisms, including the fact that the three of us are hardly a representative sample of early adolescent boys or of the ways that early adolescent boys manifest their spirituality. After all, we are three white males who come from solidly middle-class backgrounds. Not only that, we all went to church when we were in our early adolescent years, and our church backgrounds fall within that narrow swath of what is commonly called "mainline" or "mainstream" American Protestantism. Furthermore, as early adolescent boys, we were the beneficiaries of intact families living in stable neighborhoods.

One important difference between us is the fact that we grew up in different cultural eras. Allan Cole was an early adolescent in the late 1970s and early '80s, Robert Dykstra was one in the late 1960s and early '70s, and Donald Capps was one in the late 1940s and early '50s. This very difference, however, was also what gave us the insight that however disconnected the men of different generations may be, and however different the social and cultural settings of their boyhoods, there is a tough thread, however imperceptible it may seem, that binds men of different generations together, the thread for which the word *spirituality* does as well as, or better than, any other.

Our readers, of course, will be the ultimate judges of whether the three of us merely represent a *type* of early adolescent boy, and one who has little if anything in common with the boy of today or the boy of earlier generations than our own, or whether our experiences point to something more general, even, conceivably, universal. As we have suggested, we ourselves believe that early adolescent boys today (and early adolescent boys who predated us) are like us in one fundamental respect: for them, too, their spirituality is—and was—expressed in their personal identification with the loser, the loner, and the rebel.

This brings us, finally, to a question: For whom is this book intended? Whom did we envision reading this book when we were writing it? It should be obvious that this book was not written for early adolescent boys to read. Even if we had been able to write a book on spirituality that they *could* read, we knew that they would not do so. One of us conducted an informal study of what sections in a large local bookstore early adolescent boys tend to gravitate toward, and made the unsurprising discovery that they congregate around the sections on humor, sports, automobiles, adventure, and biography. They do not gravitate toward the sections on psychological development, education, or Christian spirituality. Readers of books about early adolescent boys are much more likely to be their mothers, teachers, ministers, counselors, and maybe—underscore maybe—their fathers.

We are under no illusion that this book will succeed in reaching a different readership than this predictable one, and we certainly have no desire to dissuade those who traditionally and faithfully read books on boys from reading ours. But neither do we wish to conceal our fervent hope that men like ourselves will read this book, and do so for the purpose of discovering the roots of their own spirituality, and, in making this personal discovery, use it to connect with their own sons and the sons of other men. If in the course of reading this book they conclude that the experiences to which we credit the formation of an early adolescent boy's spirituality are not the ones that formed their own, we will not consider this a repudiation of our efforts. Instead, we will view it as confirmation of our basic conviction that the spirituality of men, however this spirituality is understood or conceived, has its origins in the experiences of early adolescent boys.

OUR SPIRITUAL FATHER

When we were early adolescent boys, we assumed—confirmed by paintings on our Sunday school room walls and pictures in our Sunday school books—that the boy in the following biblical story was our own age, despite the fact that he is referred to as a "child":

> At that time the disciples came to Jesus, saying, "Who is the greatest in the kingdom of heaven?" And calling to him a child, he put him in the midst of them, and said, "Truly, I say to you, unless you turn and become like children, you will never enter the kingdom of heaven. Whoever humbles himself like this child, he is the greatest in the kingdom of heaven." (Matt. 18:1–4 RSV)

Jesus, we felt, was one adult who "connected" with us, who was, in his own way, the loser, the loner, and the rebel, and was therefore the one who manifested the self-awareness, the self-transcendence, and the self-sufficiency that were beginning to form inside of us.

If this made Jesus our spiritual Father, we cannot imagine him having become this for us if we had not also considered him to be the paradigmatic boy. As Robert Dykstra suggests in chapter 2, the story in the Gospel of Luke about the twelve-year-old Jesus in the temple in Jerusalem, "the sole available narrative episode from Jesus' boyhood," is "somehow normative in a boy's coming of age." It may seem a bit strange for us to say that this book is dedicated to that twelve-year-old boy in the temple in Jerusalem, but not, we think, when we consider that the word "dedicate" means not only "the inscription of a book to someone as a sign of honor or affection" but also "an expression of devotion, especially to a sacred purpose or work" (Agnes 2001, 377). May this book play a role, however modest, in enabling other men to see the boy who continues to live in them in that boy who came to know himself "in the temple," the temple to which he himself returned many years later and declared that it belonged to his own spiritual Father.

PART I

Losers and the Struggle for Self-Awareness

Robert C. Dykstra

1

The Birth of the Born Loser

Though it is awkward to admit this, this book is autobiographical at its core, having been written by three men not only drawn since boyhood to spiritual and religious interests and concerns but who know firsthand something of what it means to be a loser, loner, and rebel. It builds on troubling moments in the years surrounding each of our entrances into adolescence and how these moments shaped what we consider to be crucial aspects of our own spiritual self-understanding. We describe male spirituality in this book in a particular way, specifically as a boy's, and later a man's, capacity for self-awareness, self-transcendence, and self-sufficiency. These three capacities suggest a spirituality with which we as men can most identify and toward which we continue to strive.

As noted in the introduction, at the outset of this project we tended to think of our own boyhoods between the ages of 11 and 14 in the idealized way of many other men we know, that is, as among the best years of our lives. When we began to recall and talk among ourselves about more specific memories of those years, however, we were surprised by how many of them centered on embarrassing, anxious, even painful events and feelings. Threatening sorts of memories that we had previously suppressed or forgotten kept surfacing and pressing for our attention.

We eventually came to realize that those times in early adolescence when we felt most like losers, loners, and rebels proved far more instructive for understanding our present spiritual sensibilities and struggles than any number of our more pleasant memories from boyhood. We wondered whether there might be a connection between a tendency among men to downplay or even forget traumatic moments from those early years and their tendency to think of themselves as not being inherently religious or spiritual. Would other men's conceptions of their spirituality begin to shift, as ours had, if they too were to revisit their early adolescent years with as much courage and candor as they could muster? Would they come to share our emerging conviction that a man's unique approach to religious faith and his spiritual awareness and concerns, though rarely recognized or named as such, take shape in large part by way of a crucible of painful moments surrounding his entrance to puberty, times when he experienced himself as a loser, loner, or rebel?

These are often the very moments, of course, that a boy would prefer to forget. As he grows into manhood, he in fact usually does forget them. As he becomes more and more adept at this strategic kind of forgetting, however, something in addition to the shame and pain he intends to lose may also get lost in the process. What else gets lost, we submit, is a boy's unique and inherent sense of intense spiritual interest and sensitivity, of being in his own right a spirited sage, seeker, pilgrim, fool, or guide. As a man loses conscious track of his boyhood status as a loser, loner, or rebel, he may find himself losing track of the religiously inquisitive boy he once was and, in some secret part of himself, continues to be.

Even those men who, like my coauthors and myself, remain self-consciously interested in spiritual matters or focused on religious concerns as adults still tend to gloss over the most troubling aspects of their boyhood. Overtly religious men are as likely as any others to lose sight of those unsettling events that we suggest are most apt to cultivate a boy's unique spiritual sensibilities. The shame and pain of the boy-as-loser remain as palpable a threat to men who are ministers or committed Christians as to those who claim little or no such spiritual prowess.

TAKE ME OUT

This point was driven home to me recently in a conversation with three close friends, all ordained ministers, as we watched a baseball game during an annual pilgrimage to Yankee Stadium. The same conversation could have occurred elsewhere. That it happened where it did, however, is telling to me personally, in that some of the most threatening memories from my own early adolescence concern my utter lack of success at playing baseball. Despite my heroic efforts and spiffy youth-league uniform at eleven and twelve years old, I was forever the proverbial right fielder, at best tolerated by coaches and teammates and at worst suffering abject humiliation at their hands. Baseball for me as a kid was one major arena in which I experienced myself as, and by almost any measure surely was, a loser.

So there I was in Yankee Stadium, still smarting with ambivalence about the game, when one of my friends asked me what I had been working on of late. In barest detail (we were watching a game, after all), I told him about this book and how my coauthors and I were speculating that boys' and men's most formative spiritual sensibilities derive from painful experiences around the onset of adolescence. I said we suspected that boys who eventually become ministers, as had the four of us there at the game, are likely to experience themselves as losers, loners, or rebels more often or more intensely than other boys, but that as adults, we ministers too, like other men, tend to neglect or suppress those painful earlier memories.

The fierce intensity of my friend's immediate response took me by surprise. "Those were the happiest years of my life!" he protested. He then turned to the others in our group, who to that point had been oblivious to the conversation, told them what I had said, and asked them, "Weren't those the happiest years of your lives?" Without a moment's hesitation they too agreed that those had been among the best.

By this point I had begun to feel a little defensive, the early adolescent boy once again dissed and dismissed by his peers at a baseball game. I found myself thinking: *Couldn't we just get back to watching the game?* I also wondered whether our present book project had ventured too far off base. Were those years of my friends' lives as unambiguously happy as they made them out to be, discrediting a major premise of our work? Or did their instant, almost visceral reactions instead reinforce its validity, proving just how readily men idealize the good times of those early years while losing sight of the bad?

I was reassured a few days later, however, by an e-mail from my friend. He mentioned that he had shared what we had discussed at the game with his wife, a fifth-grade teacher with decades of experience working with ten- and eleven-year-olds in public schools. She challenged his perceptions of those years in his own life and agreed with what I had said about boys' silent suffering at that age. She went on to tell of a recent parent-teacher conference she had had with the mother of the reigning, in her words, "alpha male" of her classroom—the boy who stood out as the most popular, good looking, athletic, and intelligent among his peers. His mother told of a time a couple of weeks prior to the meeting when her son got into the car after school and immediately began sobbing. The pressure and confusion that had been secretly weighing on him as a result of discrete bullying by another boy in the class—feelings no one could have suspected in this particular boy—came pouring out of him. My friend's wife concluded by saying that if boys like him were facing so intense an inward struggle, how much more the case for boys with far fewer advantages and abilities.

I was glad for this confirmation from my friend's wife, someone who has played intense daily witness to boys on the cusp of adolescence. Her story also underscored how one consequence of our romanticizing boyhood—my friend's reflexive "Those were the happiest years of my life!"—is that we ministers and other religiously interested men are as likely as most everyone else to miss the subtle, often unconscious cues by which boys encode their searching and struggles. Rarely are ministers and other concerned adults adept at reading the signals of boys in their care. We simply don't understand or even consider attending to the peculiar ways that early adolescent boys experience and express their spiritual interests and longings.

Thus, whether we lose sight of the possibility that we as men are in any sense religiously or spiritually attuned, whether we forget how we came to those religious interests and convictions that we somehow *have* managed to retain, or whether instead we simply neglect the silent spiritual quests and questions of early adolescent boys in our midst, we do injustice not only to the spirit of all boys everywhere but to the spirit of that boy who continues to live, however furtively, within every man. This book seeks to reverse this forgetting and neglect among men as a means to counter this injustice to the spirituality of boys.

ON STANDING IN FOR LOSERS

It is one thing to acknowledge that a book on losers, loners, and rebels is in large part autobiographical, but quite another to be assigned to write the chapters on losers. *Why me?* I wanted to protest to my colleagues after coming up with the short straw. *Why do I have to be the loser who gets stuck writing about losers? What are you guys trying to tell me?* In American iconography, after all, both the loner (Thoreau on Walden Pond, the cowboy of the Wild West, Batman in Gotham) and the rebel (Teddy Roosevelt, James Dean, Martin Luther King Jr., Hawkeye Pierce, Bart Simpson) often command a good deal of respect. Rarely is this the case, by contrast, with the loser.

To be sure, many men can identify with well-known losers, the likes of Willy Loman, Charlie Brown, Dilbert, or the lovelorn crooners of most country songs. As Scott A. Sandage points out in *Born Losers: A History of Failure in America*, "Losers have occupied something of a market niche," particularly in the popular media, in recent decades of American life (2005, 267). No matter how much we identify with losers, however, no man strives to emulate their lot. As Arthur Miller suggested in an interview at the time of the revival of his *Death of a Salesman* on Broadway in 1999, there is something contagious or contaminating about the loser, putting him beyond even "the blessing of God":

> The whole idea of people failing with us is that they can no longer be loved. People who succeed are loved because they exude some magical formula for fending off destruction, fending off death. It's the most brutal way of looking at life that one can imagine, because it discards anyone who does not measure up. It wants to destroy them. You are beyond the blessing of God. It's a moral condemnation that goes on. You don't want to be near this failure. (Sandage 2005, 277)

We grow anxious around the loser, fearing that whatever led him to fail may also rub off on us.

This fear of guilt by association—here more likely shame by association—has become a familiar companion as I have prepared to write these chapters. This has been the case despite, or because of, my awareness that the loser whose contamination most concerns me in this instance is in large part myself, specifically that gangly early adolescent boy I once was. Though by the looks of old photographs there is little in his outward appearance that would suggest his posing much threat, and though decades separate him from my adult self, his anxiety around being deemed a loser, then and now, remains potent enough to give me pause. A sensitive, spiritually attuned boy, he nevertheless still possesses the capacity, even within the adult man, to resist his denigration. He portends to remove from the man I have become even the blessing of God.

This may be why I somehow knew, even at the outset of this project and despite inner protests to the contrary, that my coauthors were right in assigning the loser to me. It was time for the two of us to get reacquainted, to take stock and seek to reestablish common ground. We had some unfinished business between us, and neither of us, I think it's fair now to say, regrets our having attempted to tackle it.

GETTING STARTED

The first two chapters of the book focus on the spiritual threats and potential spiritual gains that come to early adolescent boys derided as losers. This group includes every boy at some time and some boys at most every time in the years surrounding the onset of puberty.

The present chapter highlights several observations shared in common by otherwise quite distinct recent works on losing and losers—one, already mentioned, written by a historian of failure in American culture, the other by a clinical psychologist who for decades has studied peer rejection among school-age children. Sandage in *Born Losers* (2005) and Karen L. Biermann in *Peer Rejection: Developmental Processes and Intervention Strategies* (2004) variously suggest that the epithet *loser* and the phenomenon of peer rejection in childhood are (1) *contextual*, arising out of a particular historical context and carrying greater stigma in some social settings than in others; (2) *gendered*, impacting boys and men more severely than girls and women; and (3) *malignant*, showing tremendous staying power both in the conceptual longevity of the loser as a character type through decades of American social life, and in the emotional residue that lingers for decades in many who experience peer rejection in childhood. To be deemed a loser, Sandage and Biermann can be read to agree, is a context-specific, gendered, and malignant affront to one's character.

In chapter 2 I consider ways in which the experience of losing or being demeaned as a loser takes its toll specifically on the spirits and spiritual proclivities of early adolescent boys. I also claim that these very same threats contain seeds for potential spiritual growth, specifically for the loser boy's moving beyond a flood of sudden and shameful self-consciousness to a more hopeful and empowering place of deepening self-awareness.

A positive outcome, however, is not a sure thing. The stakes in losing and being perceived as a loser are high, sometimes life threatening, not only for the boys themselves but for those in their emotional and social orbits. The shooters at Columbine High School in Littleton, Colorado—almost universally regarded by other students as "losers"—were described by their peers to the press as having "dressed oddly and listened to strange music" (Sandage 2005, 275). Thus, it is never appropriate for adults to collude in the shaming of early adolescent boys in some misguided effort to spiritually enlighten or fortify them. Nor may we glibly suggest to those who face derision that "it will all work out for the best" or that "this will make a better man out of you." No one knows enough to make claims such as these.

First, however, we turn to recent cultural and psychological perspectives on the birth of the born loser in contemporary life. For this, we focus on several common themes in diverse recent scholarship on so-called losers in American society.

THE BIRTH OF THE BORN LOSER

Unlike losers themselves, *loser* as an epithet has enjoyed considerable success. It approaches its work with stealthy precision, having attained high status as among the most penetrating, thereby the most effeminizing, of weapons of male verbal warfare. It takes no prisoners, even while holding sway over most every contemporary American male. Totalitarian in its designs, *loser* never approaches its mission halfheartedly, never contents itself with partial victory. It wants *all* of who we are as men and boys, refusing to rest until we come to know ourselves as *complete* losers, *total* losers, *born* losers. Often enough, it gets what it wants.

In *Born Losers*, Sandage traces the history of this term of derision that strikes fear into hearts of schoolboys and men alike:

> Today we speak an adolescent language of exclusion; contemporary synonyms for failure include nerd, dork, dweeb, geek, wimp, freak, jerk, slacker, weirdo, and even fag. "Loser," however, remains the epithet of choice. [The loser is] a misfit or outcast—as in a 1994 hit by the alternative musician Beck, who sings the refrain, "I'm a loser, baby, so why don't you kill me?" (275)

The Historical Emergence of the Born Loser

Sandage shows that this "epithet of choice" did not arise in a vacuum but developed along its own peculiar historical lines. That we are now able to dismiss persons summarily as complete losers, he argues, has come about as a distinct by-product of a particular social context, that of the rapidly expanding industrial economy of nineteenth-century America. In postcolonial America, *to fail* referred initially only to a discrete episode of failure in someone's life, usually in some business enterprise, not to the nature of that person's character. "Falling in business," he writes, "was not so calamitous as falling from grace":

> In early America, fear of failure loomed largest on Sunday. Monday morning dawned about the year 1800. By then, "failure" meant an entrepreneurial fall from grace—"a breaking in business," as Caleb Alexander's *Columbian Dictionary* duly noted. Failure was an incident, not an identity, in lexicons and common usage. (11)

By the middle of the nineteenth century, however, things had begun to change. Sandage notes that while the 1828 and 1855 editions of Webster's dictionary define *failure* as "a breaking, or becoming insolvent," that is, as going bankrupt in business, in an 1857 revision the term began to acquire more expansive psychological significance, suddenly reflecting "some weakness in a man's character, disposition, or habit" (Sandage 2005, 11). In 1800, a man could lose his business or otherwise fail in one or another aspect of his life but could not have been personally epitomized as a loser. By the dawn of the twentieth century, however, the psychological characterization had come to hold full sway. It was as though by 1900, Sandage writes, "a man would be nothing more or less than his occupation." By that point he could not only fail but could *become* a failure (13).

This trajectory, in which the concept of failure has come to define the essence rather than a mere moment of a man's life, continues to this day. Countless "misfits of capitalism" are now casually dismissed as thoroughgoing "born losers." No longer are a man's failures attributed to the inevitable downturns of a market economy, to a string of bad luck, or to tragic circumstances beyond personal control. Instead, they are thought to reflect an inherent flaw in his character, whether laziness, ineptitude, dishonesty, conformity, or the "disgrace of being 'merely' average" (5, 256). The language of capitalism permeates the language of the self, such that we no longer give second thought to speaking of " '[taking] stock' of how we 'spend' our time," " '[taking] credit' for our 'gains,' " or trying to "balance" our lives so that we will "amount to something" (265).

A Designation for Boys and Men

Sandage also notes that the epithet *loser*, having emerged from a particular historical and cultural context, is also typically gendered, applied originally almost exclusively to men, not women, and increasingly over the course of the twentieth century to younger and younger boys as well. He links the term specifically to the rise of the American myth of the "self-made man," a masculine ideal he traces to Henry Clay in 1832 and that retains prominence in Grover Cleveland's 1897 book, *The Self-Made Man in American Life*. Sandage writes:

> The bootstrap myth defined contemporary masculinity even though few captains of industry had started life poor. A gendered ideal, self-made manhood implied not only that success was a male arena, but also that great men were born of themselves and triumphed without the aid of women. In contrast, men who failed were passive, weak, dependent, and broken. . . .
> . . . The self-made man and the broken man represented the poles of an ideology of manhood based on achieved identity—the conviction that all men earned their fates and thus deserved whatever credit or disgrace they accrued. (236–37)

Protests against such views by Henry David Thoreau, W. E. B. DuBois, Ralph Ellison, Arthur Miller, James Baldwin, and countless other prominent apologists for a more complex and realistic manhood have done little across two centuries to quell the tide of the bootstrap myth in the psyches of American men and boys (12, 18, 265). "The problem," Sandage writes, "is not that our bootstrap creed is a bald-faced lie, although it is. The real problem is that failure hits home; we take it personally. To know a 'great loser'—a father, a neighbor, a classmate—is to glimpse our own worst future. Failure imperils the future even more than it taints the past" (19–20).

Thus, the *born loser* was conceived and given birth not only in the context of a capitalist and industrialized economy, as Sandage points out, but in a patriarchal and misogynist one as well. The characterization of the loser derives its outsized power not only from its link to a pervasive fear of death, as Arthur Miller suggests, but to an intense fear and consequent derision of the feminine within and among boys and men. Even the youngest schoolboy today understands that implicit in his being derided as a *loser* is the disgrace of being regarded as a *girl, woman, pussy, fag,* or *queer.*

A Thin Layer of Protection

Two moments from my own life are relevant in this regard. One occurred recently and concerns what I thought at the time would be a lighthearted classroom exercise with my seminary students but that, in fact, proved to be far more sobering. The second involves some shameful memories of ultimately tragic events concerning my treatment of a childhood friend just prior to our entering adolescence. Both stories, I suggest, reveal subtle connections between the fear of being characterized as a loser and the fear of the feminine as these play themselves out in the lives of men and boys.

Among the assigned texts in a seminary course on the pastoral care of men that I offered a few years ago was one written by a social psychologist, James McBride Dabbs (Dabbs and Dabbs 2000). Dabbs's research over several decades has focused on correlating men's testosterone levels with their various social and psychological characteristics and tendencies. Among the thousands of men he sampled across many vocational groups, for example, Dabbs discovered that professional football players and professional actors possessed on average the highest levels of testosterone. On the other hand, Presbyterian clergymen as a group had the lowest levels (142–43). Though this finding seemed to come as no surprise to the half dozen women enrolled in my class, it did appear to be unwelcome news to nearly all of the thirty or so men, many of whom were aspiring to become Presbyterian ministers. Dabbs makes clear in the book that higher-testosterone men, on the whole, are more combative and abusive, are less likely to marry, have higher rates of sexual affairs, marital dissatisfaction, and divorce, and tend to die at an earlier age than lower-testosterone men (36, 109). Despite all this, however, he also points out that "almost everyone—men, women, high school dropouts, college graduates, reporters, prisoners, and stockbrokers—wants to have a lot of testosterone" (4).

The men in my class proved to be no exception. In an exercise designed to generate additional interest in the book, I suggested early in the semester that we measure the testosterone levels of any students in the class, men or women, who wanted to participate. On the appointed day, all but one of the students offered a saliva sample for testing. I placed the test tubes containing the samples next to the ice cream in my freezer and on the following day packed them in dry ice and sent them off to a lab.

Several weeks later, on the day appointed for discussing Dabbs's book in class, the students received a confidential reading of their testosterone levels at the time of the original sampling. They also received a graph on which were charted, though without naming names, the levels of the rest of the class, with separate lines recording men's and women's scores. In this way students could anonymously compare their own levels with those of the class as a whole. In addition, I had scheduled a conference telephone call with Dabbs himself later in the same class period, during which students would be encouraged to discuss the book and our little experiment with the author.

It would be an understatement to say that, as a result of these exercises, the students had a great deal of investment in the topic of the day. There was a palpable sense of anxiety among the men of the class in particular as they opened the envelopes containing their own results and proceeded to locate their scores on the graph of the class as a whole. Despite their anonymity, there was a highly charged atmosphere among the men in the room, as if this were some great contest in which there would be clear winners and losers. Their anxiety stood in striking contrast to the relative indifference of the women to their scores, who at most appeared bemused to learn that some of their testosterone levels had been higher than those of some of the men.

Even more striking was that the men who had the highest and lowest testosterone levels, and who could have chosen to remain anonymous, instead revealed who they were in the telephone conversation with Dabbs that followed. Though not the type to flaunt his status, the student with the highest level—a Pentecostal man whose testosterone reading was off the charts, outdistancing those levels ordinarily found in professional actors and athletes— seemed to brim with pride and confidence, even as he spoke with Dabbs of his "concern" about the correlation of high testosterone levels with interpersonal and vocational difficulties. Should he, too, expect such problems? he wondered aloud, though with little apparent sense of urgency.

By contrast, the demeanor of the student with the lowest level among the men in the class—a Presbyterian, as it turned out, whose results were lower, remember, than even those of some of the women—spoke with a sense of urgency bordering on desperation. In what struck me as a no-win situation, he appeared to seek, by way of a paradoxically "unmanly" plea, whatever support for his manhood that Dabbs could muster. Dabbs reminded him that trends in average testosterone levels among various population groups can never account for behaviors of individual men; that a man's testosterone levels fluctuate throughout the course of any given day and even seasons of the year; and, most significant, that men with lower levels are, in general, more content in love and work than men with higher levels. These reassurances appeared to calm the student to a degree.

However, when I asked at the end of the class session whether students, given what they now knew, would prefer testosterone levels at the lower or higher ends of the spectrum, every student indicated a desire for a higher level. In other words, a single, fleeting hormonal reading trumped for them the alternative prospect of a longer and happier life. More revealing was that their choice came as no surprise to me, their teacher, for I too would have responded the same way.

This exercise underscored for me how enduring are messages about manhood and masculinity that boys and men have assimilated since childhood. Such messages are inescapably—perhaps necessarily—entrenched by the time boys enter adolescence, and they remain close to the surface thereafter. For the male seminarians in class that day, being perceived as a winner or loser hung with all manner of gravity on a very fragile thread indeed, their manhood wrapped in a remarkably thin protective sheath. The threat of being a loser appeared to remain ever at the ready to overwhelm even the adult minister and man.

A Contaminating Friendship

A second set of memories exposes a shameful series of events from my childhood, though the circumstances are perhaps not unfamiliar to other boys on the edges of puberty. Like the testosterone exercise among my students, these events too reveal how subtle and how costly are the stakes involved as boys distance themselves from the feminine.

On one specific day in my life as a sixth grader, I made a deliberate decision, revealed to no one at the time or after, to reject a classmate who for years had been one of my closest friends. Curt had moved into my neighborhood several years earlier. We shared common interests and quickly became fast friends. At age eight and nine we both played the piano, though he with greater promise—the one who would first introduce me to the music of Bach and Beethoven. We shared strong academic interests and abilities and were front-and-center participants in our respective church congregations, his Pentecostal, mine Presbyterian. Our church involvement didn't lead us to rule out occult interests, however, as we occasionally attempted to summon spirits with a Ouija board—until, that is, his Pentecostal parents found out, at which time I was left to commune with the dead on my own. We roamed our town on foot or bikes to see what we could see. Curt wasn't my only, oldest, or even best friend (though it's possible that he would have called me his), but for many years we shared nothing less than a spirited and even spiritual camaraderie.

That changed one day when we were twelve. After what must have been a long period of internal deliberation on my part—I certainly consulted no adults or any other friends—I decided to sever my bond with him. I was aware of just one reason for my decision at the time: he bordered on being too effeminate for what I thought would be my own good. With dawning urgency, perhaps spurred by the faintest rumblings of puberty, I came to believe that if I didn't reject Curt, others might in turn reject me. His considerable musical and dramatic interests, which to that point I had shared, coupled with some mysterious congenital kidney ailment that we never discussed but that kept him from roughhousing or playing sports, along with his parents' religious convictions that prevented him from going to movies or in other ways engaging popular culture, all conspired to make me calculate that my own implausible efforts to that point to pass muster as a man could only be further contaminated by this friendship.

My own status among the other boys had long been marginal, though more in the sense of standing in-between rather than fully outside. While I never came close to reaching the inner sanctum of the most popular and athletic among them, neither was I ever banished to the outer darkness. My place among the up-and-comers was in no way secure, but I escaped being relegated to the down-and-outers. The brass ring tended to be close at hand but also always just beyond grasp. A winner? A loser? I was never quite sure. Apparent enough to me at age twelve, however, was that the boundary between them seemed unstable and porous. To one on the margin, there was no margin for error. I could no longer risk a friendship that threatened to weigh me down.

In a naive effort to inflict as little damage on my friend as possible, I chose one day simply to have nothing more to do with him. It would be a clean, surgical break. I would attempt nothing dishonorable, would not be overtly cruel, would not talk behind his back, would not poke fun at him to other friends. Neither, however, would I acknowledge what I was about to do. No words about my one-sided decision would ever be exchanged. In the months that followed, the sudden, silent cutoff after several years of friendship must have led to a good deal of confusion on his part, though I have no way of knowing for sure. I had decided that Curt was dead weight, and, friend or no friend, he had to go.

In a striking twist of fate, as dead weight he did indeed go. He died of kidney failure the following year.

Near the end of his life, during one of what must have been his many long hospital stays, my parents—who knew that I no longer ran with Curt, though they never pressed me why—asked if I would want to visit him there. I was anxious at this prospect, fearful in part of seeing him sick but also, I knew, of revisiting my shame for having abandoned him, suddenly now even to terrible illness. But I reluctantly agreed to go.

My parents and I stood with his mother around his bed, the adults carrying the conversation. I can't remember saying anything at all to him. I distinctly recall, however, that he himself would not, perhaps could not by that point, say a single word to me—his silence, I felt at the time, was completely justified and even oddly redemptive. He died a week or two later. My parents asked whether I wanted to attend his funeral. I said no, and that was that.

There is much that goes unsaid among boys, and adults in my community did nothing to dissuade the silence. Taking roll not long after Curt's death, Milo McCoy, our kindly seventh-grade drafting teacher, commented on Curt's many absences and asked whether any of us, all boys in that particular class, knew how he was doing. Stunned at such a question from a teacher, we shifted in our seats and looked down at our tables. Then one of the boys—I think Jonathan Solstad, the only Baptist and boldest Christian among us—said, "He died."

Mr. McCoy chuckled, as if Jonathan were joking. We stared at him in silence during the awkward moments that followed, he looking to us for rescue. Someone finally obliged him: "He really died." Then we got back on task, picked up our nifty mechanical pencils, and practiced drawing our letters and numerals in the controlled, artful script of architects.

An Entrenched and Malignant Epithet

The sense that there were clear winners and losers among the men in my class in the aftermath of the testosterone exercise, and my own conscious conviction as a boy that I might be perceived as a loser on the basis of a valued friendship, both hinge in part on the unspoken assumption and fear among boys and men that we may share far more in common with girls and women than we usually care to admit. These glimpses into my own recent and distant past underscore how vigilant boys and men learn to be in steeling themselves against infiltration by feminine influences that threaten our sense of distinctiveness as males.

That even young schoolboys today commonly refer to themselves or their peers as losers, as Sandage cogently claims, is a result of grim but usually unexamined circumstances peculiar to American social and economic life. If this is the case, however, then we might also conclude that the notion of the *born loser*, though entrenched in the collective American male psyche for nearly two centuries, has no fixed essence or unyielding reality of its own. If factors of historical and social context proved to be key to the development of the conception of the born loser, then changes in such circumstances could plausibly alter its influence. Sandage's book, by raising this cultural history to collective consciousness, can be read as a crucial first step in undermining its impact, if not on a grand communal scale then at least in the lives of individual readers. By raising to conscious awareness the particular historical origins and effects of the notion of the born loser, Sandage increases the possibility that men and boys may better equip themselves to resist its relentless psychological and spiritual grip. His work destabilizes and relativizes what most boys and men assume to be a fixed and inviolable staple of masculine humiliation.

PEER REJECTION IN CHILDHOOD

A similarly subversive intent appears to guide Karen L. Biermann's clinical and empirical work in *Peer Rejection: Developmental Processes and Intervention Strategies* (2004). In decades of studying the impact of peer neglect and rejection specifically among school-age children, Biermann's efforts lend support, from the distinctive perspective of clinical psychology, to what I have described in Sandage (2005) as the context-specific, gendered, and malignant conceptualization of the loser in American social life.

Sandage laments that what began as a concept of failure initially confined to an isolated incident in a man's business career then expanded to reflect the whole of his character, only to drift over time developmentally downward to encompass the lives of younger and younger boys. Biermann, in turn, provides graphic testimony to the malignant psychological impact of peer rejection on those most vulnerable among us. She notes, for example, that though peer rejection reaches a kind of frenzied boiling point in the years just prior to puberty, longitudinal studies have shown that even first-grade children now prove adept at identifying which of their classmates will be riddled with rejection and labeled as losers in later childhood and adolescence (Biermann 2004, xiii, 24–26).

Like Sandage, Biermann too speaks to the significance of contextual factors in peer derision, offering nuanced evidence to suggest that not all children who are neglected or rejected in one social context—by peers or teachers at school, for example—are perceived or treated the same way in others, such as at church, among cousins, or away at summer camp. Her work likewise lends support to Sandage's claim that peer rejection is weighted by gender, affecting boys in mid to late childhood and early adolescence more than girls (9, 13–14, 21–22). Perhaps most telling for our purposes, however, is that even as Sandage demonstrates the malignant staying power of the loser as a character type over decades, even centuries, of American social life, so Biermann, citing empirical research that tracks particular individuals over time, shows how the psychological and social consequences often linger well into their adult lives for those targeted by peer rejection in childhood.

Neglected versus Rejected Children

Biermann begins by distinguishing between children who are *neglected* and those who are *rejected* by their peers (170). She then further subdivides the rejected group into two specific types: *aggressive-rejected* and *nonaggressive-rejected* children.

Neglected children, though shy and withdrawn from their peers in at least one important context (usually, for Biermann's subjects, in school), are often more outgoing and accepted in other social settings. A child who remains at the edge of the playground at school, for example, uncertain of just how to enter a group game already in progress, may be much more capable of engaging his peers in a Scout group or in gatherings of his extended family (19, 27). Though in the more troublesome contexts these children are seldom named by others as friends, their isolation stems from benign neglect rather than active disdain on the part of their peers. They go unnoticed, unseen, and unheard by others, but this status is fluid and can be quickly reversed according to social context. Neglected children are amenable to social coaching by concerned adults or peers and tend to improve in self-esteem and in their capacity to interact with others simply with increasing maturity over time.

This typically is not the case, by contrast, for rejected children, who in many instances may suffer the consequences of their rejection for the rest of their lives. Biermann observes:

> Children who are rejected by peers often grow up lonely and alienated, suffering through their school days, struggling with feelings of anxiety and inadequacy. As they grow into adolescents and adults, many experience continuing insecurities and difficulties in interpersonal relationships, and suffer depression and other psychiatric difficulties. (xii)

She reports that rejected children, like neglected children, fail to receive nominations of friendship from their classmates. Unlike their neglected peers, however, rejected children do not go unnoticed by classmates. Rather, they are actively disdained by them (5–7).

Aggressive-rejected children are rejected specifically on the basis of their expressions of physical or verbal aggression toward others (20). Rather than remain on the sideline of a group game already in progress, aggressive-rejected children are apt to rush right in, inserting themselves into peer activities in inappropriate or disruptive ways (5–7). Carrying what seems their dependable formula for rejection into every social setting, aggressive-rejected children find no alternative haven of acceptance at summer camp, in escaping to a new school, or by finding a more amenable peer group. Nonaggressive-rejected children, on the other hand, typically are rejected for being socially fearful or anxious, or because of some evident physical or social marker related to race, ethnicity, obesity, physical disability, native language, or gender identification that makes them stand out from the majority (14, 28).

Biermann reports that rejected children are "more likely than neglected children to express loneliness and social dissatisfaction" and are less likely than neglected children to experience improved status as a result of changing social environments, coaching and intervention by concerned others, or maturation over time (6, 170–79, 185–218). The long-term consequences tend to be severe. In retrospective (follow-back) studies of adults with serious psychiatric disorders, patients typically recall problematic behaviors and poor peer relations in childhood. In prospective (follow-forward) studies, "a disproportionate number of rejected children grow up to experience mental health problems and antisocial behavior." Biermann cites a letter from thirty-seven-year-old "JW," who wrote, "I did try [not to be afraid of other children], but people confused me and still do. The more the rejection and name calling, the worse I felt. I put on a smiley face, as I do today, but I knew in my heart that people just don't like me and never will" (xiii, 171).

Of the two subgroups of rejected children, however, *nonaggressive*-rejected boys, those actively rejected for reasons of a physical or some other readily identifiable difference usually beyond their control, appear to be among the most vulnerable to the enduring emotional residues of peer rejection—of being cast as a loser—over time. This group tends to be even lonelier than their aggressive-rejected peers, in part because nonaggressive boys ordinarily hold themselves accountable for their situation, whereas aggressive boys pin blame for their rejection on others.

Nonaggressive-rejected boys therefore find themselves in a position of double jeopardy: unlike their neglected peers, they suffer the agony of being actively targeted for rejection; unlike their aggressive-rejected peers, they remain highly sensitive and self-conscious, blaming themselves for their fate. Active disdain from others coupled with heightened self-scrutiny intensify their vulnerability to severe loneliness and shame, often for decades beyond the boundaries of childhood and adolescence (62–64).

The Malignant Consequences of Peer Rejection over Time

Bill O'Hanlon offers a sobering, though ultimately encouraging, account of the lingering aftermath of childhood peer rejection experienced by his friend and fellow psychotherapist, Ernest Rossi. Rossi had a learning disability as a boy that made it hard for him to learn to read. His story provides a glimpse into the malignant, decades-long effects of active peer rejection in a nonaggressive child. O'Hanlon writes:

> Because learning disabilities were unheard of during his boyhood, when [Ernie] fell seriously behind the other children, he was taken out of his classes and put with the kids who were called "retarded." On the playground, his former classmates teased him mercilessly, chanting, "Ernie's a retard, Ernie's a retard." He was terribly ashamed. When Ernie entered high school, his family had moved, and he had a chance to escape his old shame. Though he could now read, on that first day of high school, he began to doubt himself. *Maybe I'm not smart enough to hack it in high school*, he thought. After classes were over, he wandered around the big school library, feeling overwhelmed by all the knowledge contained in those books. His attention was caught by one particular thick tome. *If I could read a book like that and understand it*, he told himself, *it would prove I wasn't stupid.* He plucked it out of the stacks and read the title: *Critique of Pure Reason*, by Immanuel Kant. He sat down to read it. He stared at the first paragraph and could not make heads nor tails of it. He read it again. And again. And again, until he finally understood what the author was saying. He did the same with the rest of the first page and finally, after understanding it, walked home with a deep feeling of satisfaction. Ernie visited the library every day after school and read that book until he had understood the whole thing. By the time he had graduated from high school, he had read the book three times. (2003, 27–30)

Rossi went on to pursue a PhD in pharmocognosy, a field that involves deriving medicines from plants, until while in graduate school a friend handed him a copy of Freud's *The Interpretation of Dreams*, which so captivated him that he decided to get a PhD in psychology instead. He became a successful psychoanalyst and has since written more than a dozen books on mind-body healing, hypnosis, and most recently on the psychobiology of gene expression. Most tellingly, O'Hanlon says that Rossi, now in his sixties, has finally settled the issue within himself that he is not stupid (see Dykstra 2003a, 5–6).

ANTICIPATING THE SPIRITUAL CONSEQUENCES AND POSSIBILITIES OF LOSING

The fateful, sometimes fatal, combination of active rejection by peers coupled with self-blame for that rejection, evident in the childhood plight of Ernest Rossi and countless other nonaggressive boys targeted by their peers, makes for an enduring and often devastating flood of shame, vulnerability, and self-consciousness. Rossi's case also makes clear, however, that the intense scars of self-exposure and self-consciousness for boys in this subgroup in particular can also give way to an urgent and unrelenting spiritual quest in later adolescence and adulthood. The very conditions that intensify their own suffering as early adolescent boys not infrequently lead to what I describe in the following chapter as a generative awareness of their own complexity, eroticism, and vitality, all crucial components of a self-awareness not so readily realized in the lives of more effortlessly "successful" boys and men.

In his struggle, the loser—especially the nonaggressive-rejected early adolescent boy—inadvertently finds himself with a running head start in having to come to grips with one of the more forbidding of Jesus' spiritual claims, namely, the necessity of *losing one's life in order to find it*. Rossi's boyhood rejection led first to his immersion in profound philosophical complexities and ultimately to a depth of self-awareness and wisdom essential for healing others in his care. As the loser boy loses himself in ecstasy and sorrow, no doubt at times to his own spiritual peril, he also occasionally hits pay dirt, the very qualities and strength of character essential to his own and others' spiritual gain.

To be sure, this trajectory—from debilitating self-consciousness to therapeutic self-awareness—is hardly inevitable and never proceeds without fits and starts. Much hangs in the balance for countless vulnerable boys on the cusp of puberty. Like other paths to spiritual enlightenment, the way of the loser boy is riddled with struggle. But it nonetheless holds the seed of promise that gives rise to what I consider a uniquely male, usually unrecognized, and therefore typically undervalued style of spirituality and care.

2

The Spiritual Quest of the Loser

We saw in the previous chapter that few contemporary American boys and men escape the treacherous waters of losing or being deemed a loser by their peers and culture. A single failure, a moment's hesitation, or a simple miscalculation threatens to determine their whole essence or character, even for a lifetime. As the research of Sandage (2005) and Biermann (2004) suggest, it is not unusual today for boys as young as six years old, and commonplace for those entering adolescence, to find themselves derided as complete, total, or born losers, before ever having had a chance to identify their strengths, fashion their dreams, even live their lives. The challenges posed to boys dismissed as losers are severe.

One focus of the present chapter is to consider several related ways in which losing or being regarded as a loser may dampen or destroy an early adolescent boy's inherent spirit. Losing threatens to do this in part by *oversimplifying* the boy's inner experience, pressuring him to draw rigid distinctions between himself and others that can lead to intense loneliness or rebellion; by *splitting* a sense of his body from that of his mind and soul, forcing him at decisive moments and considerable cost to choose one over the other; and by *deadening* or *depleting* the boy's sense of self, diminishing his awareness of being a distinct subject in his own right and enticing him to sacrifice personal interests, opinions, curiosities, and desires on the altar of what his culture conceives as normal.

The oversimplifying, splitting, and depleting of the self accumulate over time as unconscious reactions against what the boy all-too-consciously experiences as excruciating shame or self-consciousness in the immediate present. It seems that all eyes are focused on him, the complete failure, the total loser.

45

He stands exposed, he wants to hide, he tries to forget. He seeks, so to speak, to lose the loser within, to bury parts of his memories, experiences, interests, and desires. Rather than embrace the newfound complexity of body and soul that invariably accompanies the onset of adolescence, a boy flooded with shame and self-consciousness instead finds himself fragmented and torn, convinced that he is unworthy of the interest of God, self, and others.

For some, perhaps many, among this group of early adolescent boys, however, the experience of losing gives rise not only to negative consequences but to a number of desirable traits as well, qualities that may be less apparent in boys fortunate to have avoided the loser's shameful dilemmas. Despite painfully real and in some cases life-threatening dangers to body and spirit that stem from his predicament, the so-called loser boy may discover in his very losses some unexpected gains.

FROM SELF-CONSCIOUSNESS TO SELF-AWARENESS

Chief among these gains is a heightened sense of self-awareness. It is not difficult for us to imagine that the same self-consciousness that boys inevitably experience in losing could begin to shift ever so slightly, given the right conditions, to become a proving ground for deepening self-awareness. This potential for increasing acumen in self-understanding constitutes the other main focus of this chapter. The loser's enhanced capacity for self-awareness, along with capacities for self-transcendence among loners and self-sufficiency among rebels discussed by my coauthors in subsequent chapters, comprise the crucial components of what we consider the enviable, though almost always unrecognized or underappreciated, kind of spiritual struggles most common to early adolescent boys.

I characterize self-awareness in this chapter as consisting of three overlapping aspects that correspond to, and serve to neutralize, the three threats to self of oversimplification, splitting, and self-depletion. Specifically, self-awareness entails the early adolescent boy's growing awareness of (1) his own internal contradictions and complexity; (2) his physical body and sexual interests as integral to, rather than as contradicting, his spiritual understanding and expression; and (3) his so-called abnormality not only as burden but as gift, paving a specific, if often confusing or mysterious, path to his own unique calling and creativity. Put differently, the shame and self-consciousness of the loser sometimes gives way to a studied, spiritually precocious awareness of his own *complexity, eroticism*, and *vitality*.

Shifting somewhat from the historical and social psychological lenses that Sandage and Biermann trained on losers and losing in the previous chapter, the present chapter draws especially from evocative writings in contemporary psychoanalysis on loss and failure. Specifically, I consider reflections from the clinical work and essays of Adam Phillips, a noted child psychoanalyst practicing in London, and of his close friend and similarly prolific American colleague Christopher Bollas. Their works, along with additional memories of my own and other men's boyhoods, shed light on what I hold to be the three spiritual threats and three potential spiritual gains of early adolescent boys dismissed as losers.

ROBBED OF COMPLEXITY, CONTROL, CURIOSITY, AND CONNECTION

In an essay entitled "On Being Laughed At," Phillips describes the schoolyard taunting or mockery faced by boys identified as losers as a form of thieving or robbery. To ridicule boys as losers is to steal, or to attempt to steal, something from them. And adolescence, Phillips points out, is "the high noon of ridicule" (2002a, 36).

Mockery, according to Phillips, threatens first to rob the boy of his *complexity*. For a boy to be led by peers or others to believe he is a complete, total, or born loser is to reduce to a monochromatic still life the vast kaleidoscope of colorful characters, personalities, voices, teachers, interests, desires, cultures, and experiences that come together to form his completely original, ever changing self. Ridicule threatens to reduce him to a rigid, uninteresting, disinterested caricature of himself. We will consider this threat of oversimplification in greater detail in the next section.

In addition, the mocked boy faces being robbed of *control* over the way he presents himself to others, as though some peer paparazzo had snapped a photograph of him emerging from the locker room showers and circulated it on the Internet. What is being stolen, Phillips says, is the boy's "freedom to supervise, to control the representations of [himself]," and particularly, as an emerging adolescent, representations of his "unpredictable sexually and emotionally developing bodily self" (41). We will consider this threat to the boy's relationship to his own body in the section below on "splitting."

Finally, ridicule threatens to rob the so-called loser boy of his *curiosity* and, as a result, of his *connection* to others. This is because, in Phillips' words, "curiosity is a threat to the self as idol; each new person we meet may call up in us something unfamiliar" (1994, 57; 2002a, 36, 43). The boy assailed as a loser is tempted to reject or repress those traits or interests that have led to his rejection. But to accede to this version of himself may be to engage only a small portion of his own inner experience and to risk becoming a parody of his increasingly complex adolescent self. He may stop being interested in what interests him—stop trusting where his curiosity may lead—given that curiosity often leads to new relationships that may further complicate his life.

To be robbed of one's own curiosity is thus, in effect, to lose human connection and sociability. When boys participate in so thoroughly rejecting one another, Phillips argues, they foster a "grand illusion of disunity" between them, attempting to convince themselves that they have nothing in common. What we find to be so funny in ridiculing another person is the sense of "just how different we are," of how unbridgeable is the boundary between mocker and mocked (2002a, 42–43). We will consider more fully the consequences of a boy's losing his curiosity and connection to others in the chapter's final section on the threat of self-depletion.

These various forms of thievery—being robbed of complexity, control, curiosity, and connection—represent the gravest of threats to self and soul of early adolescent boys. But those who somehow marshal the internal or external resources needed to face, resist, or overcome these very obstacles—recall Ernie Rossi (O'Hanlon 2003), mocked by other kids as a "retard," struggling to read Kant as a boy—find themselves in a stronger position than other boys to forge a precocious self-awareness and burgeoning spiritual sensitivity that could come by no other way.

THE THREAT OF OVERSIMPLIFICATION AND THE POTENTIAL GAIN OF INNER COMPLEXITY

In a chapter entitled "On Success" in his collection of essays *On Flirtation: Psychoanalytic Essays on the Uncommitted Life*, Phillips stresses that our conceptions of success and failure are not always as different from one another as they may at first appear. The slightest change in inner or outer circumstances often makes all the difference in tipping us toward one or the other (1994, 42–58).

Phillips begins by considering the extraordinary childhood education of John Stuart Mill, arguably the most influential British philosopher of the nineteenth century. Born in 1806, Mill was taught as a child "exclusively by his father and [had] no contact with other children apart from his own siblings," whom the boy himself was required to teach (42). Mill began learning Greek when he was three, Latin at age eight, and was well versed in geometry, algebra, and calculus by the age of twelve. At that point he began studying the logic of Aristotle and Hobbes, and at thirteen his father had him turn to " 'a complete course in political economy.' " Mill concludes in his autobiography that "I started, I may fairly say, with an advantage [in education] of a quarter of a century over my contemporaries," meaning, Phillips says, that at age fifteen,

Mill "had the learning of a man in his late thirties" (Mill 1873/1989, quoted in Phillips 1994, 42).

Success as a Form of Failure

Phillips suggests that to this point, Mill's own account of his childhood education appears to have all the marks of a classic success story. He goes on to note, however, that "the ultimate success of the story seems to have depended on its breaking down: at the age of twenty Mill suffered a catastrophic disillusionment" (Phillips 1994, 43). Until that time, Mill's definition of what would constitute success, that is, the passionate goal he laid out for his life's work, was for him to become, in his own immodest words, "a reformer of the world." He wanted to be able to achieve the greatest possible happiness for the greatest number of people. This and this alone, Mill determined at age sixteen, was what would be required of him in order to consider himself a success.

But at the age of twenty, Mill, the prodigy, found himself going through an emotional breakdown, a major depression that lasted many months. He came to this breakdown by way of engaging in a conscious exercise of the imagination, in which he envisioned having finally reached his ultimate goal; he had now, at last, reformed the world. Allowing himself to imagine having achieved ultimate success, he proceeded to ask himself whether, as a result, he would be happy. When the shocking answer that came to him was no, he suffered what he later likened to a religious awakening or conversion, to emerging from a trance or spell, and to what he called a Methodist's "conviction of sin." He experienced this awakening, however, not as a moment of sublime satisfaction but as a traumatic realization that everything he had worked so hard to achieve had been in vain. He found himself overcome by what he called "an irrepressible *self-consciousness*" that, he said, "made my heart [sink] within me; the whole foundation on which my life was constructed fell down. . . . I seemed to have nothing more to live for" (Mill 1873/1989, quoted in Phillips 1994, 45).

When Mill dared to envision himself as the ultimate *winner*, in other words, he was startled by a bout of extreme self-consciousness, followed by long-term depression and despair, not unlike what one might find in other adolescent boys derided as losers. To achieve great social success, of which he had long dreamed, would make of him, he suddenly realized, a great personal failure. For the young Mill, success and failure, it seemed, were intimately intertwined.

Trauma Oversimplifies the Self

Phillips's psychoanalytically sensitive eye discerns that Mill's "breakdown—like most breakdowns, given a sufficiently attentive environment—was also a breakthrough. And one of the many things that tend to break through in such crises are repressed questions addressed to the parents, or to the parents internalized as parts of oneself" (45–46). In other words, Phillips says, one plausible reading of Mill's crisis at age twenty is that it "was a protest against the life his father had organized for him" (45). Or, in the words of Phillips's friend and fellow psychoanalyst Christopher Bollas, our "core catastrophes" as individuals often involve "being trapped in someone else's (usually the parents') dream or view of success; psychically paralyzed for self-protection in a place without the freedom of perspectives" (158).

For Mill to discover a kind of success more true, we might say, to his own self or spirit, he had first to come to the realization that he consisted in more than his father's aspirations for his life. To succeed in coming to his own new fantasy of success, he had first to fail, in a sense, at his father's dream. By the age of twenty, a success story different from his father's ideal somehow had managed to seep its way into the young Mill's soul. He was, he suddenly came to learn, a much more complex person than he had previously realized. He was, in an entirely appropriate though still personally terrifying sense, a *multiple personality*. To be sure, he contained within himself others' voices and ideals. But he contained something more than these as well, namely, interests and desires uniquely his own.

In coming to the realization that we carry within us multiple selves, we should not be surprised to discover that we likewise carry within us multiple, often competing, versions of what it means to be a success and failure, a winner and loser. At our best, meaning at our most complex, we are both winners and losers at one and the same time.

The vital self, for Phillips, resists the anxiety that presses for absolute certainty or oversimplification, or what Bollas calls "the Fascist state of mind" (2002b, 56; cf. 1994, 158). In this totalitarian state, the mind attempts to kill off dissenting voices or put to rest all internal opposition. "For Bollas," Phillips says, "trauma is that which oversimplifies the self; it is that which, because of the suffering entailed, leaves people with an aversion to their own complexity" (2002b, 57). This risk of losing track of their inner complexity or multiplicity of selves is perhaps the greatest threat to the spirits of adolescent boys rejected as losers by their peers, parents, or others. It appears as a recurring theme in the discussions on the additional threats of splitting and self-depletion later in this chapter.

By contrast, for Bollas, emotional or spiritual vitality "entails the tolerance and enjoyment of inner complexity; the ability to use and believe in . . . a kind of internal 'parliament,' full of conflicting, dissenting and coercive views" (56). The purpose of psychotherapy—and, as the following look at Jesus' own boyhood suggests, the path to enhancing spiritual maturity in early adolescent boys—becomes in this light "to elicit, and enable a person to use, their essential complexity" (57). It involves not so much helping "people make more competent choices as [showing] them how many choices they are (unconsciously) making" (50).

Anxiety and Affirmation "In My Father's House"

We are offered just a single glimpse of Jesus' own boyhood beyond infancy in the Gospel narratives. Fortuitously for our purposes, it happens that this account depicts Jesus as an early adolescent, a boy being ushered into a world of increasing complexity. The Gospel of Luke recounts that at age twelve, Jesus accompanies his mother and father, along with a large group of fellow travelers, on an annual Passover pilgrimage from Nazareth to Jerusalem. On this particular occasion, however, the group is well on its way back home after the festival before Jesus' parents realize that he is nowhere to be found amid the crowd of travelers. Suddenly facing one of every parent's worst nightmares, Mary and Joseph return to Jerusalem to continue their frantic search. After what must have been for them three agonizing days, they finally find the boy in the temple, oblivious to their concern, "sitting among the teachers, listening to them and asking them questions." The Gospel writer goes on to say, in what could only add insult to the parents' injury, that "all who heard him were amazed at his understanding."

Despite whatever relief she must have felt, however, Mary is clearly agitated: "When his parents saw him they were astonished; and his mother said to him, 'Child, why have you treated us like this? Look, your father and I have been searching for you in great anxiety.'" From his parents' perspective, Jesus' attempt to explain himself in response—saying to them, in effect, that they should have known all along he would be there in the temple—appears to fall flat: "They did not understand what he said to them." For the writer and readers of the Gospel account, however, Jesus' response is the story's central claim and climax: "Why were you searching for me? Did you not know that I must be in my Father's house?" (Luke 2:41–52).

The Boy Jesus as Loser

There is much of interest in this rich biblical text. In a chapter entitled "The Child Jesus as Endangered Self" in his book *The Child's Song: The Religious Abuse of Children*, Donald Capps considers possible ways that Jesus' childhood, including his boyhood experience in the temple, may have influenced his adult ministry and understanding of God. Capps especially wonders how Jesus may have responded as a boy to what appear to have been widely circulating reports of scandalous circumstances surrounding his birth, questions of his illegitimacy that pursued him well into his adult years (see John 8:41–47). Capps examines in considerable detail ongoing speculation among scholars about Jesus' biological father. But he notes that none of these scholarly works raises the question of "the effect that awareness of his illegitimacy would have had on Jesus himself":

> While it is impossible to know at what age Jesus would have become aware of the circumstances surrounding his birth, we may assume that he would have learned them as a young child, and that he would view his illegitimacy as a personal tragedy, and himself as the innocent victim of a situation he could do nothing to alter or change. (Capps 1995b, 108)

If Capps is right about this, then one could make a plausible case that the social and psychological contours of Karen Biermann's category of nonaggressive-rejected boys in particular, discussed in the previous chapter, may fit Jesus' own boyhood as well. I noted there that boys in this group are usually actively rejected on the basis of physical or other readily identifiable and socially shameful differences beyond their control—factors such as race, ethnicity, language, obesity, or gender identification. They are also the boys, Biermann found, most vulnerable to ongoing emotional consequences of their rejection over time. Recall again Ernest Rossi, his distinguished career as a psychotherapist and author notwithstanding, struggling into his sixties to convince himself that he was not stupid.

Capps thus proceeds to raise questions of Jesus' boyhood vulnerability: "How, then, would knowledge of his illegitimacy affect him personally as a child? How would it influence his self-understanding? What measures would he take as a child to shield himself from the fact that he was perceived by those around him as deeply and irrevocably flawed?" (108). How, in other words, might Jesus have coped as a boy with being mocked, in today's language, as a loser?

Capps's response is again careful and detailed. Most relevant to our present concerns, however, may be his concluding that Jesus appears to have coped *by replacing negative internal images of an absent or neglectful human father with positive ones of God as intimate and loving Father.* This, of course, is the very image for God that Luke portrays Jesus as already having claimed as a twelve-year-old "in my Father's house."

This is no ordinary image or claim. Capps cites the assertion of biblical theologian Joachim Jeremias that Jesus' consistent " use of the everyday [Aramaic] word 'abba' as a form of address to God is [his] most important linguistic innovation." Jeremias further claims that " the complete novelty and uniqueness of

Abba as an address to God in the prayers of Jesus shows that it expresses the heart of Jesus' relationship to God" (Capps 1995b, 109, quoting Jeremias 1971, 36, 64–67).

That Jesus is depicted in Luke as having come to such an original understanding of God by the age of twelve, Capps concludes, accords with what we know from developmental psychology, namely, "that a relationship this profound would have its roots in Jesus' childhood experiences, especially his awareness of being an illegitimate child and his struggle to come to terms with the implications of this fact for his personal self-understanding" (100):

> As son of Abba, Jesus would thereby successfully challenge his fate, the stigma of his illegitimate birth, and insist on his right to an alternative identity, one that was more authentic, more true, because it was not based on social judgments and expectations, but on one's inherent, God-given freedom to be the self that one truly is. (114)

Capps's compelling reflections on the childhood of Jesus reinforce a central claim of this chapter. They affirm not only that early adolescent boys are inherently interested in matters of the spirit and capable of profound theological innovation, but that precocious self-awareness, as Jesus' own boyhood can be read to attest, comes to them most predictably by way of intense social stigma and rejection.

An Essential Complexity

Also worth considering in the narrative of the boy Jesus are hints of the text's implicit sanctioning of conflict and complexity "in the temple." As Jesus approaches adolescence, he finds himself in the seemingly untenable position of being cast by significant adults as at once a promising success ("All who heard him were amazed at his understanding") and as an exasperating failure ("Child, why have you treated us like this?"). In the space of just two sentences of the text, we glimpse the boy Jesus rushing headlong into increasing complexities and contradictions of adolescent and adult life, where suddenly one can be declared a winner and a loser at the same time and in response to the same series of events.

In the act of pleasing his teachers, Jesus has brought anguish to his parents. In becoming a successful student, he becomes, at least momentarily, a failure of a son. Though the narrative ends with Luke appearing to smooth ruffled feathers, saying that Jesus "went down with [his parents] and came to Nazareth, and was obedient to them," we readers remain skeptical. We have every reason instead to suspect that this incident foreshadows a life for this boy and his family that will never be far removed from ambiguity and anguish.

In this sole available narrative episode from Jesus' boyhood, we witness something of the newfound complexity that confronts early adolescent boys. The story could be read in part as showing how every boy—and certainly Jesus as the exemplary boy—stumbles upon the discovery that in adolescence, lines between success and failure, winning and losing, necessarily become less distinctly drawn. To be considered a winner in one realm invariably means being seen as a loser in another.

That this incident occurs in the temple at Jerusalem, the very epicenter of Jesus' religious universe, hints as well at how this growing complexity characteristically gets caught up with a boy's spiritual interests and concerns. The temple setting invites us to understand this newfound awareness of one's essential complexity as divinely sanctioned and integral to coming to spiritual maturity. It is "found," in Jesus' early adolescence and that of countless other boys, specifically in the realm of "my Father's house." Our only glimpse of Jesus' boyhood catches him in the act of at once frustrating some and delighting other key adult players in his life, and does so while implicitly affirming his wholly unconventional vision of God as "my Father." The text lends support to the notion that a dawning awareness of one's inner complexity—of how engrafted in winning is the act of losing, and vice versa—is somehow spiritually normative in a boy's coming of age.

Turning Contradictions into Paradoxes

We who live after Freud will not be taken completely unawares by the claim that winning and losing are intractably interlinked in every person's life. Phillips (1994) recalls Freud's (1916) positing of three internal agencies of the self or soul: the id, the super-ego, and the ego. Freud imagined that in every endeavor we are involved in at least three projects: "we are satisfying a desire, we are sustaining a sense of moral well-being, and we are ensuring our survival. In this useful fiction the id is productive of desire, the super-ego is the carrier of our ethical ideals, and the ego tries to make these often conflicting demands compatible with keeping going" (Phillips 1994, 48).

This means that whenever we are *failing*, or are perceived as a failure, in one of these aspects—by one of these internal voices or agencies—we are likely *succeeding* from the perspective or mission of another. We are our parents' dreams for us, to be sure, even as we are, in some sense, our peers' demands on us. But we are also much more than this. Thus, as Phillips points out, "If I fail as a student to have a girlfriend, I succeed at keeping myself as someone who loves only in the family. If I fail at my exams I successfully maintain myself as someone who is not ready for the next stage. If I can't write my essay, I can show myself to be capable of refusing a demand by a figure of authority" (1994, 49–50). Success and failure, Phillips concludes, are therefore inextricable: "We are always doing at least two things at once, and this can mean that the art of psychotherapy"—or, as the case of Jesus' boyhood experience leads us to add, the process of becoming a more spiritually unconventional and attuned person—"is turning what feel like contradictions—incompatibilities—into paradoxes" (50). Spirituality in this sense means becoming aware of, then learning to tolerate and even embrace, the complexity of oneself and others (cf. Rogers 1961, 172).

Finding One's Internal Temple

In light of Jesus' boyhood incident, it is possible for us to view what from his psychoanalytic perspective Christopher Bollas refers to as engaging one's "internal parliament, full of conflicting, dissenting and coercive views," as an invitation to early adolescent boys to enter their "internal temple" or their "Father's house"—a sacred, though not reliably tranquil, space within or without where complexity and contradictions are not only tolerated but are expected and encouraged. Boys who relentlessly contend against the totalitarian claims of the epithet *loser*—who are led to feel or believe, whether by parents, peers, or even religious authorities or teachings, that they do not measure up—would do well to find a sanctuary like that of the boy Jesus' temple. They need a place, within and beyond themselves, where a high degree of parental anxiety or anguish may be tolerated for days on end, on behalf of affirming their inherent curiosity, of freeing them from others' dreams of success, of coaxing from the ashes of their peculiar forms of rejection their own theological innovations.

They need an alternative Father's house, where their multiple personalities, their diverse inner constituencies, their complex multiplicity of selves can speak and be heard and affirmed. They need a safe haven where, to recall Adam Phillips, others show them not which choices to make but "how many choices they are unconsciously making."

The biblical story promotes a view of coming of age that, far from demanding cultural conformity or religious piety of early adolescent boys, elicits and enables them to use their essential complexity. Like John Stuart Mill's breakdown that became a breakthrough, the boy Jesus in the temple faces there unsettling realities in choosing against his parents' dreams of success. He chooses instead—or, more accurately, in addition—another house in which he finds himself blessed to live.

Coming of Age as Coming to Awareness

Adult men, who must regularly vie against totalitarian or fundamentalist tendencies of our own in our efforts to fend off the mark of the loser, should be equally vigilant in imparting to boys in our care the awareness and embrace of their inner complexity. We must alert them, against centuries of ingrained cultural messages, to the sheer implausibility of their ever becoming complete, total, or born losers. We need to remind ourselves, along with our sons and brothers, that we are always simultaneously *winning* at some other, entirely redemptive psychosocial project or purpose. To be deemed a loser by the voice of another from within or without invariably involves being recognized as a winner by some other, competing voice from within or without. In a similar way, we may come to discern discrete traces of losing, shame, and sorrow infused in our moments of winning.

Spiritually maturing selves are those emboldened to resist the essentializing designs of a social system that recklessly casts them as losers. The more courageous saints in our midst may even be inclined to reject, we now have cause to add, the equally debilitating and epithetical *winner*. Perhaps in the end, to be spiritually sane involves concerning ourselves less with winning and losing, and recognizing instead that in the most important things in life we are more apt simply to muddle through (Phillips 2005, 189).

Embracing our complexity is a divinely ordained task of coming of age, evident and affirmed even in Jesus' own boyhood. It is a task in many cases enhanced for boys by their experiences of losing. Losers, who through circumstances beyond their control are propelled into a flood of self-consciousness, often come to see themselves, as a result, in a new and more complex light, from multiple perspectives beyond those most immediately familiar. Debilitating self-consciousness in many cases gives way, given an optimally supportive environment "in my Father's house," to intensive self-awareness and sensitivity. As Donald Capps concludes, speculating on the impact of Jesus' boyhood stigma on his adult ministry, "Perhaps it would take a man who was considered to be illegitimate to point out that it was not himself, but the social order on which others were depending and feeding that was illegitimate" (Capps 1995b, 114).

THE THREAT OF SPLITTING BODY FROM SOUL AND THE POTENTIAL GAIN OF EROTICISM IN LOSING

Boys rejected as losers face a second threat, related to the threat of oversimplification, of too rigidly segregating their physical bodies and sexual interests from their emotional or spiritual self-understanding. The loser boy faces intense internal and external pressure to sever ties between his body and his soul, two mutually dependent and ultimately inseparable realms of his personal experience. He is tempted to regard his developing body, including his sexual questions, fantasies, and practices, as having little or nothing to do with his spiritual interests, aspirations, and expressions. Conversely, his spiritual life becomes prone to losing its grounding in his most familiar, urgent, day-to-day concerns. The young loser finds himself pressed into preventing either of these personal realms from informing, influencing, or enriching the other.

Though the boy's vital spirit is clearly at risk in this endeavor of splitting personal experience into overly discrete fragments, his physical body and sexual self often bear the brunt of its impact. This may at first seem counterintuitive, given that adults tend to perceive early adolescent boys as being relatively uninterested in spiritual matters and in the rituals and practices of their faith. But it makes sense that these boys would deny the value, needs, and desires of their bodies more than their spiritual concerns when we consider again Biermann's subgroup of nonaggressive-rejected boys in particular—those usually ridiculed explicitly for some physical difference or bodily trait beyond their own control. Boys whose bodies or sexual interests serve as the specific locus of their shame and rejection have ample reason to attempt to jettison those bodies or interests as a result. If the eye or hand offends, these boys' minds can almost visibly be read as reasoning, it must be plucked out or cut off. The loser does everything in his power to lose—or lose track of—those persistent traits and desires that others find freakish and deplorable in him.

Recall Adam Phillips's (2002a) assertion that boys who are ridiculed as losers are actually being robbed by others of their ability to control the way they wish to present themselves to others. Their "freedom to supervise, to control the representations" of themselves, and particularly for adolescents their representations of the "unpredictable sexually and emotionally developing bodily self," is snatched from their own hands. Loser boys are robbed, in this sense, of their own bodies, or, at least, of some desired control over them in the outside world.

They thus find themselves tempted to compensate for this loss of external control by striving instead for some semblance of internal bodily mastery or control. Boys singled out by self-appointed race- or gender-police among peers or society for crimes of displaying one or another physical difference—and whose body at the entrance to puberty is not in some way guilty as charged?—instigate their own rigid programs of self-surveillance or house arrest in response. They learn that becoming a man consists in an almost ascetic denial of the signals, needs, demands, and desires of their own bodies.

There are times, to be sure, when this process moves in the other direction, when so-called loser boys err on the side of overly emphasizing or displaying their physical bodies or exaggerating their sexual prowess at the expense of their own or their loved ones' vitality of spirit or peace of mind. Even then, however, the ultimate impact remains much the same: The rejected boy continues to simplify himself and his experience overmuch or to collaborate in perpetuating the oversimplification of others. His "complex multiplicity of selves" becomes rigidly compartmentalized, mechanized, categorized, organized, spiritualized, or sexualized, and ultimately, in each instance, compromised. His various inner selves no longer converse or coalesce in such a way as to energize, revitalize, or, finally more tragic, even recognize one another. He surrenders a chance to discern greater richness of self as an embodied soul, an in-spirited or *inspired* body, a sexual *and* spiritual, a spiritually sexual, boy.

Striking Out for Nonathletes

When I was fourteen and about to enter high school, the local school board issued a ballot initiative for the purpose of constructing a new high school building. To that point, the junior high school and senior high school of my small town had been housed together in an old and decrepit building, parts of which had been condemned as structurally unsound and beyond salvaging. It seemed clear, at least to us students, that a new school was long overdue. I was excited about this possibility, figuring that if the bond issue were to pass, the new building would be constructed in time for me to enjoy it for a couple of years before I graduated.

As it turned out, however, the bond issue failed, quashing my hopes that the school would be built within my numbered days and leaving me dumbfounded at what I presumed to be the shortsighted parsimoniousness of the townsfolk. More to my dismay, I learned that my minister and his wife, of whom I was particularly fond and who, from my perspective, should have known better, were among those who voted against the new school. They told me that ordinarily they did not even vote in local elections, explaining that since they lived in a church-owned manse and therefore did not pay property taxes, they felt they were in no position to say how those local tax dollars should be spent. In the case of this particular school bond, however, their strong sentiments against the project overruled their usual reticence to vote.

Hearing not only that they had voted no but had gone out of their way to do so made my blood boil all the more—until, that is, they explained the reason for their decision. Once they did, my anger and disillusionment gave way, first to a sense of disorientation, then to one of newfound realization and even gratitude.

They had voted no, they told me, because the proposed building consisted almost entirely in athletic facilities, with little space allotted for classrooms and a library, and almost none for music and the arts.

I had not noticed this before, having previously only seen an artist's rendering of the proposed building's exterior. But what my minister and his wife were saying was, in fact, the case. The new building would offer little for those considered "nonathletes," a term for describing youthful identity (or nonidentity) that betrayed the pervasive reign of athletics—more narrowly, of football, basketball, and, to a lesser extent, baseball—in my school and community. The building was to have had an Olympic-sized swimming pool, several gymnasiums, multiple sets of locker rooms, all surrounded by expansive acres of green athletic fields, including a half-dozen baseball diamonds, a football field, tennis courts, and a separate area devoted to track and field. But it would contain little or nothing by way of space for academics, art, music, or theater.

My minister and his wife had voted no, in other words, for the sake of students like me.

Hearing why they voted the way they did quietly rocked my world. It began to shift the foundations, however subtly, of my previous way of looking at things. Rarely in my fourteen years had adults I respected this much so overtly affirmed my interests and values over against those espoused everywhere around me. By the end of my early adolescent years, I had so thoroughly imbibed my community's tacit message about the significance of athletics in a boy's life—believing at some level that nonathletes were, in effect, nonpersons—that hearing their reasons for denying me this new school was at once unsettling and freeing. It allowed me to catch a glimpse of what would have been obvious to most any attentive outsider to my community but that had been hidden to me. I decided that I could easily sacrifice the possibility of a couple of years as a student in a spiffy new high school in exchange for an affirmation like theirs.

On Athletics without Balls

Reflecting on what he considered his most important insights as a man and a psychologist, Carl Rogers noted that

> the more I am simply willing to be myself, in all this complexity of life, and the more I am willing to understand and accept the realities in myself and in the other person, the more change seems to be stirred up. It is a very paradoxical thing—that to the degree that each one of us is willing to be himself, then he finds not only himself changing; but he finds that other people to whom he relates are also changing. (1961, 22)

In retrospect, my own process of coming to understand something of Rogers's paradox—that only in the affirmation of who one already is does real change become possible—may have taken root in the vote of my minister and his wife on the school bond issue. I say this because, oddly enough, their indirect elevation of my intellectual and musical gifts, of my status as a nonathlete, became for me an early step in a long journey of reclaiming my physical body and athletic self as genuine parts of who I am.

As a boy, I could outrun or outswim most anyone in my class. I spent hours tooling around in my family's little speedboat and grew confident, at times reckless, on waterskis. I threw a mean Frisbee, walked, sledded, skated, canoed, and loved every minute spent on my bike. But since none of these activities, to my community's way of thinking, required *balls*—specifically the footballs, basketballs, or baseballs that constituted its vision of legitimate athletics—the thought never crossed my mind, and no adult ever suggested, that I too might already be, or had the potential to become, an athlete.

As a consequence, from my earliest years in school I began a steady process of distinguishing my mind or soul from my physical body, elevating the former in status while devaluing the latter, a kind of splitting of self into discrete categories of which I was at least vaguely aware by early adolescence. Lacking the physical body and precise abilities specified for easy entrance to manhood by my community and classmates, I knew early on that I instead was given to develop an agile mind and spirit. If forced to choose, there was no question as to which hand I had to play.

Unexpectedly for him, I am sure, my minister's countering my community's message—that developing one's mind was a project for losers—paradoxically led to a fledgling but, over the years, personally defining effort to reclaim my physical body and sexual interests as important parts of my spiritual understanding and well-being. I figured that if my community's definition of what constituted athletics was as ill-conceived as its views on the relative unimportance of a life of the mind, perhaps it would be possible for me to be a body as well as a mind and soul, though on my own, rather than my community's, terms.

Anxiety and Affirmation in My Grandfather's House

A somewhat embarrassing memory of an inadvertent but revealing earlier expression (and momentary rejection) of my body/soul dualism recently came to mind—that of the day, as an eleven-year-old, that I spontaneously decided to shower with my grandfather.

Until I reached adolescence, my mother's parents continued to live in the farmhouse in which she had been born and raised. I cherished spending time with my grandparents on their small farm, which was located about twenty miles from my home, at points during summers for days at a time. I found endless diversions there from my usual life as a townie: feeding and watering livestock, learning to drive the tractor, building forts in the woods that protected the house, shooting BB guns, helping plant the garden, picking crab apples, and mowing the lawn with a riding mower. This would all change suddenly a year or so later, when my grandmother died of cancer and my grandfather sold the farm and moved into town. But as an eleven-year-old that summer, those storms remained at bay as one day I impulsively decided to shower with my grandfather.

After finishing his chores at the end of each day, my grandfather would go to the basement of their old house to shower before dinner. The basement was unfinished, and the bare-bones shower consisted in nothing more than some exposed pipes and a showerhead attached to a stone wall in the middle of the room, making the whole of the basement something of an early model gang shower. Without hesitation on a particular day of one of those extended visits, I followed my grandfather down the steps, stripped down, and showered right along with him. He seemed initially surprised at this (though probably less so than I was), but he quickly accommodated my presence without hint of shame or shaming and took the moment in stride. It was the first and last time we would see each other unclothed.

An Uncharacteristic Immodesty

I realize that this episode could lend itself to any number of interpretations, none likely to fully exhaust its meaning. In light of the present discussion on splitting body from soul among so-called early adolescent losers, however, this shower scene is significant to me in at least a couple of respects.

First, my decision to let my grandfather see me naked—my insisting, really, that he do so—ran contrary to an unusually severe modesty about my body at that time in my life. Throughout my childhood I took great care not to be seen without clothing by others, including by my father and mother, my family doctor, even my older brother. In my brother's case, this was no mean feat, for we shared a bedroom until I turned thirteen. A Calvinist propriety in terms of states of undress was the unspoken norm among members of my immediate family, though no one seemed especially prudish or heavy-handed in this regard—no one, that is, except me. I maintained my self-imposed "no-exposure" rule throughout childhood, assuming even then that it was my own inherent shame or self-consciousness, rather than anyone else's insistence, which fueled my reserve.

So the unscripted shower at age eleven with my grandfather was a notable exception to the rule, mystifying to me at the time, though also freeing.

A Tale of Two Families

A second observation: As significant to me now as the fact that my moment of spontaneous exhibitionism ran counter to my usual reticence to be seen is that

I chose my grandfather to do the seeing. How was it that, however uncon-sciously, I found in him enough safety to finally reveal my nakedness and thus, in a sense, my budding eleven-year-old's sexuality? Why him? Why then?

As to the latter question, I might speculate now that the timing may have involved, at least in part, my needing to face the encroaching prospect of group showers, required of all boys following gym classes and sporting events in the junior high school I would attend. The shower with my grandfather may have been a kind of practice session, a "wet run," for daily group showers soon to come. If indeed such a motivation did lie somewhere in the background, then this session with my grandfather must have done the trick. For when the time came, showering with my peers proved to be no great problem, this represent-ing a swift and major departure from my earlier undue modesty.

As to the "Why him?" question, the answer I would now give reflects some-thing of the antagonism I experienced as a boy between my body and spirit, a split manifested in part by sharply delimited images that I held of my mother's and father's sides of the family. This split, it strikes me in retrospect, would make my grandfather, rather than my father or brother, a more natural prospect as the object of my self-exposure.

As a kid I viewed my mother and her extended family, including her par-ents, in large part in terms of a raw, no-nonsense physicality or earthiness. Her kinfolk, to my way of thinking, were stocky, ruddy, beer-drinking, materialis-tic, at times raucous and emotionally expressive, even explosive, German Lutherans. My father's side of the family, by contrast, signified for me a gen-tle, otherworldly, Christian piety. His clan, it seemed to me, consisted of tall, lean, quiet, teetotaling, emotionally constrained Dutch Calvinists. I heard my father, a World War II veteran, use profanity only once in my life, uttering a word in a moment of anger that, coming from him, took me aback, though I had long grown accustomed to hearing my mother, and especially her father, use the very same word with utmost regularity and impunity.

Thus would play out my own little interior world war of sorts—the sensual, down-to-earth Germans seeming to battle the ascetic, otherworldly Dutch for my allegiance and affections throughout boyhood and adolescence. My Ger-man body was at war with my Dutch soul.

I found myself drawn to soldiering on both sides of this conflict. Though I grew anxious at my maternal grandfather's explosive outbursts, even when they weren't directed at me, I still liked the fact that, just as frequently, he would surreptitiously slip a few coins or a dollar bill into my hand nearly every time I saw him, or that he and my grandmother always had stashes of exotic flavors of soda and ice cream on hand. They never failed to lavish birthday and Christmas gifts on their grandchildren, always attentive to the specific items on our wish lists. They were the first of anyone I knew to buy a color television, at a time when that technology had just begun to appear. And I was glad that with predictable regularity my grandfather, unlike my frugal father, would always spring for a new, rather than a used, car.

By contrast, my father's mother (my paternal grandfather died when I was two) could not have seemed more different to me as a boy. She lived in the same small town of ours and far more simply than my rural grandparents. She was apparently uninterested in, and certainly out of touch with, cultural trends or fashions. Having never learned to drive a car and nearly agoraphobic, she was content always to remain in her little house, except for a weekly trip to church and the grocery store. She wore her long, straight, grey hair in the way of grandmothers, wrapped into a tight bun at the back of her head. She seemed to be truly content with herself and at peace with her place in the world, despite, or because of, having faced her share of trials, including the deaths of an adolescent son, my father's younger brother, in a car accident, and of her own husband, my grandfather, years later. She had almost no money and thus offered her grandchildren only a widow's mite, a dollar or two, for Christmas or our birthdays. But she consistently seemed delighted to see my siblings, cousins, and me on our visits to her home most Sunday afternoons. She allowed us to drink hot tea, always doctored with sugar and cream, with my parents, aunts, and uncles, and thereby led us to feel grown up. She taught me at age six to play my first, and to this day most happily morbid, piece on the piano, singing aloud with me as I played, "Doctor, doctor, can you tell / how to make poor Bobby well? / He is sick and going to die. / Doctor, doctor, tell me why." Perhaps for the reason of having cast my mortality this early in so stark a light, but more likely for the countless ways she exuded quiet faithfulness, my grandmother, more than anyone else in my family, appeared to "ordain" me for Christian ministry.

There was much, therefore, that I found attractive—but also unsettling—in each side of my extended family. What stood out in my mind as a boy, however, were what seemed the stark contrasts between them. These differences later began to soften and fade, in some respects even to reverse themselves, as I grew into adulthood. It eventually dawned on me, for example, that though I myself had never lived on a farm, my father's family had long been every bit as rooted in the soil as had my seemingly more earthy mother's. And I would learn much later that there was no love lost for farm life by my mother, either as a girl or as an adult. But at age eleven, any such ambiguities remained well beneath my conscious radar. Instead, I found it difficult to reconcile the discrepant styles of my two clans.

Despite pleasurable and insistent sensual yearnings that stirred within me as I approached adolescence, along with a natural temperament more like that of my mother than of my father, I followed what by that time had become the path of least resistance: I strove to emulate the side of my family that appeared to affirm the spirit over the flesh. I tried to align myself with what I perceived to be the asexual piety of my father's family, while believing my mother's to be somehow alien, though often more interesting, to me. I strove, at least in outward appearance, to be the "good Christian boy."

It would take many years for me even to begin to grasp, but many more to engage and attempt to live out, what in hindsight seems an inevitable conclusion, namely, that I somehow needed to allow these two extended families, and specifically what each family signified to me, to live more equably together within me. Perhaps no lesson over the years has become as important for me to attempt to convey to those in my care than this, no doubt as a way to keep reminding myself: that even as my soul and spirit are grounded in a humanity I share with all others, so too does God delight in my physical body and sexual interests.

I knew nothing of this elusive lesson within my conscious self as a boy of eleven with my grandfather in the shower that day. I knew only that I was somehow inspired at that particular moment, in an uncharacteristic impulse of joyful abandon, to see and to be seen. I had no notion that in fully *undressing* before another—a man who, I must have sensed, somehow gave me permission to have and be my body—I may have been *redressing* a longstanding and, by early adolescence, an increasingly unbearable divide within.

God as a Maternal Grandfather

It is unlikely that I would have recalled this memory at all had it not been for my later discovery of writings by distinguished psychoanalysts reflecting on the role of the maternal grandfather in a boy's psychological development. In chapter 5 of this book, Donald Capps builds on some previous reflections on the mythical power of a boy's maternal grandfather in his formative years (2002, 87–103). In the earlier work, he points out that a number of prominent early psychoanalysts and psychologists—among them Sigmund Freud, Sandor Ferenczi, Ernest Jones, Otto Rank, Erik Erikson, and Henry Murray—variously note, for example, that as a boy's mother retains childhood images of her own father as an unconscious ideal of manhood or masculinity, she unwittingly passes along this ideal to her son in the intense bond they share from the boy's earliest years (cf. Rapaport 1958; Rank 1964).

The boy thus first learns from his mother, and especially from her internalized view of her father, rather than from the boy's own father, how he is supposed to act and appear as a man. The boy's usually closer proximity to his father than to his grandfather only reinforces his mother's idealization of her father in the boy's mind; in seeing his grandfather as more distant, he views him as more awe-inspiring or fearsome than his father, a grandfather seemingly larger-than-life.

The boy's unconscious collusion with his mother's idealization of her father therefore often makes for a grandfather far more godlike than the boy's own father. In an intricate tracing of this historical conversation on the role of the maternal grandfather among psychologists, Capps concludes "that religion has its fundamental origins in the mother-son relationship, because it presents God the Father as having a claim on the boy prior to that of the boy's father and as being more clearly identified, among the boy's relations, with the maternal grandfather" (2002, 101).

Nothing, of course, could have seemed further from my own impression of my explosive and extravagant grandfather in my early adolescence. My eleven-year-old self would have said that, to the contrary, my grandfather was everything God was *not* supposed to be—earthy, boisterous, belligerent, and profane. I would have guessed, had I thought about it at all, that I chose to reveal myself to him in the shower precisely because I could not, *should* not, do so with God. How then could this grandfather be in any way a stand-in for God? This is how my conscious self, my *self-conscious* self, would have argued at age eleven, if given the chance at the time.

But seizing an opportune moment on that summer day on the farm, another of my multiple selves got in the first word edgewise, with something altogether different to say. This self, in an *unselfconscious* moment of joyful abandon, of losing itself, was saying instead that my grandfather was safe, good, and godly to me, and therefore that my own body—earthy, boisterous, belligerent, and profane—might somehow be safe, good, and godly too. For one spontaneous and boyishly erotic moment in pulling off my clothes, my body and soul, my sexuality and spirit, pulled off a rare instance of gloriously coming together as one.

Finding Sanctuary for Shame in My Father's House

Another specific instance in this process of claiming my body as integral to my spiritual life occurred in a series of events some years later and involved the same gifted minister mentioned earlier. By mid-adolescence, I had developed an unusually severe, almost textbook case of acne, though one mostly confined to areas on my back and chest and therefore mercifully hidden under my shirt from the gaze of others. I say "textbook case" because of a conversation I had with a physician friend years later, at age twenty-seven, while working as a chaplain in a hospital. As we talked one day, I happened to mention to my friend that if I were ever to develop a serious infection, I was sure there would be no antibiotics left to treat me because of a tolerance I had developed after so many years of taking them for acne as a youth. She asked me which drugs I had taken, and as I went through the list and got to the last and, at the time, most potent of them, one called Dapsone, she casually remarked, "Oh, the leprosy drug."

I went to the *Physicians' Desk Reference*, the drug bible, looked up Dapsone, and there it was—the primary drug used to treat Hansen's Disease, a contemporary (though not the biblical) form of leprosy. Acne was not even listed there among its possible indications, leading me to speculate about the desperation my dermatologist must have felt that day years earlier as he scribbled out the prescription. Though I had suspected it since early childhood, at twenty-seven a doctor confirmed that I was indeed a leper.

Back when I was sixteen, I cringed one day when my minister casually touched my shoulder, because it hurt. He asked why I flinched. I didn't respond. He had a long memory, however, and days later asked if he could see my back. I told him no. He wanted to know why, but again I would not say. We played this game for a while, so great was my shame, until for some reason—perhaps sheer exhaustion but more likely an inner desire to be known—I relented.

We were together in the church sanctuary, of all places, when I lifted my shirt for him. He told me that he was sorry I had suffered this alone, that he was proud of me for letting him see, and that he thought it would help for me to see a doctor, which to that point I had not done. Thus would begin my years of antibiotics and some tangible relief from an embodied source of my shame.

Today, of course, mentioning a minister's asking an adolescent boy to lift his shirt in a church sanctuary immediately raises eyebrows. We would be similarly concerned, unlike every previous generation of commentators, about the sleeping arrangements of the twelve-year-old Jesus during his overnights in the temple. This is as it should be, given recent revelations of the ravages of clergy sexual abuse. In ministry with adolescent boys, and with all others in our care, we must be unequivocal in maintaining appropriate sexual boundaries, no exceptions, no discussion. For this reason, it seems unlikely that any minister today would risk even the appearance of impropriety, as my minister did, in asking to see the acne hidden under my shirt.

But this, I think, would be the wrong lesson to draw, as ministers and mentors to boys, from the sobering sexual scandals—that we need to abandon any focus on the role of the boy's physical body, for the many risks such a focus entails, in behalf of his pursuit of the life of the spirit. There is no question that healing for my own leprosy, not only in its most overt form as acne but in its more invidious expression as shame, began long before I took even a single capsule of Tetracycline, the first of the drugs, and years before I took the final Dapsone, the last of them. Rather, the greater healing came in lifting my shirt before a sufficiently attentive other, and especially in doing so in the safety of "my Father's house." I found with graphic clarity in that particular space and action a God who was as concerned with my body as with my soul. I found acceptance, a sanctuary, for embodied shame. While it is absolutely the case that we as interested adults must never cross the line of violating the bodies of those in our care, it is equally the case that early adolescent boys need and long to be seen and known, by another and by God, in and for their bodies, not just in and for their souls. Ministry is, as it has always been and will forever remain, a risky endeavor, an embodied art, a dangerous and courageous calling.

Losing as Erotic Act

All this is to hint at the possibility that boys threatened with rejection on the basis of some physical trait or difference, if given what Phillips calls a "sufficiently attentive environment," may be poised to discover spiritual and ultimately even sexual *value* in their experiences of losing, for losing oneself is necessary not only for spiritual intercourse but for sexual communion. There is, in the words of Christopher Bollas, a kind of "erotic action" in losing oneself in another object, in another person, even in God. Those loser boys who somehow manage to hold on to or reclaim their bodies, despite their shame, tend to become experts of sorts in this appropriately erotic or eroticized kind of losing, of loving.

This is because the act of bestowing meaning and value on another person or object, in Bollas's words, requires that we project part of ourselves into that person or object. To engage or experience intimacy with another, he writes, "the subject must 'lose himself' in . . . a type of erotic action that must be unconscious and one in which the person is not being . . . thoughtful" (Bollas 1992, 22). A satisfying relationship of mutual intimacy in adulthood, including good sex, involves in part the experience of *losing* oneself in one's beloved, but losing as a means of simultaneously fully *finding* oneself, in Bollas's words, in "self-experiencing": "The distinction between the subject who uses the object to fulfill his desire and the subject who is played upon by the action of the object is no longer possible" (31).

This paradoxical notion of losing the self in order to find it consistently makes the cut for the short list of foundational principles not only for sexual intimacy but for spiritual wisdom—a boy or man "lost" in athletics, lost in study, lost in music, lost in love, lost in worship, lost in prayer, praise, wonder, thought, or grace: "Unless a grain of wheat falls into the earth and dies," Jesus says, "it remains just a single grain; but if it dies, it bears much fruit" (John 12:24). Such is the fruitful eroticism of losing.

So the loser boy faces the terrible threat of being cut off from his physical body, of splitting his sexual from his spiritual inclinations or practices. But should he somehow manage to hang on to or eventually reclaim that very body, that is, his sexual self in the broadest sense of the term, as inseparable from his spirit or soul, then his previous experiences of losing may enhance his capacity to lose in ways crucial to spiritual and sexual intimacy. In his unbearable history of loss, he gains expertise in the *eroticism* of losing, a powerful and intimate form of self-awareness less accessible to those boys and men who have known little suffering and shame.

THE THREAT OF SELF-DEPLETION AND THE POTENTIAL GAIN OF FINDING VITALITY IN ONE'S SHAME

Finally, and succinctly, a third but related observation: the boy demeaned as a loser faces the spiritual threat of self-depletion when he casts off those interests considered "abnormal" by others in his social sphere. If in the previous threat of splitting we found a boy ready to rid himself of aspects of his physical body deemed unacceptable to others, in the threat of self-depletion we find a boy who casts off his soul as well. He jettisons not just his body but his curiosity, interests, opinions, and desires, sacrificing them on the altar of what his culture conceives to be "normal." Sometimes, however, it is this very boy who comes to discover that hidden within what he thought were his "abnormal" interests and desires is his own peculiar variety of spiritual vitality or calling. He gains the awareness that within his wound may be found the precise source of his strength and mission.

The Tyranny of the "Normal"

In an essay entitled "Normotic Illness," Bollas describes a kind of patient he calls "normotic." If "normotic" sounds a lot like "robotic," this may be for good reason, for Bollas views normotic persons as suffering from being "abnormally normal," almost robotic in their personal style. If a psychotic person is someone who is out of touch with external reality, a normotic person is out of touch with internal reality. To be normotic is to lose touch with one's subjectivity, with that "internal play of affects and ideas that generates and authorizes our private imaginations, creatively informs our work and gives continuing resource to our interpersonal relations" (Bollas 1987, 137). It is to lose touch with one's personal vitality.

The normotic person is driven to be *normal*. He has no moods. He is overly stable, secure, comfortable, and socially extroverted. When asked to reflect on the play he just saw or the book he just read, if he can bring himself to see or read one at all, the normotic person is at a loss for how to respond. He has no capacity for reflection or introspection. He might describe Hamlet as "an unhappy young fellah." When his mother dies, he says, "Well, she's very old, you know, and we've all got to go sometime!" (140). The normotic person strikes the outside observer as "appallingly empty," though he does not experience himself in this or any other way. If we say of the psychotic's break with reality that he has "gone off the deep end," we would say of the normotic's break with subjectivity that he has "gone off at the shallow end" (146). If the danger for the psychotic is drowning in the deep end of the pool, the danger for the normotic might be in hitting his head and finding himself paralyzed in the shallow end.

Bollas attributes the origins of this character type to parents who only partly see or dimly reflect or mirror their child. Such parents refuse to affirm the imaginative capacities of their child and have a high need to keep the child focused on "reality." The child, Bollas says, "who is wanting to play murder with his father is pushed [instead] into watching TV. Programme follows programme, day after day, in a predictable manner" (145). "Above all, [the parents] are concerned that their children be normal and [not] act in a way that could be construed as inappropriate or odd. So the child is rewarded for being good, where good means ordinary, and is ignored or threatened for being imaginative" (144). Bollas describes adolescence as the most fragile time in the normotic person's life, where the child often becomes a socially cheerful and well-adjusted drug addict or suicide victim (148).

Again, as in our accounts of the previous two spiritual threats, we find in the normotic youth a shunning of inner complexity, a splitting off of part of the boy's self-experience, such that he is overwhelmed by banality. If what makes a boy a unique subject in his own right is found to be unacceptable by his parents or peers, it is again the case that he will work to cut off that unacceptable part. In the normotic person, that part is less his physical body, as in the previous threat of splitting, than his unique, subjective, imaginative, creative soul. His only choice appears to be to excise what those around him deem to be abnormal and to imitate their version of normality instead. Ridiculed for being interested in what interests him, he expunges curiosity, that which makes him a distinctive and interesting boy. He unconsciously strives to be shallow, to fit in, but at the cost of finding himself paralyzed in relationships precisely for having gone off at the shallow end, for having become so ordinary. Having surrendered his curiosity, he thus also surrenders, or rather is robbed of, a chance for intimate connection with others. This is the threat of the depletion or deadening of the so-called loser's subjective self or soul.

Out of One's Depth

But there may be a more hopeful alternative for the loser than going off the deep end and drowning (in a psychotic loss of touch with reality) on the one hand, or going off the shallow end and becoming paralyzed (in a normotic loss of touch with subjectivity) on the other. That alternative, a wonderful analogy for a boy's peculiar approach to coming to spiritual self-awareness, is *learning how to swim.*

Phillips tells of a sixteen-year-old patient, a self-described loner and one likely familiar as well with the epithet loser, who in a therapy session told Phillips "about the moment, at age ten, when he eventually learned to swim after having been terrified of water. 'I knew I was safer out of my depth,' " the boy told him, " 'because even though I couldn't stand, there was more water to hold me up.' " Phillips continues:

> One of the central paradoxes of the adolescent is his discovery that only the object beyond his control can be found to be reliable. For the boy the risk of learning to swim was the risk of discovering that he, or rather his body, would float. The heart of swimming is that you can float. Standing within his depth, apparently in control, was the omnipotence born of anxiety; the opposite of omnipotence here was not impotence, as he had feared, but his being able to entrust himself to the water. The defense of vigilant self-holding precluded his being able to swim. He needed a "generous kind of negligence" with himself. (1993, 30; cf. Dykstra 2003a, 2)

One cannot learn to swim, as this boy so remarkably determined at age ten, by standing up to one's knees or even one's neck in water, by remaining safely within one's depth and in control. One must instead risk a "generous kind of negligence," risk *losing* oneself, giving oneself over to one's terrors, surrendering to the water to find out whether it is reliable, trustworthy, and something worth counting on. "I knew I was safer out of my depth because even though I couldn't stand, there was more water to hold me up."

Only the object beyond one's control is an object worthy of desire, love, and trust, if one is ever to learn to swim, ever to get beyond mere safety, mere acceptability, mere normality on the shore. This is a painful paradox of life and love, a profound parable of the spiritual life, and a terrifying reality of coming of age. So perhaps we should not be surprised to learn that boyhood losers, should their negligence of self be of a truly gracious or generous kind, sometimes find themselves ably endowed to lose themselves—to float, to swim—in an object, a faith, a love, even a God worthy of their desire. Precisely in their abnormality, their personal terror, or the specific trajectory of their curiosity, they find their spiritual gift.

A Vocational Calling in One's Wound

Not long ago, I received a package of old black-and-white photographs in the mail from my sister, who wrote that she had found them while cleaning her basement and thought I might want them. Among them were some of my childhood friend Curt, the boy I had rejected in early adolescence and who died shortly thereafter of kidney failure. These photographs of him came as a real surprise, given that my sister had no way of knowing I was thinking and writing about him at that very time. In one of them, he and I are smiling broadly at the camera as we float on our bellies in shallow waters on the shore of a lake where my family vacationed each summer.

There was a time when seeing a photograph like this would have brought no small wave of shame and sadness over me, given what each boy had done to the other—my having abandoned him in life and he having abandoned me in death. This time, however, as I opened the package and found us swimming there, I smiled at seeing my friend again. Something was shifting in me.

What might account for the change? I would like to think that it could involve, at least in part, my intentional struggle in the intervening years to face fears of the feminine and fears of death—key aspects, if Scott Sandage is correct, of a man's fear of failure. More immediately, it also may have involved what had become for me a difficult revisiting of my own early adolescence through the lens of the loser in preparing these chapters. Many fears and losses were wrapped up together for me as an adolescent in Curt's life and death, and I have paid them a good deal of attention, consciously and no doubt unconsciously, in my personal and now professional life ever since.

Is there any connection between my conscious rejection of Curt for what I perceived as hints of femininity and the time I have spent reading and teaching historical, biographical, psychological, biblical, and pastoral literature on adolescence, feminism, men's studies, and human sexuality as a seminary student, minister, and professor? Or between that rejection of him and my increasing comfort over years of ministry in hearing and speaking of quite personal aspects of the lives of those, usually seminary students, whom I counsel?

I can't say for sure. I can say, however, that I have sought, sometimes at what has seemed my spiritual and vocational peril, to make amends to Curt, to myself, and to other boys and men and the women whom by implication we demean, at first by having attempted to tolerate, then at times having managed to embrace, what I reflexively deem as aspects of the loser in my own and other men's (and women's) lives.

In a similar way, might there be a link between that moment in my first days of adolescence when I stood silent and helpless by Curt's hospital bed and the many times since, when as a son, minister, or hospital chaplain I have stood by others near their times of death? Again, I have no way of knowing for certain. I do know, however, that even without the help of the Ouija board with which Curt and I used to play, I continue to this day to conjure the dead I have known: the little boy who accidentally hanged himself on the

Venetian blinds cord in his home; the young woman who, after taking an overdose of a painkiller, pleaded with me in the emergency room, saying she'd repented of her decision and suddenly wanted to live, only to die an hour later as the drugs took their toll; or the cancer patient in his twenties who made me proud by insisting that he be allowed to wear a T-shirt and gym shorts rather than the flimsy regulation hospital gown during the many stays before his death.

I remember these and many endings like theirs, and I am gratified by their terrible gift to me. Their deaths sometimes catch me up short in my whining, remind me of what matters most, give me reason to pick up the pieces and begin again, and make me risk speaking out for what I believe, for time is short. These losers whom I have known endeavor against the odds to make me faithful or wise. In these and other deaths that have threatened me with ultimate loss, I have come to an awareness of what gives me purpose and life. This is true of many other men I know, whose specific source of shame in childhood has claimed for them their calling later on, and this not only for men overtly religious but for those who would never consider themselves as such.

THE NERVE OF FAILURE AS PATH
TO SELF-AWARENESS

In *Born Losers*, Sandage notes that in classic sociological studies of the 1950s, David Riesman determined that many Americans lacked what he called the "nerve of failure" (rather than the more familiar "failure of nerve"): "[Riesman] explained, 'The *nerve of failure* is the courage to face aloneness and the possibility of defeat in one's personal life or one's work without being morally destroyed'" (Sandage 2005, 267, quoting Riesman 1954, 33, 55). "It is not often," Sandage concludes, "that poets, psychoanalysts, sociologists, and economists give the same advice: we fail because we have not learned to die" (271).

It seems possible in retrospect that what transpired in my childhood friendship with Curt, and in the many other ways I stood on the brink of loss and losing, may have contributed in some small measure to upping my capacity for the "nerve of failure" in adult life. If my life as a loser in early adolescence did this at all, it may have done so by teaching me, if not *how* to die, then at least *that* we die—even thirteen-year-old boys who play Beethoven better than baseball. Curt's life and death, along with my shame in adolescence for my physical body and a laundry list of abnormal interests and desires, may have provided me an inert dose of "courage to face aloneness and the possibility of defeat," of a "generous kind of negligence" with myself, in my otherwise cowardly life. They may have offered a timely inoculation against future ills and failures to come. My self-consciousness in being perceived as a loser and my fear of death were wrapped into one package at a highly impressionable time. The stakes were raised, death became real, my world grew complex, and the grace of a sufficiently attentive environment made way for an erotic and vital spirit. That spirit, I can only hope, will continue to enrich my awareness of self and life.

PART II

Loners and the Struggle for Self-Transcendence

Allan Hugh Cole Jr.

3

Loneliness as a
Condition of Boyhood

In 1994, a band consisting of three brothers, ages nine, eleven, and fourteen, began a meteoric rise to the top of the pop music industry. Using their surname, they called themselves "Hanson." That same year the band released a song titled "Lonely Boy" on their first studio record. Hanson's song shared a title with an earlier song by another artist, Andrew Gold. Released in 1976, his song became a top five hit in the United States. Both songs speak of how being a "lonely boy" feels.

Hanson describes the lonely boy as "trying to find the missing part." He is "all alone," "looking for a fresh start," his loneliness joined to a lost heart. Gold's lonely boy seems to feel similarly, "running down the hall" and "crying" over his own newfangled lonely state. Unlike the boy in Hanson's song, Gold's boy identifies both when and why his loneliness began. It began as he was displaced from "only son" status. After his two-year tenure as "a lovely boy," the exclusive recipient of his parents' desires to teach, nurture, and provide, one day he had to make room for another. A sister was born. His mother "told him we must attend to her needs / She's so much younger than you," which left him feeling betrayed and all alone. Having believed he was "the only son" and "the only one," he realized he was not.

Both Hanson's and Gold's songs speak of boyhood anecdotally. Their respective subjects are particular "lonely boys," and their songs recount specific experiences informing those boys' loneliness. Indeed, the artists' songs are quite personal and seem related to their own boyhood experiences. Gold says as much. His own birthday, August 2, 1951, must inform his song's line "He was born on a summer day 1951," and the members of Hanson were early adolescent boys when they released their song. Yet in speaking of particular

77

boys' experiences the artists actually identify something common to boys, at least to some degree. Boys feel lonely. They live their lives with a sense of isolation and disconnection that they cannot name, but they surely feel its effects (Pollack 1998, xxi). Discovering a world full of contradictions, confusion, and threats, they struggle to find grounding on a terrain that seems constantly to shift and remains uneven. Furthermore, while still needing to maintain a connection to what has sustained him thus far, namely, the nurture and support of parents—and especially his mother figure—a boy simultaneously feels the need for autonomy and distance, toward which he is often pushed too quickly and prematurely by well-meaning though misguided parents who buy into and perpetuate inaccurate myths of boyhood (Kindlon and Thompson 2000, 3; Pollack 1998, xxii, xxiv). All of this contributes to a boy's feelings of isolation, disconnection, helplessness, shame, loneliness, anxiousness, and silent suffering stemming from a sense of having been alienated from parents, siblings, peers, and himself. These feelings may last throughout boyhood and continue into adulthood (Pollack 1998, xxi). Often, to be a boy is to be lonely.

Dan Kindlon and Michael Thompson, authors of *Raising Cain: Protecting the Emotional Lives of Boys*, agree. Drawing from more than thirty-five years of combined work with boys in clinical practice, they reflect from a range of experiences that transcend the merely anecdotal and seek to shed more light on what being a boy typically entails. They believe that American culture largely supports emotional development for girls, and appropriately so, but that it fails to support boys and their emotional needs (Kindlon and Thompson 2000, 4). Boys are "emotionally *mis*educated" by parents, teachers, and the larger societies in which they live. Powerful stereotypes of "masculine toughness" serve to cut a boy off from his emotions, denying their legitimacy when they do not map onto the masculine ideal. This means that a boy is discouraged from maintaining healthy attachments and learns early in life to "hide his feelings and silence his fears" (4). Stating their reasons for writing the book, the authors say "a large part of our task was to convince skeptical parents and educators of a truth we knew from our years of experience as therapists: that boys suffer deeply as a result of the destructive emotional training our culture imposes upon them, that many of them are in crisis, and that all of them need help" (5).

In light of these findings, I take both Hanson's and Gold's "lonely boys" to be illustrative of *typical* boys, and especially those in early adolescence. Seeking in this chapter to detail why that is so, I discuss why loneliness so often characterizes boyhood and how boys experience such loneliness in ways unique to them. Their loneliness differs in degree, if not in kind, from that which girls may experience. In the next chapter, I show how loneliness may either complicate or enrich a boy's life. As an alternative to loneliness, which most persons understandably avoid and even regret, I explore and advocate for the notion of *solitude* in boyhood, which I view as a positive, adaptive kind of loneliness. Rather than something to avoid or regret, solitude is a boy's ideal response to loneliness and a sign of emotional maturity.

Additionally, I am concerned with how boys, in their solitude, seek religiously for someone to fill or replace what Hanson calls their "missing part." As concerns early adolescent boys, I suggest that, for many, and maybe most, the one after whom they seek and *must* seek is God. As noted in our introduction, the early adolescent boy's newly discovered and emerging sense of spirit joins with a quality of self-transcendence (along with self-awareness and self-sufficiency) to shape his spirituality. That spirituality includes a need to view himself as a participant in the transcendent—something larger than both himself and the ordinary world in which he lives, something that takes him beyond himself and connects him with "all that is." In light of this common—and I believe necessary—self-transcendent quality of the boy's spirituality, I advocate in the next chapter for the importance of providing early adolescent boys with kind, nurturing, supportive, and self-affirming understandings of God.

While those understandings may offer something valuable to all boys, they prove indispensable to lonely boys. They do so, of course, because they portray accurately the God of the Christian gospel. But they also assure boys that, in transcending themselves to join in the eternal and connected nature of things, they are recognized and known by their Creator. Not only that, through their self-transcendence that informs their spirituality, boys find a spirit—we could call it the Holy Spirit—that not only adheres in all things but one to which they themselves are joined in their own spirit. Jürgen Moltmann appropriately calls this spirit "the Spirit of Life" (Moltmann 1992/2001). In transcending themselves and their lonely boyhood condition to connect with that spirit, boys indeed come to find and experience life in a new, and I would say life-saving, way. Kind, nurturing, supportive, and self-affirming understandings of God, the Spirit of Life, further provide the lonely boy an answer to the often asked boyhood question that three boys named Hanson posed, namely, that there is indeed one who "at the end of the day" "could love a lonely boy," "hold his hand," and "understand."

WHY BOYS ARE LONELY

The circumstances surrounding boyhood loneliness vary widely, and we do boys an injustice if we lump their experiences together and assume that they are all alike. Even so, all boys eventually experience a time when they must separate from their first love, namely, their mothers or maternal figures, as they seek to establish their identities as boys. This is precisely what the boy in Andrew Gold's song went through, and in telling his story Gold identifies why boys inevitably feel lonely. A boy becomes lonely as he realizes another has ousted him: a sibling or someone else, even a parent. He perceives that another has taken away at least a part of what was once exclusively his own. Whether it involves a newly arrived or discovered brother or sister, or the realization that his father (or mother's partner) is also the recipient of her love and affection, a son eventually becomes aware that there is someone else who garners his mother's devotion. He, the son, is not the only one. In Erik Erikson's terms, the once "hallowed presence" becomes tainted, "paradise" is forfeited, and thus life no longer promises what it once did (Erikson 1968/1994, 101, 105). A boy then begins to grieve what he has lost.

Premature Separation and the Fear of Raising a "Momma's Boy"

This sets the stage for the boy to withdraw from his mother, separating from her both emotionally and physically. In time he will be forced to separate even further by parents and the larger society, who fear that mothers' failing to "cut the apron strings" (Pollack 1998, xxiv) with their boys sets them up to be like girls, in which case boys will neither be "real" boys nor become "real" men. As a boy separates from his mother he begins to identify more closely with his father, with other male figures, and with what the boy observes as acceptable ways of being a boy or a "little man." Yet the boy's loneliness continues. It continues because he knows that he will never again be "the only one."

Sigmund Freud explained this emotional and physical distancing that boys undergo, the basis for which lies in how boys separate from their mothers, in his well-known concept called the "Oedipus Complex." This theory holds that young children are sexual beings. By this Freud did not suggest that children's sexuality can or should be like that of adults—in degree or kind—but merely that children experience sexual desires, pleasures, and fantasies at very early ages. From around age three to age seven, boys' sexual energy centers on the mother figure. We should not find this surprising, for she has gratified him already by providing food, warmth, stimulation, and security. Assuming she will provide in other gratifying ways, she becomes the object of the boy's sexual interest. This prompts him to develop a rivalry with those perceived to be vying for, or possessing, the mother sexually. Typically, the father or other significant male person in the home serves as the chief rival. The boy begins to dream of destroying his rival so that the boy may have his mother to himself. He soon realizes, however, due to a myriad of external influences, that this is unacceptable. Internalizing the prohibition against his desire for his mother so that it becomes part of his own conscience, and having dreamed of destroying his rival (who is also loved because he has provided the boy with other pleasures and needs), the boy feels conflicted and guilty.

He also begins to live in fear. He fears retaliation on the part of his father (or other rival), which Freud said was really the boy's fear of losing his penis, but he also fears (perhaps more so) losing the love his parents have offered him thus far. His father presumably has provided him care, security, and nurture. His mother once lived with him in "paradise," when he was "the only one." Though his status has changed and he now must separate from her, he still loves her deeply. Fearing he will be found out with regard to his inappropriate feelings toward his mother and father, and thus lose his parents' love, the boy seeks to get rid of his feelings and the potential dangers they bring. Though occurring in the realm of his unconscious, these feelings of internal conflict, guilt, and fear become powerful and endure.

The boy seeks to get rid of his feelings by denying them. In Freud's terms, he represses them. He likewise increases his association with his former rival, that is, with his father (or mother's partner), and also with other males whom the boy perceives to be like his father and thus like himself. Freud believed that this "identification with the aggressor" provides the boy with a feeling of self-protection. As Michael Kahn describes it, "Freud pointed out what an interesting and adaptive form of protection this is. The danger is external. Father might punish or even castrate. . . . There is no way to neutralize father; he's much more powerful than I. But what if I protect myself where I *do* have power, inside my own head? So I institute an effective prohibition against the dangerous wish, the wish that would get me punished if acted upon" (Kahn 2002, 86). The boy thus identifies with his father, and in so doing makes maleness, in whatever qualities he perceives to be most valued by his father and others around him, his ideal. For the boy, the idea becomes "the more male I can be, the less chance there is for those former wishes to resurface." As this happens, however, he feels increasingly removed from both emotional and physical proximity to his first loves. This distancing results in a pervasive loneliness whose qualities and intensity *only* boys will experience and that impact a boy's early adolescent years and beyond.

In *Real Boys: Rescuing Our Sons from the Myths of Boyhood*, William Pollack details the exclusive qualities of boyhood loneliness, by which he means the reasons girls don't feel lonely in the same way. Citing the research of sociologist Nancy Chodorow, among others, Pollack contends that boys experience a *forced* separation from their mothers, often at the hand of the mothers themselves, sooner and more completely than girls. Cultural values pressure the boy to develop his masculinity, to become more "manly." This process involves the boy's increasing attachment to, and identification with, his father, which the culture assumes will occur *only if* he achieves separation from the mother, both physically and emotionally. Donald Capps draws on Pollack to suggest that a boy's perceived loss of his mother's love lies at the root of male melancholia in adulthood: "Pollack wonders: What would happen to girls if they were assumed to need to separate emotionally from their mothers? Would we not assume that this would likely be traumatic for them? And would we not want to be very certain that such separation was necessary, and that she could in fact 'survive' this separation emotionally?" (Capps 2001, 151).

Capps points out that, in the case of boys, those assumptions and sensitivities remain absent. In fact, with boys we assume that separation must occur but that they will be able to handle it emotionally so that it does not become traumatic (151). We thus minimize boys' difficulty in separating from their first love, which girls, because they are expected to become like their mothers, do not have to undergo nearly as early or completely. Moreover, we assume that "only the 'pampered' boy will be unable to separate naturally and easily" (151). For this reason, those boys who struggle with separation more acutely are thought to be less than fully "boy." They get dubbed "sissies" or "momma's boys," and neither they themselves nor their parents welcome that. As Pollack describes it in another book, "The worst insult a boy can experience is to be called 'wimp,' 'fag,' homo,' or 'wuss'" (Pollack 2001, 6). Widespread concern over that possibility, of raising what many call "momma's boys," results in society placing inappropriate demands on a boy to separate from his mother, which parents unknowingly encourage.

While the push toward separation may begin in early grade school years, boys often experience it more acutely in their early adolescent years, when they are no longer "babies" who require their parents' constant care but are not yet adolescents yearning for more freedom and space. Reflecting on his own early adolescence, when he moved from elementary to middle school, a young man named Taylor, age seventeen, sums up what many of his peers have experienced too: "When I was younger we were a lot closer. My mom's a teacher, so in elementary school she was always around. Then I got thrust into middle school, and that's when it hit. I felt abandoned, I guess. Parents seem to abandon boys at that age because we're supposed to be independent and manly and things like that. It really hurts when that change happens, but I think people are unaware of it because boys are so busy trying not to show it. We try to be big and tough and stand tall. But it hurts" (Pollack 2001, 56).

We must not miss Taylor's point. It is not parents' insensitivity or inattention that leads them to "thrust" boys toward separation prematurely, but rather their attention and sensitivity to what they have learned, and believe, is *appropriate* for boyhood. Parents unknowingly embrace and perpetuate inaccurate and destructive myths of boyhood. This often stems from how parents were raised themselves, and also from having been convinced that good parenting requires the same of them. But ironically, pushing the son "out of the nest" typically feels unnatural, especially for mothers, meaning that they go against what their intuition tells them and, usually, what they desire themselves. I do not seek here to engage in "mother blame" but only to raise awareness of a trend perpetuated by societal norms that both mothers and fathers buy into and that often trump a mother's own sense about what is best for her boy. Even so, this push toward premature independence, which Taylor describes as "abandonment," gives rise to a greater likelihood of separation trauma among boys and thus to eventual boyhood loneliness. As James E. Dittes describes the boy's experience, "It's as though we were haunted by the devastating psychological separation forced on a boy but not a girl. Girls may and must identify with their mothers. But to rescue and mold his identity as a male, a boy has to put distance between himself and the one who gave him life, his mother. A man has had to choose between maleness and intimacy with life" (Dittes 1996, 11).

Of course, separating from one's mother is not unique to boys. Girls also must separate as part of normal development, if typically less quickly and completely. Boys' separation has an added wrinkle, however, that often complicates the experience even more. As a boy separates from his first love and seeks increasingly to identify with men, he encounters confusing social messages concerning what being a man should mean. On the one hand, the dominant culture encourages a boy to believe that men are strong, tough, aggressive, and self-sufficient. On the other hand, a boy learns from that same dominant culture that twenty-first-century men should be vulnerable, sensitive, calm, and relational. Boys learn too that a man's success relates directly to the number of hours he works, the amount of money he makes, and how much power and influence he wields, all of which require their own kind of toughness and unwavering resolve. Yet simultaneously, boys receive the conflicting message that a man (particularly a father) should be more available to his family, more involved in his children's lives, and more relaxed at home, where he should spend longer periods of time. These mixed messages on manhood, which the boy recognizes as contradictory, add a layer of complexity and confusion to his already lonely state.

The Pressure to Get Big and to Score

Though perhaps not to the extent that girls experience it, boys also learn early in life that they are judged, and for that reason they judge themselves, according to how physically attractive and fit their bodies are. More often than not, tied to this is the boy's desire to be "big." After all, "bigness" lies at the heart of being a real and successful man, the value of which the boy has learned and subsequently embraced as his ideal destiny. Thus begins the boy's pursuit of bigness, which often lasts a lifetime. Dittes notes that it is as though boys are "taught one mantra with which to address all ills: 'just as soon as I get bigger'— an incessant conjuring we sounded for our first ten years" (11). Bigness and related qualities thus become "the panacea for all ills" (11). Eventually bigness pertains to biceps, bank accounts, job titles, cars, and one's penis, among other things (11–12). After all, to be big is to be a man.

A 2002 documentary film entitled *Body Image for Boys* confirms the importance boys place on their physical appearance and bodies. Young boys, including early adolescents, aspire to have large muscles and strong bodies because they recognize that with these come power, influence, popularity, and success—the marks of manhood. A seventeen-year-old boy, Dylan, speaks for many boys when he says, "If I get in shape, if I develop a more attractive body, I'd be more popular. It's like the way life is around here, what society shows you. It's a problem to be naturally skinny like me. You're not as athletic or muscular or attractive; you're not as good as the other kids are" (Pollack 2001, 302). Increasing numbers of boys, seemingly feeling the kinds of pressures Dylan describes, strive for the ideal body at younger ages and do so at great risk. They ingest and inject vitamins, steroids, and other performance-enhancing supplements and drugs at alarming rates. For some sports, like gymnastics and wrestling, boys starve themselves to cut weight while simultaneously exerting more and more physical effort. Boys also spend increasingly large blocks of time working out at gyms, and on courts and playing fields, seeking affirmation and adulation from peers, girls, parents, and other adults. After all, these assure the boy that he's on his way to becoming a man.

Dev, a seventeen-year-old high school wrestler from the suburban South, illustrates what is at stake for many boys with respect to their bodies, sports, and the self-esteem tied to both. Reflecting on his own experience, he says:

> I do think guys, like girls, really do care about how they look. I don't want to be fat again, so I exercise a lot. I spend at least four hours a day exercising. I would have to say that most of my friends are worried about being too fat and about being too thin. The thin guys should take creatine to build up, and the fat guys should stay off the steaks. There's this huge, three-hundred-pound guy who looks like a whale. We make fun of him all the time. He's got to want to be thin. Steroids are available but nobody really takes them. There was this senior who graduated last year. I hear he took steroids. He was pretty big, pretty bulked up. Guys use a lot of creatine also. It makes your muscles pop out. You look more powerful. You look better. . . .
>
> Guys are always trying to prove themselves by scoring with girls, or winning athletically. In weigh-ins, you're in your underwear and

looking at the other guys. It's all joking, but it's like, I have a bigger dick than you. That's definitely something. It's even down to that level. I think that's the quintessential level. How big your dick is and how many girls you get on the weekends. I want to be healthy in mind and body. Some would say that what I'm doing now with my body is not healthy. I disagree, because now that I have higher self-esteem, I can achieve more. (Pollack 2001, 305–6)

At what may be unprecedented rates, today's boys prize getting bigger and achieving more as a means to feeling better about themselves. Making those their chief goals at younger and younger ages, even as they embrace them as marks of manhood, boys seek after them with abandon, regardless of the risks or costs.

To be sure, boys' involvement in sports and fitness is not necessarily destructive. To the contrary, great benefits may be found in these activities. Sports promote comradeship, collaborative work to achieve shared goals, and even a special kind of emotional connection and demonstration. As Pollack notes, "For many boys, sports are a form of intimacy and a way to be honest," as they are "a theater for the unfettered expression of [boys'] feelings, a place where it's OK to be spirited, emotive, passionate" (Pollack 1998, 272). Where else do we see boys, and later on, men, hugging one another, shedding tears, and even patting one another on the butt as a sign of affection? Sports may also help a boy learn to lose in healthy and appropriate ways. A boy's involvement in sports demonstrates that hard work and talent do not always bring the success he hopes will come, and as a result they prepare him for coping with disappointment, both presently and in the future. All of this may foster the kind of self-awareness Robert Dykstra advocates, which remains essential for boys' spirituality. Furthermore, sports and physical activity help prevent childhood obesity, a growing epidemic, and are promoters of good general health and well-being. In and of themselves, sports and physical fitness are good for boys.

For many boys, however, the extent to which broad segments of society make the requirements to be successful at these activities marks of "maleness" and "manhood"—namely, big, strong, and fit bodies along with an undaunted competitive edge—adds yet another layer of complication to the already mixed messages boys receive. Now manhood (and thus boyhood) requires even more time and energy than previously thought. It requires working long hours to be successful, which for many men now includes extended time away from home on business travel. It demands that time be spent with family at home, meaning men must work and travel yet be at home and available. Finally, it necessitates looking a certain way and excelling in certain activities, which include working out to sculpt the manly body and, perhaps, being good at a manly kind of sport. As one fourteen-year-old boy, Chandler, put it, "A guy is supposed to be strong, tall, and fast and have the qualities of an ideal athlete. At the same time, he's supposed to be smart. He's expected to be nearly perfect" (Pollack 2001, 297). Anything less means being neither a real man nor one on his way to that destiny.

Historically, the premium placed on body shape and fitness has been the burden of girls and women. Until recently, boys and men were not supposed to worry about their appearance, and to do so was deemed to be less than masculine (297). Times have changed, however, and now boys and men, like girls and women, feel the pressure to "look good" at increasingly younger ages. Now women *and* men, girls *and* boys enlist the services of dieticians, personal trainers, and even plastic surgeons at unprecedented rates. The cynical among us may say that boys and men are finally getting a taste of their own medicine. They now merely feel the pressure and pain that they, in large part, have been responsible for inflicting on girls and women in a society that expects so much of them in the way of physical beauty. Yet, as the proverbial saying goes, two wrongs don't make a right. The pressures to look a certain way, to excel at particular pursuits, and to have the energy and desire for both places a heavy burden on boys and men just as it has on girls and women. Tragically, it has the potential to destroy them all. It should come as no surprise that the documentary film on boys' body image cites both eating disorders and exercise addiction for adolescent boys as being on the rise, conditions that historically have affected girls and women at alarming rates and something we as a society should find ways to correct. This rise in boys' eating and exercise disorders provides more evidence for the pressures boys begin to recognize, if not to feel themselves, well before adolescence, as they are pushed further away from the things of "girls" and ever closer to the ideals of manhood. And, of course, neither boys nor girls should have to bear the burdens of socially sanctioned but unrealistic expectations.

Confusion about the "Boy Code" and Its Demands

In Pollack's terms, a boy's need to adhere to the "Boy Code" drives his internal struggle. This code consists of the values and rules society sets and boys adopt, which then influence their feelings and behaviors. The Boy Code may be summarized with four stereotypes of male ideals and modes of behavior: (1) males should be independent, strong, invulnerable, and stoic; (2) males are naturally macho and full of bravado, daring, high-energy, aggressive, and even violent; (3) males must achieve power and status, and simultaneously avoid shame, at all costs; and (4) males do not express thoughts, feelings, or ideals that are "feminine," including dependence, warmth, and empathy (Pollack 1998, 24). Pollack describes the boy's struggle:

> While the Boy Code, with all of its various rules about masculinity, still tells this generation of boys that they must act in the traditionally masculine ways . . . society is also constantly broadcasting messages today about all the ways men should reform their behavior and attitudes so that they will be more emotionally appealing and better attuned to the needs of girls and women. Society seeks men who are more sensitive, men willing to help perform housework and become involved in child care, men who are more socially adept, nurturing, and empathic. These conflicting outlooks produce much soul searching and, at times, a great deal of personal pain for boys. Indeed, who wants to grow into a man if society is not clear about what a man should be? (51)

Similarly, Dittes describes boys' reactions to the mixed messages they receive and the internal dilemmas that follow: "It's as though we [as boys are] relentlessly cheered on by culture to emulate titanic heroes of great prowess and glamour, but heroes conjured out of fantasy and never reachable" (Dittes 1996, 11).

Each of these descriptions, which capture typical boyhood experience, suggests not only that boys feel lonely but also that their loneliness often comes laced with confusion over what may lie beyond it. If a boy begins to feel lonely as he separates from his mother and seeks after men to emulate, then the multitude of mixed messages and standards concerning who those men really are and what they should be like only adds a layer of emotional unrest to one who has become more vulnerable and afraid than we suppose. Often the lonely boy feels anxious, fearful, confused, and distrustful about himself, including not only who he is but also what he should strive to become. In Hanson's words, "He's looking in the spring / looking for another start / Trying to find the switch / And turn on the light in the dark."

THE LONELY BOY'S RISKS

Boyhood loneliness brings with it risks, some of which have already been identified. Lonely boys feel not only alone but afraid, anxious, confused, and distrustful. They also feel depressed, have fragile self-esteem, and are angry and sometimes violent. In adolescence, they are four to six times more likely than girls to commit suicide, which illustrates further the depth, and perhaps the duration, of their struggles (Pollack 1998, xxiii).

Silent Suffering

To make matters worse, much of boys' suffering occurs in silence. A boy learns early in life that "he must hide his feelings and silence his fears," which means he typically lacks the coping strategies that arise from working with one's feelings in more deliberate ways. As Kindlon and Thompson characterize this, the boy has "a limited emotional repertoire" with which to manage conflict, adversity, and change in his life (2000, 4). This becomes the boy's lot because most societies make normative the notion that boys should not make themselves vulnerable by sharing their true feelings. That, in turn, dictates how parents raise their boys and the norms families embrace in the home.

I have already mentioned parents' propensity to buy into inaccurate societal myths about boyhood and various misunderstandings of boys' experience that follow. Professional educators working with kids outside the home often accept and spread the same boyhood myths. Consider a junior high school principal's perspective on boys. During orientation for the new school year, the principal asked parents of girls to be especially mindful of the role competition plays in forming cliques and to actively discourage the girls from doing so. Yet the social struggles of boys were dismissed by the same principal, who said, "We don't worry so much about boys at this age because they are a lot more resilient and straightforward about it all. . . . They get mad, they push each other around a little to blow off steam, and then it's done. They don't hold grudges" (6).

The principal's perspective may identify accurately the way many boys behave. Boys often do seem more resilient and straightforward in their approach to conflict and struggle. They also tend to evidence an ability to "move on" rather quickly and completely following a conflict experience. I can recall my own experiences in boyhood when a friend and I would argue—sometimes heatedly—and perhaps stop playing together, only to pick up where we left off a few hours or, perhaps, a few days, later. The problem, however, which centers precisely on what the principal misses in his commentary on boys, is that boys' behaviors do not always reflect how they are feeling. Again, boys tend to suppress their feelings and silence their fears. One way to do both is to behave in a way that seems very different from how one truly feels, to compensate for feelings that one may sense are not warranted or welcome. I can recall feeling devastated over arguments with boyhood pals, whether our "falling out" lasted a few days or a few minutes, and the devastation was magnified in instances when I sensed two or more boys were allied against me. I am convinced that other boys feel the same way. In light of that, the principal's perspective perpetuates a myth about boyhood which results in adults' failure to recognize that boys, like girls, experience great pain and suffering over social conflicts, being rejected or ostracized, or in some way not measuring up to the ideal of the larger group.

School Struggles

Consider also what Pollack calls the "systemic" difficulties boys face in school. In recent years much attention has been paid to making school classroom environments more fair and equitable for girls. Efforts have been made to correct the historical "silencing of girls' voices" in the classroom, which has followed from a lack of attention to their unique developmental and learning needs (Kindlon and Thompson 2000, 23; Pollack 1998, 233). Surely, fairness and equity in classrooms remain necessary and important goals, as does meeting girls' educational and emotional needs. We know the injustice many girls have experienced, particularly in school, feeling frustrated and hindered by environments not conducive to their learning. Fortunately, attention to girls' needs has helped them feel more comfortable in school and perform better. Consider that whereas twenty years ago more boys went to college than girls, currently among high school graduates 67 percent of females go on to college as compared to 58 percent of males. Likewise, while historically girls have performed below boys in science and math, girls have closed that gap substantially in recent years, showing improvement in both subjects. Moreover, and perhaps most striking, research indicates that girls are more confident in their abilities to learn than are boys, and girls more actively seek to develop their careers beyond high school. In the 1990s, a U.S. Department of Education study found that more girls than boys planned to pursue graduate or professional studies, and the majority of master's degrees (59 percent) are now awarded to women, while the percentage of men engaging in graduate and doctoral studies declines each year (Pollack 1998, 235). Efforts to meet girls' and women's needs in the classroom have borne much fruit.

Regrettably, the "unchallenged assumption" continues to be that if girls have struggled in school boys have not, such that while we have recognized and attended to girls' difficulties in school we have assumed boys are breezing through (Kindlon and Thompson 2000, 23). But a variety of research, statistics, and clinicians' experiences in therapy with boys and men tell another story (23). Upon closer examination we discover that elementary schools in particular are not always perceived by boys to be "friendly" to them either. As Kindlon and Thompson note:

> Grade school is largely a feminine environment, populated predominately by women teachers and authority figures, that seems rigged against boys, against the higher activity level and lower level of impulse control that is normal for boys. As one disappointed first-grade boy remarked unhappily at the end of his first day of school:

'You can't *do* anything!' The trouble wasn't really that he couldn't do anything, of course, but that everything he loved to do—run, throw, wrestle, climb—was outlawed in the classroom. In this setting a boy's experience of school is as a thorn among roses; he is a different, lesser, and sometimes frowned-upon presence, and he knows it. (23–24)

Schools typically do not attend to boys' unique learning styles, which typically differ from those of girls, and educators fail to recognize that boys tend to develop abilities for attention span, impulse control, verbal communication, reading comprehension, and sedentary learning—among other "classroom standards"—later than girls. Moreover, due to the lack of male teachers in most elementary and middle school settings in particular, boys receive "an early and faulty message," namely, "that education and learning are primarily for girls and women" (Pollack 1998, 232).

Boys also perceive that male teachers understand them better than female teachers. As a sixth-grader, Alan revealed to his therapist what the authors of *Raising Cain* believe remains common among boys. The topic of conversation was the boy's feelings about having women and men teachers, and whether the boy preferred one over the other. The therapist asked, "Is it easier for boys to have men teachers?" Alan responded, "Yeah. They understand us more or something. They understand what we are trying to say." The therapist followed up with another question, "What do women have trouble understanding about boys?" Alan's response was, "They don't like to be gotten mad at" (Kindlon and Thompson 2000, 27–28). The authors take this opportunity to make the point that for many boys "being yelled at" is a common experience. As one school librarian—a woman—put it, "Adults often feel justified in yelling at boys because they are so 'bad' all the time" (28).

Feelings of Inferiority

Erik H. Erikson detailed why this perspective and treatment proves so destructive, particularly for the early adolescent child. For nearly six decades, Erikson's "life cycle theory" has been instrumental in helping us understand the relationship between psychological development and socialization, particularly as concerns one's self-understanding. He posited eight stages of a person's life, each of which involves a "critical psychological conflict" or "crisis" that must be "resolved unceasingly" if the human being is "to remain psychologically alive" (Erikson 1959/1980, 52). He terms the phenomenon a crisis because it involves a tension of sorts between opposing forms of psychic energy that meet at any given life stage. Out of this tension, which both physiological factors and one's sociocultural milieu influence, arises a conflict that the person must resolve. This suggests that a crisis denotes a "turning point," a potentially "radical change in perspective" or "a crucial period of increased vulnerability and heightened potential" that remains the source of both strength and maladjustment throughout life (1968/1994, 96). More specifically, during each of the life cycle stages a conflict arises "between a positive, growth-oriented strength and a negative growth-impending weakness," and healthy growth requires that the individual obtain "a preponderance of the designated strength over the weakness, though the weakness is never entirely overcome" (Capps 1983, 648). In other words, the "ratio of development" should be in favor of the growth-oriented strength if psychological health is to be realized and maintained (Erikson 1995, 596).

Erikson describes the particular crisis of early adolescence as one of "industry versus inferiority." This suggests that the kid's conflict involves the pursuit of being useful, seeking to make things and contribute to shared goals and also gaining proficiency in what the kid has identified as the wider culture's more valued commodities and technologies. Moreover, this is a time when kids, largely through formal education, are presented with opportunities to become proficient in both cognitive and social skills. A boy feels a sense of "industry" when he has, more or less, met the goals of his pursuit, sensing that he is participating in the adult world in a significant and ultimately valued way (Erikson 1959/1980, 91). Conversely, when his goals are not met, the boy may experience feelings of "inadequacy" or "inferiority," sensing that he will never be any good (91–92).

Perhaps Erikson's most telling statement with regard to this life cycle stage is that, for the early adolescent, self-understanding—which surely relates to our spiritual quality of self-awareness—may be summed up as follows: "I am what I learn." By this Erikson means that learning more and mastering the culture's commodities and technologies, so prized by the adult world, fosters the early adolescent's growing sense of self. Kids of this age have discovered that in order to be worthwhile, important, and successful, people must eventually be good at particular activities and pursuits, namely, those which at least approximate what thriving adults are good at. A kid's "industry" "provides a token sense of participation in the real world of adults" and thus informs his sense of worth (88).

Learning the Wrong Things about Boyhood

Erikson provides an important perspective in that, as has been discussed, the principal contexts for a kid's developing sense of industry, namely, the family and school environments, are packed with sources of frustration, confusion, shame, anxiety, loneliness, and silent suffering. Boys in particular find this to be the case. Both the family circle and school setting tend to perpetuate myths about boyhood that "teach" boys destructive attitudes, self-understandings, values, and uses of the commodities and technologies they seek to master. If indeed a boy at this life stage understands himself in terms of "I am what I learn," then it becomes all the more crucial that what he learns fosters healthy selfhood, relational development, and, as will be discussed further in the next chapter, a nurturing view of God. It may just be the case that we are *teaching* boys to be lonely when we could be teaching them something else. We could be teaching them solitude, the embrace of loneliness that, when understood and cultivated, may inform self-transcendence—and which surely includes a growing sense of himself as connected with others, of healthy relationships with those others, and, certainly, of communion with God.

By discussing boys' experiences in schools I am not suggesting either that all schools and teachers harm boys or that boys have exclusively negative experiences in school. Many educators and schools make noble efforts to provide all children with the skills and learning they need to flourish. Yet the data are telling. They confirm that many boys struggle in school unnecessarily, for reasons that arise out of a lack of awareness concerning their needs. As Pollack describes it:

> By looking at boys in a narrow way and failing to recognize the gentle, creative, empathic sides of many boys, I believe some teachers—though they may not consciously intend it—can seriously encumber the emotional and scholastic development of boys in their classes who do not necessarily comply with society's old stereotyped gender rules about how they should behave, learn, and grow. Unwitting as it may be, many teachers strictly enforce the Boy Code and suppress any boys who try to buck it. (Pollack 1998, 243)

In light of the data cited, and recalling the junior high principal's perspective in particular—which I too believe represents the majority view in American society—Andrew Gold's recollection of school is particularly poignant: "His mother and father said what a lovely boy / We'll teach him what we learned / Ah yes just what we learned / We'll dress him up warmly and / We'll send him to school / It'll teach him how to fight / To be nobody's fool / Oh what a lonely boy."

I draw attention to boys' struggles, both at home and in school, because the suffering of many boys is profound, many-sided, and unrecognized. Boys experience great pain over the conflicts and disappointments they face. They feel hurt over the lack of attention their sufferings receive and the widespread minimizing of those struggles, particularly by adults in whose care they live and learn. Furthermore, when their struggles are recognized, boys often wind up wounded over their inability, and lack of encouragement, to share their pain with others. As Calvin Branford, a fifteen-year-old boy, explains, "It's really hard being a guy because you're really expected not to talk about your feelings. You've got to deal with everything yourself. With girls, everybody expects they'll go off and talk to somebody. When you're a guy you're really not allowed to do that. I guess it's pretty hard being a guy because there are so many things a normal person would probably do, but you're just not expected to!" (Pollack 1998, 20).

As an adolescent, Calvin surely faces struggles and hardships that younger boys may not. Yet being expected not to talk about your feelings, and thus facing struggles alone, is a boyhood pattern put in place long before adolescence. Calvin speaks for many boys when noting the silent suffering he has endured. As Michael Lewis describes this silencing process, "From the moment a child enters into [the] social network, the rules, values, and standards of the primary caregiver, family, and culture start to be imposed. Certain behaviors are rewarded and others punished. Children are the recipients, both directly and indirectly, of standards and rules from the beginning of life" (Lewis 1992, 91). This means "emotional isolation has become virtually a reflex by the time a boy reaches adolescence. He has learned to deny his emotional neediness and routinely to disguise his feelings. Intimidated by the constant threat of humiliation presented by the culture of cruelty and the ensuing erosion of trust, boys strike a psychological bargain—a bad one—namely, that they'd rather hide out than take any more hits. The more pressure a boy feels, the more deeply he withdraws" (Kindlon and Thompson 2000, 142).

Therefore, while the boy's "first denial" of his feelings may be inevitable, as it follows from his taboo sexual desire for his mother, his subsequent denials, which seem to increase with age, are rooted in his desire to be "a good boy." When a boy's behavior could be characterized as "bad," "obstinate," "hyperactive," "reckless," "selfish," "insensitive" or "aloof," perhaps the reason is that he seeks merely to live up to the expectations for boyhood he learned early in life from the cacophony of voices around him, expectations that remain beyond reach and, thus, that perpetuate his loneliness.

So whether we are speaking of cliques in schools, a boy's place in his family, membership on a team or in a club, or any other context for boys to experience pain, loss, or disappointment, boys may not be as "resilient" or "straightforward" as we think. In fact, just the opposite may be true. Boys have needs similar to girls when it comes to acceptance, affirmation, support, encouragement, and being recognized for who they are and for what they deem important. Even so, boys' struggles typically go unnoticed, and if noticed, they tend to be minimized if not dismissed. This leads a boy to feel frustrated, sad, anxious, and lonely. As Hanson sums it up, "And at the end of the day / There is no one to hold his hand / There is no one to understand."

BOYHOOD SHAME AND SELF-LOSS

This perception that no one understands them informs two additional risks of boyhood loneliness: pervasive *shame* and its corollary, a *loss of self*. Shame may be the feeling most basic to boyhood loneliness. A boy is ashamed to feel different from the way he learns he is supposed to feel. Perhaps his first sense of shame comes with having to separate from his parents, and particularly his mother, before he feels ready or wants to do so. This shame stems from wanting, often longing for, a closeness to and connection with his mother (and father) that the boy once enjoyed, where he felt safe, secure, supported, important, and free to be himself. Even though they want these things desperately, sometimes—perhaps more often than not—early adolescent boys keep them in abeyance as they shun their parents' offers of hugs or other displays of affection; their attention to his school work and involvement in sports or other interests; and other shows of concern for his welfare, such as whether and how often he must check in by phone, where he may ride his bike, go fishing, or visit friends, and whether or not he may stay out past dark in his neighborhood. The closeness, connection, and concern he shuns are precisely what he has learned is inappropriate, akin to being a girl, and surely not what it means to be a "big and real boy" en route to being a "big and real man."

Moreover, a boy's shame tends to intensify each time he can no longer fend off his emotions and he demonstrates his vulnerabilities. If a boy voices tender feelings, as infrequent as that may be, he knows he's not meeting what people expect of him, including his peers, parents, teachers, and other adults. If he happens to cry, or to teeter on the verge of ceasing to be "tough," "independent," and "strong," he becomes even more ashamed of himself because he knows he isn't measuring up to the Boy Code. His peers, parents, teachers, or significant others, most of whom have likely been raised to embrace the same Boy Code, make it clear that when he shows vulnerability he has failed to be a real boy, which is to say he is acting like a sissy, a wimp, or the like, and certainly not like his father, whom he has come to idealize.

In his book *Fatherless Sons: Healing the Legacy of Loss*, psychotherapist Jonathan Diamond recounts a conversation he had with a neighbor, who told Diamond that his ten-year-old nephew's father had just died:

> When I asked him how his nephew was doing, he said that it was tough on him but he was impressed at how well the boy was holding up. He told me they had just come back from the funeral that morning and how proud he was of his nephew because he "never lost it." "The kid teared up a bit," my neighbor continued. "I thought he was going to lose it a couple of times, but he held it together. He's tough, just like his old man. He's going to be okay, that one."

I fumbled for something to say that might make the boy's tears more acceptable to his uncle. I told him that in my experience, it was good for children to cry at times like these, because then it doesn't come back up on them later. But it didn't matter what I said. The men in this family were simply trying as best they could to come to terms with the devastating loss they'd just suffered, and this boy, like most male children his age, knew what was expected of him. His feelings about his father's death, dutifully cast aside at the beginning of his young life, will not resurface until years later. (Diamond 2006, 21)

Psychologist Gershen Kaufman notes the kind of damage that boys have done to them when they are told, whether explicitly or implicitly, to cast their unacceptable feelings aside. When persons perceive they frequently disappoint someone significant, and especially a parent, this "immerses the self in feeling inherently deficient" and thus ashamed (Kaufman 1992, 22). Consequently, the Boy Code inflicts a twofold kind of damage. It promotes an early onset of shamefulness which, in turn, it then perpetuates.

Lest we forget or somehow minimize its pain, Pollack provides two illustrations that help remind adults of how shame feels. The first has to do with what happens when we see someone we know walking across the street and wave at them, which serves as a way for connecting with a familiar person. When the person to whom we have waved stares our way but does not return the gesture, part of us likely assumes that she simply did not see us. We think to ourselves, "Perhaps she was deep in thought." "Maybe she could not see me because of the sun's glare." Or, "It could be that she needs new glasses!" Even so, we still feel odd if not ashamed, and we will often glance around us wondering if anyone saw what happened. What we are interested in is whether we looked foolish and whether others saw it. Frequently, we respond to this scenario by wanting to "melt into the sidewalk" because we feel both isolated and humiliated (Pollack 1998, 32). We feel ashamed because we have been vulnerable, exposed, and our gesture has not been supported. Feeling as though we have looked foolish in another's eyes, we avert our own in shame.

The other illustration concerns what may happen in the workplace. We have prepared an important presentation at our supervisor's request. Following the presentation, and in the company of colleagues, the boss rejects the key points we sought to make and disparages them. We feel embarrassed, stupid, incompetent, and ashamed. We may also feel angry, mistreated, and even betrayed. But because we do not want to show our vulnerability, and risk others' responses to our vulnerability, which would only exacerbate our pain, we avoid any help offered by colleagues who reach out to us. We become emotionally disconnected from them and, perhaps, from others (33). We also become emotionally disconnected from ourselves.

While painful feelings associated with these experiences may pale in comparison to what a boy feels when he realizes he has not met the expectations of the Boy Code, these experiences confirm that shame may involve feeling so fearful of being embarrassed or humiliated that we opt to suffer in silence, all alone (33). Furthermore, unlike most girls, who may be "shame-sensitive," most boys are "shame-phobic," meaning they will do most anything to avoid shame and usually mask their shame with "a variety of behaviors that range from avoidance of dependency to impulsive action, from bravado and rage-filled outbursts to intense violence" (33). The point to stress here is that a boy feels shame that intensifies and becomes more pervasive because the Boy Code whose standards he strives to meet is not in synch with what he needs to develop appropriately. Neither does it reflect the person he truly wants and needs to become.

This suggests that related to shame, and often its result, is a loss of self. Kaufman points out that "contained in the experience of shame is the piercing awareness of ourselves as fundamentally deficient in some vital way as a human being" (Kaufmann 1992, 9). Boys who sense they are not measuring up to parents' or others' standards for boyhood begin to feel shameful in this way. They feel a lack of affirmation, not merely for what they do or refrain from doing, but for who they are. This follows from their being encouraged constantly to behave in ways that feel unnatural to them, to act in ways inconsistent with who they feel they truly are—*in their spirit*. Urged to be strong, independent, and emotionally in-check at all times, when they are not ready or able to do so, at least not to the extent typically expected, they face having to project a kind of false self, one that others may want and expect but one not reflective of their true spirit.

Kaufman says that for all people, boys included, lack of affirmation—particularly in moments of heightened vulnerability—leads one to focus on the *difference* between oneself and others, eventuating in the "invidious comparison" (69). Here one perceives that he compares unfavorably. He doesn't "stack up," because if he did he would be affirmed in who he is and what he values. This leads to the following scenario: "Rather than valuing the difference between the self and other, either we . . . feel obliged to wipe it out or we try to be all things, even things not appropriate to or congruent with the self inside of us. Beliefs, values, and practices that may be appropriate for one person transfer to another without that individual ever considering their appropriateness for himself" (69). For that reason, shame associated with a boy's socially unsanctioned feelings of vulnerability not only masks his true feelings but also his true self. He cannot accept his own feelings as being appropriate, and he cannot share them with parents, family, other adults, or close peers. Furthermore, and even more tragically, eventually boys cannot express "their genuine selves even in private" (Pollack 1998, xxvi) and thus are "turned away from their inner life" (Kindlon and Thompson 2000, 1).

Eventually many boys simply "harden" to become who they are expected to be (Pollack 1998, xxiv, xxvi). In that case, appropriate self-awareness, self-transcendence, and, as Donald Capps will discuss in his chapters, self-sufficiency, all of which tie into a boy's budding spirituality, have turned instead into painful *self-loss*. A boy's loneliness continues and deepens. If he is to recover his self—and his spirit—he must begin "trying to find the missing part." The next chapter suggests ways a boy himself might go about that and be helped by others to do so. I focus there on two resources or "allies" for lonely boys: cultivating a kind of solitude that mitigates loneliness and finding the God who promises something more.

4

Solitude and God:
A Lonely Boy's Allies

In the previous chapter I suggested that loneliness marks typical boyhood experience and that it follows from at least two common factors. First, a boy has to separate emotionally from his parents, especially his mother, and often is forced to do so prematurely, in order to become the boy society and its cultural institutions expects and values. Second, from the time he can understand them, a boy receives mixed messages concerning what both authentic boyhood and the manhood toward which he strives entail: messages from parents, teachers, other adults, peers, and most any example of mass media imaginable. These factors place the lonely boy at risk for pervasive shame and self-loss, as well as for feeling afraid, anxious, confused, distrustful, angry, violent, and lacking in self-esteem, all of which relate to, and perpetuate, his loneliness.

While loneliness may be inevitable, I suggest in this chapter that boyhood loneliness turned into *solitude* becomes the boy's ally, promoting his emotional maturity and well-being while also fostering his religious outlook. The boy's quest for solitude, which my coauthors and I associate with his need for self-transcendence, is religious in nature. It entails his embrace of the positive potentials of loneliness and helps him cultivate qualities that inform more authentic personhood—including creativity, wholeness, relationships with others, and peace and community. Yet it may also contribute to his having faith in God. As I discuss (especially drawing from my own boyhood experience), positive, nurturing, and peaceful images and understandings of God, or what I call God "portraits," foster the boy's solitude and its benefits, especially his trust in, and reliance upon, God. In fact, these kinds of God portraits further the self-transcendence tied to his budding spirituality. On the other hand, negative God portraits, especially those depicting God as harsh, unpredictable, judgmental, and wrathful, circumvent solitude and thus perpetuate loneliness. Not only that, those kinds of God portraits kill a boy's spirit. They further weaken his capacity for self-transcendence and thus for connection to the Spirit for which he strives and with which he seeks communion. This suggests that, as with solitude and perhaps as a component of it, a boy's trust in a nurturing and faithful God may keep his loneliness at bay as it nourishes his spirit. I conclude this chapter by offering for consideration four God portraits lonely boys may need and that adults, including parents, pastors, Sunday school teachers, and others with responsibilities for their spiritual lives are encouraged to provide.

SOLITUDE AND THE CAPACITY TO BE ALONE

Though inevitable and surely risky, boyhood loneliness holds potential for healthy outcomes, particularly when it leads a boy to embrace solitude. By *solitude* I mean an experience similar to what the British pediatrician and psychoanalyst D. W. Winnicott called "the capacity to be alone." Identifying this capacity as among the most important signs of emotional maturity, Winnicott characterized it as a "paradox" in that it describes the infant's or small child's ability to be alone while in the presence of another, specifically the mother or mother figure (1965, 30). Drawing from his experience in psychoanalysis, he likened this capacity to what happens to an adult in psychotherapy when she becomes comfortable sitting with the therapist in silence. She feels free to be herself with herself, without anxiety over having to fill the silence with speech. She is alone while in the presence of another.

Winnicott believed that, ideally, this capacity finds its roots in the mother-child bond, which provides a consistently secure milieu. This security provides the child with a "holding environment" that allows for developing the ability to tolerate the mother's absence, without anxiety, for longer periods of time. Influenced by the work of psychoanalyst Melanie Klein, Winnicott held that as the infant experiences the mother's nurture, provision, and security through consistent interactions, the infant "internalizes" the mother so that she, in a real sense, lives within the infant. As the child uses mental images or representations to take into himself the mother's positive qualities, she remains with the infant psychologically even when she is not physically present. In other words, since the mother has been consistently present and caring, the child learns to feel nurtured, supported, and secure when the mother is not present. The child senses that "Mother is still with me, even though she's not here right now." This internalization allows the mother to be away for increasing periods of time because the infant continues to "have" the mother with him at all times.

Winnicott thought that a child at play best illustrates this capacity to be alone. As he plays, a child becomes absorbed by his activity. In a sense, he becomes *lost* in play. Not only does he lose himself, he also loses his mother. Both move outside of the child's awareness and thus no longer exist. But when he ceases playing and returns to himself he discovers nothing has actually been lost. His mother and he remain intact. Though forgotten by the child, the mother has not abandoned him. Consequently, the child grows in his confidence "that the person who loves [him] and is therefore reliable is available and continues to be available when remembered after being forgotten" (Winnicott 1971/1989, 48). As Winnicott describes it, the capacity to be alone requires having a "good object"—by which he means the mother's positive qualities—in one's memory, so that one may "rest contented" when external stimuli are absent (32). The adult equivalent to this capacity to be alone in childhood is the ability to relax (34).

The Role of Creativity

The capacity to be alone informs the eventual embrace of solitude, by which I mean one's penchant for welcoming being alone and appreciating what it offers. Whether in childhood or adulthood, Winnicott thought that solitude is essential for discovering and maintaining one's own "personal life" or authentic self (1965, 34). He links solitude with self-discovery and self-maintenance by means of "creativity." This has less to do with producing some item or "thing" and more to do with "non-purposive being," or what children experience as they engage in play. Creativity shapes one's attitude toward the whole external world. It provides a way of living *as oneself*, so that the external world is not determinative for the internal world, and it greatly influences a person to feel that "life is worth living" (1971/1989, 65). Creativity's opposite is compliance, wherein one seeks merely to fit in with, or adapt to, what the external world demands. As Winnicott describes it, "Compliance carries with it a sense of futility for the individual and is associated with the idea that nothing matters and that life is not worth living. In a tantalizing way many individuals have experienced just enough of creative living to recognize that for most of their time they are living uncreatively, as if caught up in the creativity of someone else, or of a machine" (65). This suggests that creativity, or "non-purposive being," is solitude's companion. The capacity to be alone, which may become the ability to embrace solitude, creates a space for creativity to do its ongoing work. Creativity's work informs and maintains a personal life of integrity, which lies at the core of experiencing life as a true self.

Solitude and Our Brain

Religious thinkers, mystics, and artists, among others, have known the value of solitude for centuries. They have made us aware of the connection between solitude and personhood, creativity, wholeness, faith in and relationship to the Divine, peace, and life in community. Yet in recent years, modern brain science too has found that people need solitude. In fact, scientists now believe that proper neurological development and lasting health require solitude. As psychiatrist Daniel J. Siegel explains, "Solitude is an essential experience for the mind to organize its own processes and create an internal state of resonance" (1999, 235). Solitude prompts one to focus inwardly, to attend to one's true self, and to "alter its constraints by directly reducing the input from interactions with others" (235). Siegel goes as far as saying that we must recognize and respect a person's need for solitude, which alternates with the need to feel more of a connection to the external world, because solitude allows the mind "to 'heal' itself" (Siegel, 235). Along with our emotive and surely spiritual need for solitude, then, we are also physiologically predisposed toward it. This need is "hardwired" into our brain, and our cognitive well-being requires that we attend to it.

The Problems of Overcompliance to External Influences

In *Solitude: A Return to the Self,* British psychiatrist Anthony Storr notes that Winnicott believed that many of his patients' problems stemmed from the lack of ability to reduce external influences on the self, particularly the influence of other persons. His patients were trying "to live in ways which were expected of them, or which pleased others, or which were designed not to offend others" (Storr 1988, 20). Particularly telling is that many personal problems were said to follow from having learned to be "over-compliant" *as children* with respect to others' expectations. At a very early age, the self had become "false," based not upon the person's own authentic feelings and needs but on what was believed to be best for others. When this happens, a person eventually feels that his life lacks meaning and authenticity, and rather than seeing the world as a place where his needs can be discovered and met, he seeks instead to adjust his needs to its prescriptions (20–21).

Solitude Is Not Separation or Isolation

As Robert Dykstra has noted in an earlier book, solitude must not be confused with separation or isolation. One can be all alone, like a prisoner in solitary confinement, and not experience a sense of solitude (Dykstra 2001, 23). Conversely, one can be with others, living in connection to them in meaningful relationships, and even be in physical proximity to them, and yet still experience solitude. The distinction lies in solitude's embrace of being alone *while still remaining connected to others*. In solitude we relish the opportunity to tune in to our personal inner life as we resist the external influences bombarding us—those which encourage the reign of another, false, self. As Donald Capps puts it, solitude must not be confused with "a defiant declaration of one's capacity to go it alone" (1995a, 51). Instead, solitude recognizes and embraces one's occasional need to be alone *in order to* remain joined with others in meaningful relationships.

Theologian Paul Tillich gets at the distinction by differentiating between "essential aloneness" (solitude) and "existential estrangement" (loneliness). He claims that the English language has wisely sensed and differentiated between two ways of being alone. The word *loneliness* expresses "the pain of being alone," while the word *solitude* expresses "the glory of being alone" (Tillich 1963, 17–18). The latter is an expression of the human being's complete self-centeredness, by which Tillich means an appropriate and essential focus on the self, which has both positive and negative potential. Positively, this self-centeredness, when joined by love, empowers the individual to take part in the world "without limits," meaning that one has the capacity to engage the world and others in it without the fear of rejection. This state recalls the biblical notion that "perfect love casts out fear; for fear has to do with punishment" (1 John 4:18). In more psychological terms, a healthy sense of self (centeredness) frees the self to engage in the work of living without the kinds of limits it places on itself when fearful of being abandoned. Calling abandonment one of the most feared kinds of punishment, Tillich concludes that we ultimately find it "intolerable."

The negative potential of this self-centeredness, which results in "existential estrangement," follows from the individual, in his loneliness, being driven to participate in life and the world by "surrendering" his lonely self to the "collective" (Tillich 1957, 72). The "collective" refers to the dominant group's will, norms, and self-definitions, which depart from an individual's own but are nevertheless imposed on him against his desires. Among the problems with the "collective" is that it consists of other individuals who have surrendered themselves in the same manner. All of them live life looking for communion with others but cannot find it. Each individual lacks the ability for solitude because she has surrendered herself (72). Tillich recognized that true relationships, or what he terms "communion," require solitude, which suggests that solitude lies at the heart of a shared life (71). It necessarily precedes and informs a life of true selfhood—but also a life of true communion, with others and with God.

Solitude and Hope

In *Agents of Hope: A Pastoral Psychology*, Capps points out that living with a sense of hope also requires solitude. In order to hope, a person must be confident, that is, nonanxious, about waiting for someone or something that has yet to come. This confidence comes from having acquired the capacity to be alone, which, again, finds its roots in experiences of having "internalized" the mother figure so that she remains psychologically present even when physically absent. Without this confidence, one feels separated, abandoned, and lonely—without hope that the loved one will return. Solitude prompts hope because it requires that we have already figured out sufficiently how to "internalize the object of our desire . . . [which] is 'out there' and 'in here' at one and the same time" (Capps 1995a, 51). As we internalize what we desire—what we hope for—we make it part of ourselves so that we live with it at all times. In theological terms, to embrace solitude indicates that we have learned to live nonanxiously in both the "already" and the "not yet."

Although Winnicott describes solitude most often as an achievement of infancy, meaning it begins in early life with the mother-infant relationship and with the infant's capacity to internalize the mother and thus keep her present, solitude may also be discovered later. In fact, the capacity to be alone and to embrace solitude may be thought of in at least two ways: as occurring in infancy and thus becoming "the foundation on which sophisticated aloneness is built" or as "a highly sophisticated phenomenon" that a child discovers in school age or beyond (Winnicott 1965, 30). This suggests that, in a similar way, some persons begin to embrace solitude in infancy, though surely this capacity becomes more sophisticated in time. For others, though, solitude may be a much later achievement, occurring in later childhood or, perhaps, even adulthood. Regardless of when a person develops this capacity, childhood remains the ideal time for cultivating solitude and its benefits. Children must be helped to learn how to live in a manner that enriches their inner life and encourages their ability to embrace their own will, norms, and self-definitions, especially in the face of external "threats" that seek merely to have them comply with the "collective," the dominant group who, in the case of boys, imposes an impossible and utterly destructive Boy Code. A boy should be encouraged to be appropriately *self*-centered, a quality that joins with his self-awareness, self-transcendence, and, as Donald Capps will discuss in the next two chapters, self-sufficiency to nourish and sustain his spirit and spiritual life. Without this self-centered focus, a boy tends to lose his hope and his self.

I am not suggesting that his own life should become the boy's exclusive focus, or that it alone holds value. But neither should that life be sacrificed merely for the sake of what others value, especially when many of those values contribute to a boy's loneliness and loss of self. Reckless or coerced self-sacrifice does not prompt self-transcendence, but rather self-destruction. While all persons require solitude, and while adults should encourage it for both boys and girls, early adolescent boys stand in particular need of its benefits. For reasons already cited, they often live lonely lives marked by fear, anxiety, confusion, distrust, fragile self-esteem, anger, violence, shame, and silent suffering. As a result, they live with a great deal of risk to their spirit and spiritual life.

THE LONELY AND LONGING EARLY ADOLESCENT BOY

To the extent a boy can develop and enrich his capacity for solitude, he may turn his loneliness into an ally. Far from being harmful, when loneliness becomes solitude it enriches a boy's life and promotes emotional maturity. I now want to discuss further why early adolescent boys may be particularly lonely and thus in dire need of solitude. My own boyhood experience suggests that early adolescent boys may benefit from being presented with, and eventually accepting, particular understandings of God as a means for assuaging their loneliness and cultivating their solitude, thereby promoting their self-transcendence and spiritual lives.

Psychiatrist Harry Stack Sullivan, who practiced psychoanalysis and trained others in the same during the early to mid-twentieth century, was among the first to pay close attention to the period of early adolescence. As part of his "interpersonal theory" of psychiatry, Sullivan held that, in the case of both boys and girls, with early adolescence comes a kid's need for a new kind of intimacy with other persons, and particularly those he deems to be like himself. The "chum," as Sullivan called this newfound interest, becomes the one with whom the early adolescent discloses his most intimate and deeply held personal feelings, thoughts, and ideas (1953/1997, 245).

Typically, an early adolescent and his chum will share many things in common, including age, social status, and sex—such that boys' chums will typically be boys, and girls' chums will typically be girls. That enables the early adolescent to experience, "often for the first time, genuine love, loyalty, opportunity for self-disclosure, and intimacy" with a peer, "but in an atmosphere still uncomplicated by the lust dynamism" (Muuss 1988, 128). The emotional and physical complications of puberty have not yet begun, which suggests that the early adolescent may put the lion's share of his energy into cultivating this peer relationship without the "complications" that tend to come with intimacy during subsequent developmental periods, meaning adolescence and beyond.

Among the most valued qualities of this new relationship—this chumship—is that the early adolescent finds approval from one who values him and finds him appealing, which works against the low regard he may have for himself and believes that others have for him. Moreover, "this process of revealing virtually everything about oneself—and especially things that had previously been kept secret—can relieve the sometimes morbid, egocentric thought: 'I am quite different from everyone else'" (129). In the chum, an early adolescent finds a comrade—a kindred spirit—with whom to experience intimacy in a new way. Sullivan defines intimacy as "that type of situation involving two people which permits validation of all components of personal worth" (1953/1997, 246). In the chum, an early adolescent boy finds intimacy with one who joins him as an ally, with whom he can share himself fully and confidently, and with whom he may attempt to be most authentically the person he wants and needs to be.

The connection between this newfound comradeship and loneliness is striking. Such loneliness reaches its peak in early adolescence, when a kid's need for nurture, affirmation, and support becomes profound, and also when, particularly in the case of boys, a kid becomes increasingly aware of difficult, if not impossible, cultural norms he is expected to meet. Precisely because that need for relationship with a trusted peer, best friend, or chum *is* so powerful at this age, when the need goes unmet a kid feels intense loneliness and disconnection. This follows from the deeply social nature of persons. From the earliest moments of life, and continuing throughout the rest of it, persons need to be in relationship with others in order to thrive. Infants require touch and tenderness. Toddlers and older children need adults to share in playing and other activities. Younger school-age children need to form relationships with a wider circle of peers. Early adolescents need the chum. Finally, from adolescence on, we need maturing forms of love, sexual intimacy, and mutuality with others (Muuss 1988, 130). This relational quality of personhood recalls Tillich's view that we seek communion with others in order to be most fully ourselves.

But because early adolescents tend to locate what they need as coming from a single person, namely, the chum, much more rides on that primary relationship. When that relationship does not develop adequately, or is otherwise impaired, the boy experiences a great deal of pain and insecurity. Although younger children, adolescents, and adults may compensate for a lack in *any* given relationship of importance by making more of an emotional investment in other relationships, this may be more difficult for the early adolescent. Why? Because, in a real sense, he has put his faith entirely in a *particular* peer (the chum), whom he believes will help him fend off the loneliness that seems always to be so near. In fact, Sullivan stresses the chum's value by saying that the "quiet miracle" of this period is that one's interest in the happiness and well-being of another will rival one's interest in securing the same for oneself (Muuss, 128). As Sullivan remarks about this phenomenon:

> If you will look very closely at one of your children when he finds a chum—somewhere between eight-and-a-half and ten—you discover something very different in the relationship—namely, that your child begins to develop a real sensitivity to what matters to another person. And this is not in the sense of "what should I do to get what I want," but instead "what should I do to contribute to the happiness or to support the prestige and feeling of worth-whileness of my chum." So far as I have ever been able to discover, nothing remotely like this appears before the age of eight-and-a-half, and sometimes it appears decidedly later. (245–46)

ONE LONELY BOY'S FEAR OF GOD

Having detailed solitude's bearing on selfhood and interpersonal relationships, and also the early adolescent boy's particular need for solitude, I now turn to the relationship between a boy's loneliness/solitude and his religious outlook, particularly his view of God. My interest in this subject is deeply personal. It surely relates to an experience I had when I was eleven years old that had a profound effect on me for many years.

My Cousin Frank and His Frightening God

A distant relative in his thirties, "Frank," was what I would today call a fundamentalist Christian. He and his family lived near where my family and I moved during my sixth-grade year. Though I had never met him before, I discovered that in many ways Frank was a generous man whom I quickly came to appreciate and admire. While only a few years younger than my father, he seemed much younger to me. I now recognize that this may have been a sign of his immaturity that escaped me at the time. In any case, he seemed more to me like an older brother than one of my father's peers.

Frank gave generously of his time, seemed to enjoy having a good time, and was an avid sports enthusiast, just as I was. While I remember him liking various sports, he was particularly proficient at a game called foosball, a kind of table soccer, that was popular at the time. I had played it before myself, at a skating rink, and had watched older boys excel at it. In fact, to this day I can recall vividly the way those older boys at the skating rink could "push" and "pull," and "snap" and "pop" the sliding handles on the foosball table, sending the ball into the goal at such a quick pace that one had a hard time following it. Needless to say, I was impressed to discover Frank's foosball interest and skill, perhaps thinking that he could teach me how to push, pull, snap, and pop like the older boys I admired. Given that I was new to town and had not yet made as many friends as I wanted in my middle school or in the neighborhood, I suspect I envisioned learning how to play foosball better would be a good way to spend time during the summer between the sixth and seventh grades.

As I recall, Frank was a foosball champion of some sort, having won a series of tournaments and gaining his share of notoriety along the way. Looking back, the notoriety I picked up on may very well have been self-generated, meaning that Frank may have been nearly as adept at self-promotion as he was at playing foosball. Even so, I have vague memories (which I believe are accurate) of him having come very close at one point to being a national champion. Though his skills had diminished a bit since his "playing days," he was still outstanding, and he surely endeared himself to me as he helped me become both a bigger fan and more skillful player of this game. I recall him demonstrating on many occasions the finer points of play on the slick, top-of-the-line foosball table in his home.

For all his generosity, I eventually discovered that Frank was inflexible in a number of ways, particularly with regard to his religious views. I do not recall how or when I first became aware of this, but I know it had something to do with discussions he had about religion with my parents, some of which I overheard on more than one occasion. My parents and I were Episcopalians, and my sense, both then and now, is that Frank was suspicious of our tradition. In what may have been well-meaning attempts at enlightening all of us by sharing his own, presumably superior, theological commitments, more often than not Frank's behavior was simply off-putting and even harmful.

My Introduction to Frank's God

One talk I had with Frank, when neither of my parents was present, is particularly memorable. On that occasion Frank used words and images that I had never before heard or encountered, at least as related to my church or faith. He used words such as "antichrist," "beast," "rapture," "accept Jesus," and "saved." Though these were new to me, I got the gist of what he was saying because he linked those words with others I did understand: "be ready," "ask for forgiveness," "resist the devil," and "avoid the eternal fires of hell." Needless to say, Frank put "the fear of God" in me, literally, as he so confidently told of the antichrist's imminent reign on earth, the trials and tribulations of the rapture, and what those who follow Jesus must do not only to be "ready" for these events but to come out of them in good shape, which I soon learned is what he meant by "accepting Jesus" and "being saved."

Though that was nearly thirty years ago, I recall as if it were yesterday how terrified, confused, and anxious I became. I began seeing (or so I thought) images of "the beast" in the woods behind my home. I became fearful of the dark, of being alone, and avoided at all cost the basement in our home, where it just so happened that my own foosball table, which my parents had recently purchased, was located. None of this was a problem for me before chatting with Frank. In fact, my experience with him prompted my regression to more common fears and anxieties of *earlier* childhood. I remember also becoming obsessive over professing my desire to follow Jesus, which meant I would be "saved." This did not take the form of a public profession, mind you, but became an internal one instead as I repeated over and over again in my mind: "I love God, and I hate the devil. I love God, and I hate the devil." One time I got it mixed up and reversed the mantra's order. The result was that I experienced what I now believe was an anxiety attack. My heart beat rapidly. I was short of breath. I began to feel hot, then clammy, all over. I also had difficulty sleeping because of what I was convinced was my unpardonable sin. During the same period, as it began to rain quite heavily one day, I recall wondering if God was going to end the world by flooding it again. I knew about Noah and his ark and assumed this could be another of God's deluges on what Frank had called a "sinful" and "wretched" world. Though I was surely relieved to discover that the Bible tells us that God said this would not happen again, all that assurance did was help me worry less about rainstorms, for I remained convinced that God would simply use some other means to unleash God's wrath—on others and, I assumed, on me as well.

By the Busload: Meeting Additional Devotees of Frank's God

Around the same time, I recall a busload of college-aged missionaries being dropped off in my neighborhood and "witnessing" door-to-door. I don't recall the full name of their church or organization, but I think it had "New Life" and "Tabernacle" in it, and I'm certain it had a millennial orientation. Riding my bike with a friend that day, I encountered one of the group's members, a man in his early twenties, who quickly cut to the chase. He told me about the approaching end times—which he said were imminent—and ultimately reinforced what Frank had said using the same kinds of images and understandings of God, the world, and most importantly, me. This young man urged me to take very seriously what he was "sharing" with me because "it's a matter of eternal life in heaven or hell." He then added, "Make sure you are saved!" Before he left, he gave me a pamphlet that detailed "God's Plan for My Salvation," and I was encouraged "not to let another day pass" before I prayed the "saving prayer" that was included. God only knows how many times I prayed that prayer.

Thinking back, I find it interesting that the friend with whom I was riding my bike that day and I never talked about this incident again. On the one hand, this seems puzzling, as he and I did lots of things together and would have had numerous occasions to chat, if only briefly, about the busload of college students, the pamphlets they were passing out, and how we each experienced this event. In fact, this kid and I were as "chummy" as we could be. On the other hand, talking about this experience, which for me, and maybe for him too, cut to the quick of a budding spirit, would have been more than either of us could bear. Why? Because we were *boys*! And as boys we had learned not to talk about things that hurt, were scary, or called for admitting that we were upset. Even a chum could not be trusted with *this* experience. The Boy Code had done its job!

The Lasting Imprint of Frank's God

Both of these formative experiences, with Frank and with the college group in my neighborhood, resulted in my having a very negative view of God for several years. God became for me someone to be distrusted if not feared, though, of course, I was afraid to admit this because of what God might have done to punish me. I grew increasingly anxious about my standing before God and longed for God's comfort, assurance, provision, and companionship when I encountered the typical life struggles of an early adolescent boy. Truth be told, I wanted God desperately, and yet I didn't! I am reminded here of Kierkegaard's depiction of his own struggle with God and his faith: "I acquired an anxiety about Christianity and yet felt powerfully attracted to it" (1844/1980, 172). That was my experience too. I had long been drawn to Jesus and my faith, even recalling at a very early age my deep admiration for my priest, the Rev. Henry Sommerall. I felt "at home" in the church as a very young boy, and fixed upon watching Father Sommerall preside at the liturgy in the little Holy Cross Episcopal Church in Simpsonville, South Carolina, where I was baptized and where my family belonged. I even remember thinking that someday I would myself like to be able to do what he did. But through my experiences with Frank and the twenty-something missionary, my comfort and longing for God turned to anxiety and running from God.

Of course, my parents, who were attentive and nurturing, continued to present me with positive images and understandings of God, and we continued attending a church that reinforced them. As a matter of fact, neither my parents nor anyone else was aware of how troubled I became over the things of God and my standing before God. Like most boys, I had learned early in life not to share my feelings, particularly those related to my fears, anxieties, or vulnerabilities. In spite of what I consider to have been a safe and inviting home life, where I could have shared my troubles, in the end I could not do so. Once again, the Boy Code had done its work!

A few years later, in high school, I recall seeking discretely to discuss the matters over which I continued to struggle with my pastor, the Rev. Harvey G. Cook—or "Gerry," as he was called. He served as rector at Trinity Episcopal Church in Myrtle Beach, South Carolina, where my family had moved the summer before I began ninth grade. I remember calling Father Cook one evening from a pay phone at a 7-Eleven across the street from my high school. I had just finished football practice and was worried about something having to do with my standing before God. While the details are sketchy, it had to do with my experiences with Frank and the missionary being stirred up again. That happened after a parachurch organization, complete with a charismatic young leader, made its presence known among students at my high school. Many of my friends and I initially found this group and its leader attractive, but I soon began hearing things having to do with God that reminded me of Frank's views and my experiences with him. So I disengaged from the group but needed to readdress my longstanding concerns having to do with God and my standing before God, and I phoned Father Cook.

Like my parents, Father Cook presented me with a God who was quite different from the one Frank believed in and touted. Father Cook assured me that I did not need to be afraid of God, because God's nature is love, not wrath. He also encouraged me by saying that God wanted good things for people and that God's love would always be present with them, including me. He also suggested that I worry less about when the world may end and more about how I might serve God for as long as I am in the world. This conversation surely helped alleviate my fears and struggles to an extent. But a great deal of damage had been done in my early adolescent years at the hand of Frank, damage that was not easily repaired. The residue of my conversations with Frank remained and continued to inflict injury on my spirit, even if less frequently and intensely than in earlier years.

Saying Goodbye to Frank's God

It was not until I reached my early twenties, as I was nearing the end of college, that I began to feel that my spirit had recovered. I was fortunate to have been befriended by a wonderful man, William H. Terry, who was then the dean of students at Davidson College. Will was a Presbyterian minister and among the most inviting and hospitable persons I have ever known. Though much older than me, he became, in a sense, a kind of early adulthood "chum," one with whom I was able to share a number of struggles and ask many questions, particularly religious ones. It was during this time that I began giving serious thought to going to seminary, and more important, that I was able to come to terms with the God whom Frank had introduced to me. For about twelve years, the time between being introduced to Frank's view of God as an early adolescent and settling into my own alternative in young adulthood, I was, to varying degrees, scared of God, distrustful of God's motives, and surely lonely in my spiritual life. I often wonder what life would have been like for me, in my spirit, had I met Father Cook or Will Terry before meeting Frank. Surely it would have been less painful and spiritually destructive.

I share my own story for two reasons. First, I am convinced the kind of God a kid encounters, imagines, and comes to understand has a powerful impact on his life, for better or worse. God can be a source of comfort, courage, peace, and solitude as well as a basis for fear, anxiety, confusion, and despair. Furthermore, how adults present God goes a long way in determining what kind of God a kid will meet. Second, there are plenty of alternatives to destructive images and understandings of God that are biblically based, psychologically healthy, and surely illustrative of the God known in Jesus Christ. The last section of this chapter provides examples of these. I discuss there how they helped me, and I hope that they will help other boys to fend off the despair associated with destructive views of God. Before that discussion, however, I need to point out the importance a boy's view of God has for his psychological and religious well-being, and thus for promoting his solitude and its fruits—not the least of which is his budding spirit and spiritual life.

THE GOD OF LONELINESS VERSUS THE GOD OF SOLITUDE

Solitude and religion are inherently connected. William James held that solitude is the condition that influences one to become religious (1902/1982, 36). Similarly, Paul Tillich recognized the necessity of solitude for communion, with others and God. While I agree with these claims, solitude and religion relate to one another in a more mutual way. Solitude gives rise to religion, by which I mean a seeking for God, but religion may also foster a richer kind of solitude. This is particularly true for boys. How a boy comes to imagine and understand God, and more specifically, his acceptance and internalization of a certain kind of God, enables him to keep his loneliness at bay as he uses solitude to become a boy more true to himself and to God.

Understandings of God as Distinguished from Images of God

I want to distinguish here between "understandings" of God on the one hand and "images" or "representations" of God on the other. Understanding connotes a more conscious and cognitively grounded and shaped notion of God. Understanding requires an ability to think more conceptually, reflectively, and abstractly and may not have much if any emotional effect on the one holding the understanding (St. Clair 1994, 23). In other words, understanding is typically characterized by a more emotionally distant relationship to its subject. Children tend not to begin forming understandings of God in the stricter sense until they are school-aged, when their capacities for more abstract thinking arise and develop through formal pedagogies. Recognizing the school-aged child's growing capacities, religious communities capitalize on these with catechesis or formal religious instruction.

Prior to gaining understandings of God, however, children form God images or representations. These are subjective in nature, deeply emotional in quality, and arise primarily out of the child's earliest and most significant relationships, especially with parents. Anna-Maria Rizzuto, a physician and psychoanalyst, has authored an important work on God images and representations, *The Birth of the Living God: A Psychoanalytic Study*. This book describes in psychological terms how persons come to think and feel about God, including who their "private" God is for them and also how myriad relationships, experiences, instructions, and subjective factors influence their perspectives on God.

Rizzuto embraces Freud's view that a person's current significant relationships tend to be influenced, even shaped, by memories of earlier significant relationships, so that the quality of a child's early relationship with her parents continues to play a substantial role throughout life in influencing subsequent relationships. Rizzuto goes further, however, claiming that the quality of a person's early relationships with people has a strong impact on how that person comes to imagine and relate to God, both as a child and as an adult. Unlike Freud, who identified the child's father as the exclusive source of God images, and specifically the idealized all-powerful and protective father, Rizzuto argues that *both* parents inform the child's formulation of God images, that other sources beyond parental relationships also play a determinative role, and that a person's God images change over time in light of new experiences, relationships, and influences. She writes, "The very pressure of living makes us rework, over and over again, consciously and unconsciously, the memories of those we encountered at the beginning of our days—the time of the heroic, mythic reality of childhood[,] . . . [and] it is out of this matrix of facts and fantasies, wishes, hopes, and fears, in the exchanges with those incredible things called parents, that the image of God is concocted" (Rizzuto 1979, 7).

As the Jesuit psychoanalyst W. W. Meissner has noted in drawing on Rizzuto's work, there may be a close similarity between a child's parental images and God images, so much so that they can be used more or less interchangeably as equivalents or substitutes, especially in moments of concern or struggle. Conversely, a child's parental and God images may also be diametrically opposed and even antagonistic toward one another. In this case, God may be "utterly good and protecting, while the parents are regarded as mean, ungiving, or unloving," or the parents can be idealized and God devalued (Meissner 1984, 141). For our purposes, I wish to highlight two things. First, while God images surely relate to early parent-child relationships, they are not informed by those relationships exclusively; other significant relationships and experiences also contribute. Second, God images change over a lifetime, being shaped and reshaped by virtue of new experiences, relationships, and contexts in which a person lives.

As a boy reaches school age, he is often introduced to more formal religious instruction or, at least, to more cognitively based and conscious "understandings" of God. Those understandings, which institutional religion and systematic religious instruction formalize, eventually meet with the child's currently held God images, and he begins developing his own understandings. Subsequently, each has an ongoing influence on the other. A boy's God images inform his newfound understandings of God, and those understandings, which continue to be affected by others' understandings of God presented to him, will influence, and perhaps reshape, his own God images. This means that the boy alone does not create his view of God. Rather, he observes his parents praying, attends church where he encounters official ritual, and hears different adults speak of God in various ways, all of which we expect will further shape and expand his image of God (St. Clair 1994, 23). An additional observation must be stressed, namely, that a boy already has a God image in his possession when he is exposed to the influences of official religion and its understandings of God (Rizzuto 1979, 10). Religious education, therefore, does not contribute significantly to one's images of God. Rather, it builds on (and perhaps alters) the God images already formed.

Presumably, both images and understandings of God will affect persons of any age and gender. Girls and boys, women and men alike will typically have their experiences, feelings, thoughts, relationships, values, and goals shaped by who they understand and imagine God to be—even if they understand and imagine God *not* to be. But early adolescent boys, because of their propensity for loneliness, will be particularly vulnerable to fears and anxieties having to do with God. This follows from the fact that fears and anxieties often grow out of a boy's more basic state of loneliness. A harsh, unpredictable, judgmental, and overly demanding God will reinforce precisely what many boys experience in their world. Conversely, a kind, nurturing, supportive, and affirming God, who accepts a boy for who he is as opposed to who he *should* be but in fact *cannot* be, may serve to help a boy fend off the pressures he feels to conform to others' understandings and expectations—powerful influences that lead him to sacrifice his true self, injure him spiritually, and surely perpetuate his loneliness.

The Boy's Quest for God

The kinds of God images and understandings a boy comes to hold take on added importance in that an early adolescent boy seeks in religious quest something, or someone, to meet him in his loneliness. Specifically, he searches for one who will respect that loneliness and thus his boyhood. A boy's quest is for one who understands him as a boy, a truly real boy, which means not the kind of boy his culture seeks to impose on him. Calvin Branford's words sum up the early adolescent boy's experience well: "I guess it's pretty hard being a guy because there are so many things a normal person would probably do, but you're just not expected to!" (Pollack 1998, 20). An early adolescent boy searches, often feverishly, for one who truly understands the straitjacket in which he often lives. Recalling Hanson's take on the boy's struggle, in seeking for that other—whether it be the chum or God—it is as if a boy says, "Love me, hold me—is there no one?"

Sullivan pointed out that the chum becomes a primary object of the early adolescent boy's quest. The boy may believe that in finding a best friend with whom to share the boyhood journey, he will have found the one to share, and perhaps alleviate, his loneliness. Harking back again to Hanson's song, the lonely boy "is looking for another lonely heart." But I contend that the boy soon discovers that he needs more than a chum. He needs solitude. He needs an emotional space in which to explore his true boyhood more fully, a space in which he can become more the self he desires to be, wherein his spirit may be healed and nurtured. This is when the boy's quest becomes particularly religious in nature. He recognizes that he needs someone to fill the void in his life more completely than the chum, someone who can love him unconditionally, who can hold him up as valuable for who he is *as* he is, and who thus can substitute for the "missing part." As Hanson tells us, the boy seeks an answer to the question: "Is there anyone who could love a lonely boy?" In other words: Is there anyone who can love a lonely boy who may not meet others' expectations of him but who is, nonetheless, a good boy?

I suggest that the "someone" after whom an early adolescent lonely boy ultimately seeks is God. A boy hopes that God will indeed love him and help him feel like "the only one" again. That kind of love and affirmation cannot be provided by the chum, as important as a boy's relationship to him may be. The chum, after all, is a lonely boy himself who seeks his own ultimate solution. He too searches for the one who can love *him* as he needs to be loved. Boyhood chums surely may help and comfort each other, but they cannot satisfy one another's deepest spiritual needs. Only God can do that. In relationship to God a boy finds the fullest self-transcendence. In communion with God he senses in his spirit a connection with all that there is, something beyond the ordinary world in which he lives and strives, so often unsuccessfully, to meet the standards of the Boy Code. God provides him with a way to be and to become most fully himself, which is to say that communion with God nourishes and sustains his spirit. Therefore, it's difficult to name anything more important for boys and for those who care for them than the kind of God images or understandings a boy encounters and eventually embraces. No less than a boy's spiritual life is at stake.

Why God's Qualities and Character Matter So Much to Boys

Rizzuto goes as far as to say that how one imagines God, at any age, will have an effect on whether one holds to belief in God. Following the rubrics of Erik H. Erikson's life cycle theory, Rizzuto suggests that for the school-aged child in the "industry versus inferiority" stage of development, the following can be said about the child's relationship to God. First, the "type of God" the child typically imagines is one who has some similarities with the child's parents, meaning that God is, in part, a projection of the parents, though less so than at earlier ages. In other words, a child holds that "God is both like and not like my parents." Second, the God representation that leads to belief, by which Rizzuto means the child's conscious, positive view of God, is one that prompts the child to think about God in this way: "You are my protector," come what may. In the next life cycle stage, adolescence, a young person will need to view God more than simply as "protector," seeing God especially as "the beloved and the loving." Surely early adolescent kids need that too, if to a lesser degree. However, the quality in God that the early adolescent needs most in order to believe in God is God's ability and desire to protect. An early adolescent boy needs assurance that God will protect him in the face of any threat or adversity. He needs assurance that one will meet and provide for him in his most vulnerable condition. According to Rizzuto, when this need goes unmet, a boy, like any other kid, will struggle to believe in God.

A God representation that leads to unbelief or a negative view of God prompts one to view God in this manner: "You are destructive. You won't spare me" (Rizzuto 1979, 206–7). When presented with a God who is harsh, judgmental, unpredictable, or overly demanding, a child will have no reason to believe in God, or to want to believe. The child will see in God essentially what has already been discovered as threatening, unpredictable, and repugnant in the world. Thus, certain God images and understandings will actually lead a child to reject God and thus will rob the child of the gains a "positive" view of God offers to anyone encountering life's difficulties.

One may respond by noting that a plea for nurturing, supportive, and comforting God images and understandings is nothing new. We have long known of the importance for persons of all ages, and especially children, to form and hold positive views of God. One may add that mainstream Christians tend not to be inclined to imagine or understand God—let alone speak of God to children—in the ways of my relative Frank. Some may assume, therefore, that children of mainstream Christians will be protected, by and large, from the kind of negative experience I had. I understand that presumption. Had I not experienced what I did as a child, I would have assumed the same. But my family was religiously mainstream too. We did not embrace millennial theology or "hellfire and brimstone" Christianity; neither did we espouse a judgmental, unpredictable, harsh, or overly demanding God. We were Episcopalians, after all! Moreover, for quite some time my parents remained unaware of what Frank was exposing me to with respect to God, and they were quite angry when they discovered what had happened. So despite good parenting and being raised in an environment informed by positive views of God, by virtue of being exposed to profoundly negative images and understandings of God as an early adolescent I had a very painful experience that proved damaging for many years.

I don't think that my experience is extraordinary. Despite parents' and church leaders' best intentions and care, children are presented with loads of harmful God images and understandings, ones that may indeed injure them spiritually. These come by way of various media and include televangelists who thrive on reminding viewers of "the fear of God," which curious children may stumble on. These views also may be presented by people with whom children are in regular contact: extended family members, family friends, teachers, other children in the neighborhood, even persons within the so-called mainstream congregation who, for whatever reason, hold to images and understandings of God that approximate those Frank held and presented to me. Speaking from personal experience as a pastor of mainstream congregations, it is not unusual for well-meaning, though misguided, church members to present a kind of God to children that proves harmful, if not destructive, to their spirit. If not the God of the pending rapture, it may be the God who "hates their sin," who is "jealous" or "wrathful," who endorses corporal punishment by reminding parents that "sparing the rod means spoiling the child," and who certainly "knows and sees everything," especially what one does not want God to know or see. Children will fear, dread, and ultimately reject—or want to reject—that God as well.

I suggest further that the need for raising awareness and intentionally teaching more positive God images and understandings is *immediate*. "Apocalyptic" views of God are alive and well. Due in large part to the popular *Left*

Behind series of books and similar literature spawned by its success, "the God of the apocalypse" now saturates popular reading circles and has even been made into television movies and motion pictures. A recent trip to my local bookstore revealed not only copious volumes in the *Left Behind* series but also such book titles as: *When Will Jesus Come? Compelling Evidence for the Soon Return of Christ*; *Are You Rapture Ready? Signs, Warning, Prophesies, Threats, and Suspicions That the Endtime Is Now*; and *The Shadow of the Apocalypse*. There was even a workbook one could use to plot the events leading to the "endtime" and gauge one's readiness for the pending "rapture." Similarly, a recent survey of Sunday morning cable ministry programs confirmed that "the endtime" remains a hot topic for sermons, musical offerings, and various paraphernalia being offered in return for "a small donation"—all of which play on fear, anxiety, and confusion about God.

The subject of millennialism is not new, to be sure, but never has it garnered so much attention in mass media. I am convinced this means that a significant number of children are being exposed to, and affected by, images and understandings of God similar to the God introduced to me by Frank. Even if children are not reading these books or seeing these movies or televised ministries themselves, sales statistics, as well as the frequency of debate on the subject in both mainstream and parochial news and talk programs, indicate that many adults are reading and seeing them. That includes adults who parent, worship with, and possibly teach children in mainstream congregations. Thus, we who serve as leaders of mainstream congregations cannot ignore or dismiss the kind of thinking that permeates the *Left Behind* series and its sibling genres, which inevitably impacts many children with whom adults, mainstream and not, relate and ponder God. While my concern centers on all children, I am particularly mindful of the needs of the early adolescent boy. His propensity for loneliness, as well as the fear, anxiety, shame, and loss of self that often accompany it, is exacerbated by the Boy Code and its power to prevent him from speaking his feelings. Likewise, confusion and struggle over the One he needs to know will protect and support him in the face of any adversity only adds to his loneliness and pain. In Hanson's words, he feels as though "there is no one to hold his hand. There is no one to understand."

PORTRAITS OF GOD FOR LONELY BOYS

With that in mind, I offer three types of God "portraits" that are nurturing, peaceful, and therefore full of potential to fill a lonely boy's need, especially his quest for solitude. In using the term *portrait*, I recognize the distinction between God images and understandings previously mentioned. I combine the two here, however, because, as noted, by the time one reaches early ado-lescence one possesses both images and understandings of God that relate to and inform each other in mutual and ongoing ways. Consequently, "God por-trait" refers to the interplay of God images and understandings, and further-more captures God's qualities or characteristics that we may present to children for them to internalize and make their own. My discussion seeks not to be exhaustive but merely suggestive. These portrait "types" can be expanded, nuanced, and surely made use of in light of one's own context and perceived needs. Moreover, each type overlaps with the others and also with additional ones that I have not identified but that surely remain consistent with those I cite. I hope simply to offer God portraits that both parents and leaders in faith communities may intentionally embrace, cultivate, and consis-tently impart to all children in their care—especially lonely boys.

The God Who Values Everyone

The first type of God portrait depicts "the God who values everyone," includ-ing those who at times live unfaithfully toward what God or others desire of them. This type depicts the God who loves all people and seeks after them unceasingly for relationship, for no other reason than their intrinsic value. We find biblical illustrations of this God in numerous places, but perhaps the best example comes in two parables: "the lost sheep" and "the lost coin" (Luke 15:1–7, 8–10). In both parables we hear of Jesus' response to a group of judg-mental religious leaders. They condemned persons they identified as "sinners" and criticized Jesus for "welcoming" and "eating" with them. These "sinners" had sought to listen to Jesus and, presumably, to hear about God. Jesus takes this as an opportunity to tell the religious leaders who judged him and the oth-ers about particular qualities of God. Jesus assures them that God seeks after the lost, just as a shepherd will go and look for one lost sheep. As Jesus explains, the shepherd cares so much for each sheep that he will leave a multitude of others in order to find the lost one. Furthermore, when the shepherd finds the lost sheep he demonstrates his profound joy. He embraces the lost sheep by laying it on his shoulders and "rejoicing." The shepherd's joy reaches such a state that he announces the good news and invites others, his "neighbors" and "friends," to join him. Having been reunited with a "lost" one for whom he has great love and concern, his exuberance can't be contained.

Similarly, the parable of "the lost coin" likens God to a woman who loses one of her ten silver coins, all of which, like the shepherd's sheep, are valuable. Like the shepherd, she goes to great lengths to recover what she has lost. Find-ing it, she responds just as the shepherd did: with great celebration. Summing up both parables' teaching, Jesus assures his audience that there is joy in heaven and among angels when one who belongs to God is found. God values those God loves, so much so that God will search for those who are lost.

This portrait of God is especially important to convey to lonely boys in need of solitude, who often feel lost themselves, who are told both implicitly and explicitly that they fall short of others' expectations, perhaps even those of God, and who seek for a God who values them enough to look for and indeed rejoice over them. In the parables mentioned, both the lost sheep and lost coin become the singular focus of the one searching after them. The one sought after is, for a time, "the only one," the one who is the searcher's exclusive concern. A lonely boy who learns of the God who responds in the same way to him, especially when he feels lost, may gain strength and, when needed, renewal with respect to his belief in, and relationship to, the God who rejoices.

The God Who Is Deeply Compassionate

The second type of God portrait depicts "the God who is deeply compassionate." Related to the God who values everyone, this is the God whose enduring concern joins with steadfast kindness, forgiveness, and care. Among the more vivid portrayals of this kind of God is the parable of "the prodigal son," which I prefer to call the parable of "the compassionate parent" (Luke 15:11–32). The familiar story recounts the "lost" son who asks his father for his inheritance before he dies, uses it to support a lavish and morally bankrupt lifestyle, and eventually finds himself destitute and performing the most menial of tasks in order to stay alive. Deciding he will return home, ask for his father's forgiveness, and request to be treated as one of his father's hired hands—whose lifestyle and provision now far exceed his own—he appears prepared for rejection and, perhaps, even an "I told you so" response. Neither would be an unreasonable assumption. The lost son had made his own bed, as they say. What he discovers upon returning, however, is the father's unconditional welcome and embrace. Luke tells us that when the father sees his son coming, the father is "filled with compassion." He "ran and put his arms around him and kissed him," ordered the best robe, sandals, and ring to be given to the son, and also that the "fatted calf" be slaughtered and a banquet be thrown. All of this is to celebrate the one who was lost but then found.

In this parable too, which follows the two previously mentioned, Jesus seeks to convey what God is like. God offers compassion, extends hospitality through generous offers of welcome, and remains eager to rejoice over God's children, especially when they have been "lost." God is tender, one who, like the waiting father of the parable, will put his arms around his children and kiss them, love them, nurture and celebrate them, not for who they should be and for what they should have done or not done, but merely for who they are, with all their warts as well as their beauty marks. The God portrayed here is not harsh, punitive, or eager to point out failures. Rather, this God is loving, concerned, and eager to embrace. Brenden, age 18, describes that God this way: "God never says, 'Oh, you are such a jerk,' or 'You are a wimp,' or 'Why aren't you doing better in school?'" (Pollack 2001, 101). Instead, like the welcoming father in the parable, God remains the loving parent who awaits the son's return, with open and compassionate arms.

It is significant too that the father in the parable is not content with being the only one who feels this way toward his child. Indeed, he urges his elder son, who has little patience or appreciation for his younger brother and for how the father is treating him, to embrace the lost one as he, the father, has done. Yet the father simultaneously embraces the elder son, even as he struggles with his father's decision and, in a real sense, falls short of the father's expectations. The father says to the elder son: "Son, you are always with me, and all that is mine is yours" (Luke 15:31). This implies, of course, that God feels the same way toward others who are lost, who question, struggle, make poor decisions, and otherwise fall short of expectations—like typical boys.

Lonely boys who need solitude may find in a compassionate, welcoming, rejoicing God a balm for their struggle: with schools that seem "unfriendly" and "unwelcoming"; with a society that asks more of them and of the men they are destined to become than is possible to fulfill; with the threats of pervasive shame and loss of self that follow from what boys perceive as a lack of empathy, understanding, and love from those on whom they depend and love most; and perhaps too with those who inflict them with notions of a harsh and unpredictable God that poison their spirit. Pollack writes:

> In the realm of God and spirituality, many boys seem to be seeking, and finding, a source of unconditional love and empathy. Especially for boys who struggle with some of life's most searing kinds of emotional pain—loneliness, depression, abuse, sickness, death, and loss—turning to a caring and loving God for support often feels like their sole salvation. . . .
>
> Many boys do not feel capable of removing the shackles of the Boy Code. They don't feel that they can "be themselves"; they don't always sense that it is safe to talk to parents, siblings, teachers, or friends about their sadness, fear and longing. As we have seen, their pain often grows more acute, turns inward, or simply explodes. Believing in God . . . enables many boys to open up their pain outward and to be heard in a positive, peaceful, and constructive way. (Pollack 1998, 87)

Holding up the God we find in the parable of "the compassionate parent" provides one way to facilitate lonely boys' meeting and embracing precisely the kind of God whom Pollack claims that boys need.

The God Who Is Faithfully Present

The third type of God portrait depicts "the God who is faithfully present." This God may be called upon in time of need but also remains present unceasingly, even prior to being called upon. Yet unlike the negative, "apocalyptic" image of the God who remains present in order "to see everything" and waits in the lurch to mete out justice when one errs, this "faithfully present" God stays dependable, predictable, and constant in one's life *in order* to bestow support, provision, and protection. Pollack witnessed boys needing this kind of God too: "One of the most inspirational experiences I had in my recent trek across the country, listening to and learning from America's boys and young men, is the large number of them—individuals from all walks of life—who feel a meaningful connection with a *spiritual* or religious force, an all-powerful presence outside themselves, a deeply caring being who is always there to listen to, love, and protect them." Furthermore, "from dealing with sparring parents or managing a neighborhood bully, to handling abuse, coping with depression, resisting addiction, or trying desperately to feel good about who they are as people, scores of boys emphasize just how important a spiritual being is to their happiness and survival" (1998, 86). Reflecting out of his own experience and need, fourteen-year-old Cedrick describes that kind of God in this way: "God is the person who is there when nobody else is" (Pollack 2001, 96).

There are numerous biblical accounts that portray God in this way. I think of the writer of Psalm 139, who muses, "Where can I go from your spirit? Or where can I flee from your presence?" (Ps. 139:7). Similarly, the author of Isaiah portrays God as a mother who abides in provision, comfort, and concern: "For thus says the LORD: 'I will extend prosperity to her like a river, and the wealth of the nations like an overflowing stream; and you shall nurse and be carried on her arm, and dandled on her knees. As a mother comforts her child, so I will comfort you" (Isa. 66:12–13). Jesus also speaks of this faithfully present quality of God in his postresurrection words to his disciples, commonly called the "Great Commission," at the end of Matthew's Gospel: "And remember, I am with you always, to the end of the age" (Matt. 28:20).

Hearing These Words Again for the First Time

These particular words from the Great Commission have been critical for my own spiritual life. The first time I recall hearing them was during my first year of seminary, though surely they must have been uttered in my presence before. Perhaps I had heard them during a baptismal liturgy or even read them on my own. But when a professor spoke those words that first year of seminary, which was when I had just come to terms with my own history and spiritual pain, I heard them as never before. I now believe that the power of these words of Jesus related centrally to what had happened to me as a boy, when, seemingly by accident, I mixed up the mantra I could not keep myself from repeating, "I love God, and I hate the devil," and reversed whom I loved and hated. My ensuing anxiety, which I previously detailed, while enormously painful, seems to have provided a positive outcome. Specifically, my deepest fears, which stemmed from the belief that I had committed the unpardonable sin, were not actually realized. The sky did not fall on me. God's "righteous wrath" did not sweep me up "in the blink of an eye" in the way Frank described would happen to "the wicked." Nothing catastrophic came to pass. I was anxious. I worried about my error. I was lonely, to be sure. But I had survived, and so had God.

Winnicott pointed out that a necessary part of a child's development is the ability to "destroy" objects, things external to the child that are simultaneously loved and hated, but nevertheless have those objects "return" or remain alive. This process typically begins with the mother's breast or its substitute. The child needs to be able to love it but also to be ambivalent about it, hate it, and thus psychologically "destroy" it, only to have it return and be ready to be loved, hated, and treated again in the same way. At work here is what psychologists call "object constancy," which relates to the child building trust in both himself and his external world and which relates also to what the child needs in order to develop the capacity to be alone. Winnicott held that throughout childhood, and particularly among adolescents, loving and destroying objects remains necessary and normal. In their anger and "hatred" for their parents, to cite perhaps the most important example, children need to be able to "destroy" their parents, that is, to convey their negative (even hateful) feelings toward them and have them not only "survive" but also return again and again, in order to love and be loved, but also, at least potentially, to be hated and destroyed once more (Winnicott 1971/1989, 86–94; 1994, 238–40). When I inadvertently reversed the order of the one I loved and hated with respect to God and the devil, I was destroying the God I indeed hated and needed to destroy, the one Frank told me about and who terrified me. But this was also the God I loved, or wanted to love. My parents and my church, among others, had helped me learn that God had good qualities, ones that were very different from Frank's portrayal of God. In attempting to destroy the God I hated, however, I was able to see that not only did God survive my attacks (among other things, I still believed in God and it seemed that others did too) but God remained there *for me*. In other words, God stayed present, faithfully present like the "compassionate parent" of the parable, regardless of what I had done or failed to do. Furthermore, by not attacking me for what I had done, God proved to be something other than who Frank described. As a result, God was one I could truly love and to whom I could devote my life.

That day in class, as the professor repeated Jesus' words that end Matthew's Gospel, I heard something remarkable, even life changing. God is for us, forever, "to the end of the age." "I am with you always," Jesus promised, and in that I heard him to say, "God will not let you go." I am now convinced, however, that these words which so moved me that day in the classroom were ones I believed *first* as a boy. While Frank's view of God crippled my spiritual life, it did not destroy it. I still sensed that God was different from what Frank said. I knew that Jesus was once a boy himself and also was what God is like. And perhaps I thought to myself, "If he says 'I am for you,' he means 'I am for *you!*'" So maybe I don't need to be so afraid or confused about God anymore." Somehow, and God only knows how, amid my boyhood loneliness and fear of God I found a way to hold on to that. To be sure, I held on to it more tightly on some occasions and less so at others, but it must have sustained me in my journey through a spiritual hell. As the apostle Paul put it, I now think I made it through that time—spiritually and maybe otherwise—because somewhere in my boyhood I had learned that "if God is for us, who can be against us?" (Rom. 8:31).

My Adult Chum's God Portrait

A recent conversation with a colleague, who is also a dear friend and a kind of adult "chum," provided still one more way of thinking about, and offering to others, the God who remains "faithfully present." I asked him if he would share with me an image or understanding of God that he remembered finding comfort in as a boy. He told me that he did not recall much in the way of thinking about God as a child, something he attributed to growing up without a religious tradition, and thus had not come to embrace religious faith himself until adulthood. He added, however, that the most meaningful and comforting way he thinks of God *presently* is in terms of Mary as *Theotokos*, or "God-bearer." He explained that he finds encouragement in the idea that Mary was able to carry God inside her, as part of herself, and that God was nurtured in and by her. Equally important, eventually Mary gave birth to God in the person of Jesus and, in a sense, the rest was then out of her hands. My colleague added that thinking of ourselves as being "God-bearers" in our own right—meaning that, like Mary, we "carry" God with us, nurture what we carry, and then let it go by "delivering" it to be what it will be on its own—proves meaningful for him and serves as a model for living out his own faith. He said, "In this way, God is part of me and not part of me," such that "God is the one I carry privately and who grows inside me but also the one I eventually birth by sharing God with others." As a result, life consists of "constant transactions between God-bearers" that occur not merely because of human choices but principally by virtue of "a divine gift." He concluded that this serves as an important reminder to him that "a seed of the divine lives within me to be nurtured."

I am convinced that my colleague's personal portrait of God, though not realized until adulthood, has something to offer a lonely early adolescent boy. First, like those previously mentioned, this God remains "faithfully present," a part of the boy himself, living within him and connecting him with God in a personal and trust-filled way. Among other things, this reminds the boy of how special he is to God. He is a kind of "only one," just as Andrew Gold's "lonely boy" desires. The boy is so special, in fact, that God chooses to live inside him, to be nurtured in him and by him, as preparation for the boy's sharing God with the world. Moreover, this God remains compassionate, trustworthy, and also trusting of the boy, and pledges to be *for* him at every moment. Harking back to Hanson's song, this God, who becomes part of the boy by living inside him, may thus be seen as taking over for the "the missing part," replacing a part of the boy that has been lost. Consequently, this view of God further encompasses what the previously mentioned portraits may offer.

Second, this God may provide the boy with two essential connections he needs: to a new life source, namely, God, but also to his first life source, meaning his mother. Specifically, as a boy views himself as "God-bearer," the life-giver and sharer of God with others, he enjoys a connection to the source of all life. The boy knows God as the Great Provider, who, as previously discussed, offers life and abundant love and concern to all whom God loves. But the boy may also recognize, and should be helped to recognize, that in a certain way he is like God. He is like God in that not only has God created him in God's image, as orthodox Christian theology would affirm, but he, the boy, is also a kind of life-giver himself. Like Mary as *Theotokos*, he may allow God to live and be nurtured inside him for the purpose of then sharing God, who gives life, with others. Additionally, as God-bearer the boy enjoys a semblance of what he senses his mother experienced with him. In a sense, the boy thus becomes like his mother too, as he also now "nurtures" and "gives birth" to one inside him. Though the roles have reversed, this is reminiscent of what the boy experienced from his mother earlier in life, and it leads to him identifying with her in a new way. The boy finds a new connection with his first life source. In a different though still meaningful way, he finds "paradise" once again. If boys are encouraged to identify with their fathers as they seek to live up to the Boy Code, this image of God-bearer encourages a countervailing identification with their mothers. If mothers have a natural "interiority," enabling them to carry "life" within them, so boys may vicariously experience a similar interiority and connection to life.

Boys' Primordial Sorrow

This last point takes on added importance in light of what James E. Dittes says about male experience, namely, that an increasing "sense of primordial sorrow" informs it, one that grows out of awareness that women are the ones who carry, give birth, and nurse new life. Characterizing what many males will experience, he writes, "Confronting a nursing woman may, paradoxically, be like confronting a corpse, because both encounters are face-to-face confrontations with a man's own mortality, with a man's apprehension of his unwanted but unavoidable separation from life" (Dittes 1996, 22). As a result, "it does seem likely that, at some primitive level, men are aware of an irremediable deficit that is their lot as men, some unbridgeable separation from life, rawly and plainly experienced" (23). If Dittes is correct, this recognition of "an irremediable deficit" occurs first in boyhood, at precisely the time when the boy discovers he is losing, or has lost, his first love and his own source of life. Providing a boy with a portrait of the God who lives within him, which the boy, as God-bearer, nurtures and births, joins the boy with both his original and his new "life source" simultaneously. In my own case, such "God-bearingness" would have been a welcome alternative to "God-fearingness."

A Possible Critique

I anticipate a possible critique of my proposal being that these types of portraits provide a limited and even one-sided view of God, one not faithful to the entire biblical witness and that perhaps may set up the boy for later disillusionment when he discovers the Bible's presentation of a more complex and mysterious God. I simply do not believe this is true. In fact, one could argue that the more positive images and understandings of God a boy has at an earlier age, the more these will serve to fend off any later disillusionment. Moreover, the assumption that we should prepare a boy for disillusionment itself runs contrary to who Christians understand God to be, namely, the One who conquers disillusionment in Jesus Christ. My primary concern here is a *pastoral* one. It centers on an exceedingly vulnerable group of God's children—early adolescent boys—who tend to stand desperately in need of imagining and coming to understand a particular kind of God. If lonely boys require solitude, and if religion and solitude are inherently connected, with each enriching the other, then those of us in positions to expose boys to God and educate them on what God is like have the responsibility of offering God portraits that enhance their spiritual well-being. We must "err" on the side of bathing a boy in images and understandings of God that will protect and preserve him from the vicissitudes of boyhood, for this is the only viable pathway for a boy into God's mysterious and complex nature. To fail to do so results in making the mistake that Pollack attributes to the secular educational system, namely, that of failing to recognize and provide for boys' unique vulnerabilities, concerns, and needs.

While all children require this protection and preservation, the God a boy imagines, is introduced to, comes to understand, internalizes, and ultimately embraces as his own object of faith and devotion has a particularly deep and lasting impact on his life—for better or for worse. As I have suggested, a boy's experience of loneliness, the feelings tied to it (such as anxiety, frustration, and confusion, to name a few), and also his subsequent needs for God remain uniquely his own. In sharing part of my own story, I have sought merely to describe the kind of boy I was and the kind of God I needed. In a sense, my long search to reunite with that God after being presented with another was in itself healing. In other words, I now believe that while it took years to come to terms with Frank's God, years that involved loneliness and spiritual pain, my being able finally to do so indicates that solitude and God did their work. Granted, I did not have the degree of solitude I could have enjoyed if Frank had not come into my life, but I found enough to sustain me, for many years, in my loneliness. After all, I survived, and so did God.

The God portraits I advocate here were a salve for me as I sought healing, once and for all, from the pain I endured over Frank's God. These portraits may not be sufficient for everyone, which is to say that I do not know if they will provide for what all boys need. But they provided for me. They gave me something to hold on to as my very spirit got tossed around in a spiritual storm. These God portraits were no less than a lifeline to the God I wanted, and needed, to know would be with me, even to the end of the age. Helping another boy to know and embrace the God I have described may not only permit but also encourage him to be a boy more true to himself. With this God a boy can express his genuine self, "even in private," and thus "turn back toward his inner life" that has been thwarted. A "true boy," he can maintain fidelity to his true self as he maintains fidelity to God, even in the face of powerful cultural, interpersonal, and theological "forces" that encourage him to do otherwise. Though a degree of loneliness is every boy's inevitable lot, my own experience shows that God seeks quietly to transform that loneliness into solitude. Becoming the boy's ally, God helps him believe that he too has "found the answer" about which three boys named Hanson sing, "You can prevail, through the darkest nights, coldest winters, and the fires of hell."

PART III

Rebels and the Struggle for Self-Sufficiency

Donald Capps

5

The Making of the
Reliably Religious Boy

Boys who grow up in different decades (as the three authors of this book did) have very different cultural experiences. They don't watch the same movies and videos, they don't listen to the same types of music, they don't tell the same jokes, they don't have the same athletic or military heroes, and so forth. But there are similarities in the experiences of early adolescent boys that transcend cultural differences. All early adolescent boys identify to some degree with the loser, the loner, or the rebel. Many identify with all three.

As an early adolescent boy, I identified with all three labels. But as I think back, the one that stands out is the rebel. This is because it was the part of me that I had the most difficulty understanding. Probably because I had had a few loser and loner experiences before I became an early adolescent, they were sort of familiar to me. The rebel, though, was something new, and it puzzled me. I doubt I was ever self-conscious enough to ask myself, "What has gotten into me?" But I felt there was something happening to me, or inside of me, that didn't seem right. Because it had some pretty negative consequences at school and at home, I certainly didn't think of it as something positive. If I had thought to use the language of spirituality to describe or make sense of it, I am sure I would have thought of it as a bad spirit instead of a good one. Maybe I would have identified with the boy in Mark 9:14–29 who had a demonic spirit. But I didn't make this connection. After all, it didn't seem *that* bad. But neither did it seem a normal part of growing up, and it certainly didn't conform to my self-image as a boy who was a good citizen at school and a dutiful son at home. In fact, the feeling that my self-image had become tarnished troubled me a lot more than the consequences of my rebellious spirit—the disapproval and the punishments my behavior received from adults. In fact, most of the time I felt that my rebellious behavior was justified because I could see that adults' exercise of authority was sometimes unfair and that it was unevenly applied. I simply didn't think of myself as a rebellious kid.

I don't want to exaggerate my early adolescent rebellion. By most standards, it was pretty mild. I was certainly no flaming sociopath. I was never in danger of being sent to reform school. The basic issue, though, isn't whether a kid's rebellious spirit is massive or mild, exaggerated or understated, for even mild expressions of rebellion can tarnish the self-image that a younger boy has so easily and effortlessly developed. This self-image is the important thing, and to see it get tarnished for no apparent reason is a troubling experience.

What I didn't realize at the time is that this rebellious spirit has a positive side. In fact, it was many years before I realized this. As we said in the introduction, the positive side of this spirit of rebellion is that it gives a boy a sense of self-sufficiency, the sense that, as *Webster's New World College Dictionary* defines it, he has "the necessary resources to get along without help; independent" (Agnes 2001, 1302). A boy's rebellious spirit is a reaction to the vicissitudes of adult forms of support and beneficence. By expressing and exercising the spirit of rebellion, a boy also discovers that there are limits to how far those who have the power and resources to help and assist him are willing to go. By trying and testing these limits, he becomes more aware of his own power and resources, his own capacities for making good things happen. He discovers the futility, at times, of relying upon the support and beneficence of the adults who have authority over him. No doubt there are better, less painful ways to learn this important lesson. Still, whatever the negative consequences of the spirit of rebellion may happen to be, it teaches him to look to himself for the strengths and resources that he will need to make his way in the world. For some boys, rebellion is the best teacher in this regard. (Other boys may learn it the harder way, by adult abandonment.) I include myself among the rebels, but I am thankful that my rebellion was pretty mild, because more extreme expressions of rebellion may lead to a sense of self-sufficiency that is not grounded in reality but instead based on an inaccurate appraisal of the resources and strengths that one possesses. It may also lead to an unnecessarily cynical view of adult (and therefore institutional) forms of authority and to the equally inaccurate view that all authority is suspect and unworthy of one's support and confidence.

RELIGION AND SPIRITUALITY

Let's begin by clarifying some terms. Many people these days make a distinction between being religious and being spiritual. They say they are not religious but spiritual, or spiritually inclined. They dislike the word *religion*, usually because they got too much of it, or too much of the wrong kind of it, when they were growing up. I believe this distinction is a good one, and I will be using it in this chapter, but my point will be that we shouldn't think of religion and spirituality as competitors. Religion needs spirituality so that it doesn't become stultified and merely ceremonial, while spirituality needs religion so that it doesn't get esoteric and ethereal. Spirituality "works" not because it opposes religion but because it "plays off" religion. The word *religion* means (in Latin) to "bind back." The same Latin root word for *religion* is also the root word for *ligaments*, which *Webster's New World College Dictionary* defines as "bonds or ties connecting one thing to another" and "a band of tough tissue connecting bones or holding organs" (Agnes 2001, 829). I associate the word *religion* with one of the hymns I sang as a boy, "Blest Be the Tie That Binds."

Then there is the word *spirituality*. When I was a boy, I would not have thought of myself as "spiritual." The word *spirit* had mostly negative connotations. I saw it on medicine bottles, I associated it with my uncle's alcohol abuse, and I heard the word used in church as a synonym for something demonic, as when King Saul was said to be possessed by an "evil spirit" when he threw the spear at young David (1 Sam. 18:10–11). The Holy Spirit in my early adolescent years was the "Holy Ghost," so I didn't associate "spirit" with "God." On the other hand, a positive connotation of *spirit* was communicated through the study of American history at school. We learned about "the spirit of '76," which enabled the American colonists to throw off British rule. Significantly, the "spirit" in this case was the spirit of rebellion, the refusal to knuckle under British authority. We also learned about the *Spirit of St. Louis*, the plane the young aviator Charles Lindbergh flew across the Atlantic Ocean. Because this was a solo flight, his achievement was the very epitome of personal self-sufficiency, of drawing on his own skills and inner resources, because there was no one else in the plane to rely upon if something happened to him. Given my boyhood adulation of him, Charles Lindbergh (in spite of what I have since learned about his politics) remains more of a model for me of spirituality than, say, Saint Francis of Assisi. Because I learned religion in church and spirit in school, the two terms were not incompatible. But neither is their connection to one another obvious. I have to work at relating the two, and this, I suggest, is because both have their roots in early adolescent experience.

THE RELIGIONS OF HONOR AND HOPE

To complicate matters further, I believe that early adolescent boys develop not one but three types of religion. I call these the religions of honor, hope, and humor (see Capps 2002). My basic point in these chapters will be that the spirit of rebellion was, in my case, an expression of the religion of humor at the expense of the religion of honor.

Men like to say that they are not very religious, certainly not as religious as their wives, mothers, pastors, and priests. When a man says this, he does a disservice to the boy who continues to live inside of him, because this boy really *was* religious. In fact, he was so desperately religious that he needed a strong dose of spirituality to save him from the oppressions that his religious nature imposed upon him. For me and lots of other religious boys, the spirit of rebellion was especially important in this regard.

How did we men get religious? By listening to hot-headed preachers? By squirming for an hour on hard church pews? I think it was more subtle than this, that what made us religious was an experience that did not seem to have anything to do with religion. This is the emotional separation, described by Allan Cole in chapter 3, that takes place between a boy and his mother when he is three to five years old. All boys go through this due to powerful social and cultural expectations that a boy will begin at this age to identify with his father and become a man like him. This separation is unique to boys, for a daughter's continuing identification with her mother is considered appropriate and desirable at this age. As Cole noted, this separation is an important theme in William Pollack's *Real Boys* (1998), though for Pollack the separation from mother occurs around age six. I suggest that it begins earlier, and this seems to be the general consensus of developmental psychologists. What I want to emphasize here, though, is not so much the separation itself but the fact that boys develop two types of religion in their effort to cope with the separation.

First, there is the religion of *honor*, which is based on the boy's assumption that he is to blame for the separation. This assumption is false, because the real reason for the separation is that mothers are under considerable social pressure to ensure that their boys identify with their fathers and the world of male activities and pursuits. Also at this age, boys are developing in ways that encourage greater independence from their mothers. When I was growing up, none of the boys in our neighborhood wanted it said of him that "he's a mama's boy" or "he's tied to his mother's apron strings." (Mothers actually wore aprons in those days!). We worried a lot about a boy on our block whose mother kept him in the house all day and only reluctantly allowed him to play with other boys because she was afraid that he would get hurt. In a way, her fears were effective, because the fact that the rest of us knew about her fears led us to be especially careful that he not suffer injury. This was partly out of concern for him, but it was also because we did not want his mother to phone our mothers and tell them that we mistreated her boy.

The religion of honor takes the form of a vow—and the determination to live up to it—that one will try to be a good or better boy. By making this vow and sticking to it, a boy seeks to get back into his mother's good graces. Sometimes this vow is elicited under pressure or duress. In my day, a spanking would result in a reluctant—though appropriately tearful—promise to be good. More often, though, it is a vow that boys make to themselves, a silent pledge to avoid the behaviors that cause mother to become upset, angry, or, worst of all, hurt—a hurt that says, more powerfully than words ever could, that she is deeply disappointed in the boy she has taken such pains to bring up and for whom she has sacrificed her own aspirations in life.

Second is the religion of *hope*. In one sense, this religion evolves out of the religion of honor. After all, there is a strong element of hope in the anticipation that a boy's intention to be good will be rewarded and that his mother will welcome him back into her good graces. But in another sense, the religion of hope is very different from the religion of honor. The religion of honor involves winning mother back. In contrast, the religion of hope involves setting one's sights on other objects and objectives, especially ones that remind us of our mothers. After all, there were other women in the world besides our mothers, and some of these women, especially those who are loving and kind, offered what we came to desire from our mothers—the four "A's" of affection, approval, affirmation, and admiration. If the main purpose of the emotional separation from our mothers was so that we would identify with our fathers instead, this plan was compromised by the fact that teachers in the lower grades were women. As small boys, we transferred some of our desires to be the apple of our mother's eye to one or more of our teachers, and this set the stage for other such transfers over the course of our lives. As we moved through early to late adolescence, we undertook the stressful process of transferring these desires from our mothers and other older women to girls (and perhaps boys) our own age. Typically, a struggle would ensue between our longstanding loyalty to our mothers and our new, intense devotion to a special girl our very own age.

In effect, the religion of hope basically involves an emotional displacement. The original object of a boy's desire for affection, approval, affirmation, and admiration, is not relinquished, but as they say on Wall Street, he learns to "diversify" as a defense against the loneliness and emptiness that occur when mother is angry, upset, or hurt. Thus, the religion of hope involves seeking in the outside world what the boy previously experienced at home. Over the course of a lifetime, there will be other objects of desire and longing. Some of these will respond as he hopes they will, others will not, and still others will respond with such ambiguity that he will experience confusion, uncertainty, and doubt. Although women, being the closest analogue to his mother, are likely to figure prominently as the objects of such emotional displacement, he may be attracted to other men or to objects in the world—such as natural or created objects of beauty—that remind him of what he originally experienced in relation to his mother.

I call these religions. True, they lack holy scriptures or writings, a prescribed set of formal rituals and observances, a moral code and ethical ideals, a set of doctrines or beliefs, and so forth. But I use the word in an experiential sense. In *The Varieties of Religious Experience*, William James makes a distinction between institutional and experiential religion and defines experiential religion as "the feelings, acts, and experiences of individual men in their solitude, so far as they apprehend themselves to stand in relation to the divine" (1902/1982, 29). He added that there is a profound seriousness about this:

> For common men, "religion," whatever more special meanings it may have, signifies always a *serious* state of mind . . . . It favors gravity, not pertness; it says "hush" to all vain chatter and smart wit. . . . There must be something solemn, serious, and tender about any attitude which we denominate religious. If glad, it must not grin or snicker; if sad, it must not scream or curse. But if hostile to light irony, religion is equally hostile to heavy grumbling and complaint. (37–38)

For me and the other boys I knew, religion certainly signified "a serious state of mind." Later, though, when I introduce the religion of humor, I will suggest that we also allowed ourselves a few grins and snickers, and some light irony, at its expense.

Back, though, to the serious religions of honor and hope. Since I will be emphasizing the religion of honor in the course of this chapter, a couple of poems will illustrate how a boy gets hooked on it. William Stafford's "Mother's Day" illustrates how he tried to ensure that his mother would never get mad at him again (1998, 226–27):

Mother's Day

Peg said, "This one," and we bought it
for Mother, our allowance for weeks
paid out to a clerk who snickered—
a hideous jar, oil-slick in color,
glass that light got lost in.

We saw it for candy, a sign of
our love. And it lasted:
the old house on Eleventh,
a dim room on Crescent where
the railroad shook the curtains,
that brief glory at Aunt Mabel's place.

Peg thought it got more beautiful,
Egyptian, sort of, a fire-sheened
relic. And with a doomed grasp
we carried our level of aesthetics
with us across Kansas, proclaiming
our sentimental badge.

Now Peg says, "Remember that candy jar?"
She smoothes the silver. "Mother
hated it." I am left standing
alone by the counter, ready to buy what
will hold Mother by its magic, so
she will never be mad at us again.

Here Stafford suggests that his sister had known all along what he had not understood, that the jar did not possess the magic he hoped it would have. There is a sense of desperation in the concluding lines, as if to say that surely there is something that "will hold Mother by its magic," some gift that will permanently ensure that she will never get upset with him again.

While Stafford wrote his poem as an adult looking back on the boy standing alone at the counter, I wrote a poem when I was twelve years old for my mother on Mother's Day. Like Stafford's candy jar, a material gift probably accompanied the poem, designed to ensure her continuing favor—the equivalent of a gift offering to win the favor of the gods. The poem itself, however, was like a hymn of praise, extolling the virtues of the honored one, and doing so in much the same way that the adoration of the human mother, Mary, was made an integral part of the Christian religion and that Mother's Day has become an integral part of the church year. Here is the poem:

To Mom

God made the wondrous mountains,
God made the billowy sea,
And then, to me, he showed His love
When he gave me at birth to thee.

God looked down from the heavens
And saw you'd be a mother
Whom I would love and cherish,
Who'd care and tend like no other.

God gave *His* son a mother
Who was kind and good and sweet,
But then He gave to *me* a mom
Who's the finest a soul could meet.

So today I'm trying, Mom,
To express my adoration,
And say that you're the brightest star
In God's wonderful creation.

I found this poem in an old scrapbook that I had begun to compile at the age of
ten. The fact that I saved it indicates that I thought well enough of it to have
kept a copy for myself. Because it is addressed to my mother and not to God, it
differs from the hymns of praise that are collected together in a church hymnal.
Yet, like these hymns, the language is that of adoration. There is also a tone of
determination and effort throughout the poem, but especially in the first line of
the fourth verse—"So today I'm trying, Mom"—as if I had assigned myself a task
that did not come altogether easily, as if I had to work at it. There might even
be an unintended irony—which sometimes happens when one is engaging in an
act of praise—in the third verse, where Jesus' mother is described as "kind and
good and sweet" (everything that a boy wants in a mother) whereas *my* mother
is "the finest a soul could meet." There is an elevated tone to this line—"finest,"
"soul," even "meet"—that implies an emotional distance between the youthful
poet and the one upon whom he is bestowing all this honor and praise. Maybe
this elevated tone is simply because this is a Mother's Day poem and the poet is
attempting to respect the formalities of this special occasion. Even so, the poem
seems similar, in its emotional tone, to what the adult Stafford captures so beau-
tifully in his Mother's Day poem, namely, the desperate effort to find whatever
will hold Mother by its magic—a gift, the right words, whatever it takes—so that
she will never be displeased with her son again.

THE RELIGION OF HUMOR

If the religions of honor and hope are the primary religions to develop out of
the emotional separation from one's mother between the years of three and five,
there is a third religion that begins to come into its own in the early adolescent
years. This is the religion of humor. This religion reflects the boy's growing confidence in his ability to cope with the consequences of the original separation,
but it also reveals his growing impression—and suspicions—that the religions of
honor and hope are not all that they are cracked up to be. (I use the phrase
"cracked up" advisedly, as this phrase is often used to apply to our response to a
joke we find especially funny.) The religion of honor—being a good boy—is not
always rewarded. Sometimes a boy finds that he has been, literally, "good for
nothing." Maybe mother is depressed or distracted and simply doesn't notice
that he is trying to regain her favor. Or maybe she favors one of his siblings, and
there is nothing he can do to gain a similarly favorable position. Or maybe she

secretly prefers him to be a somewhat mischievous boy, one who is prone to get himself into trouble at school, perhaps because she knows that such a boy will continue to need her assistance in bailing him out. Or she may want him to be a good boy but worries that his very goodness will make him unfit for the competitive world that he will enter one day. Or maybe she isn't very good at hiding her true feelings regarding the gift that he has given her (Stafford's candy jar). Whatever the explanation may be, the boy has difficulty figuring out what would make her happy and proud to be his mother. He may even begin to feel that regaining her favor isn't worth the effort required.

The religion of hope may also create its own disappointments. When his hope relates to his mother, he may find that the gift intended to soften her heart and win her over does not have its intended effect. When his hope is directed toward others—the diversification strategy—he may discover that a teacher who has a whole classroom of children to contend with cannot give him the personal attention that he covets for himself. In fact, if he is also committed to the religion of honor and therefore determined to be a good boy, the teacher may take his reliability for granted and give greater attention to a boy who is giving her a more difficult time in class. As he grows older and enters the early adolescent years, the boy who has become the object of his boyish affection may instead have *his* eye on another boy, and he experiences his first lesson in unrequited love.

When either or both of these religions fail him, the religion of humor comes to his rescue. The religion of humor is not merely a religion that takes its place alongside the other two. Instead, it is a religion that stands over against them, calling their convictions and assumptions into question. Judging from the jokes that early adolescent boys tell one another and the jokes about boys that men tell, the religion that it initially challenges is the religion of honor. A typical joke in which a boy plays a key role is one where he "misunderstands" a teacher's question and gives an answer that, although technically in error, is funny, clever, or both. While overt misbehavior is likely to lead to some form of punishment, punishment is unlikely in this case unless the teacher believes the boy intends to undermine her authority. The most successful expressions of humor are those that cause the teacher herself to laugh, as this enables the whole class to experience a moment of mirth.

HOW ONE BOY BECAME RELIABLY RELIGIOUS

In my case, the religion of humor was the donkey the spirit of rebellion chose to ride. Before I tell that part of the story in the following chapter, though, I need to tell the part about how I became a "reliably" religious boy in the first place. This will take the rest of this chapter. If telling my story may seem a bit self-indulgent, my hope is that it will trigger similar recollections in other men. As Carl R. Rogers, founder of "client-centered" psychotherapy, wrote in his autobiographical essay "This Is Me":

> There have been times when in talking with students or staff, or in my writing, I have expressed myself in ways so personal that I have felt I was expressing an attitude which it was probable no one else could understand, because it was so uniquely my own. . . . [But] in these instances I have almost invariably found that the very feeling which has seemed to me most private, most personal, and hence most incomprehensible by others, has turned out to be an expression for which there is a resonance in many other people. It has led me to believe that what is most personal and unique in each one of us is probably the very element which would, if it were shared or expressed, speak most deeply to others. (1961, 26)

The word "reliably" refers to the fact that the early adolescent boy (ages 11–14) has developed a religious habit of mind, a habit reflected in his embrace of the religions of honor and hope. Three experiences in my early adolescent years loom especially large. One was listening to my mother tell me about her father's death. The other was listening to a Sunday school teacher tell my class that Jesus was coming again, and very, very soon. The third was listening to my father's ironic comment about a dead robin. It seems significant to me now that in all three experiences all I did was listen as adults said what they had to say (as though, perhaps, I was destined to go into the professional field that I did).

My Mother's Tragic Story

The story my mother told involved my maternal grandfather, a man I never knew. He was a Swedish immigrant who fathered four children (three daughters and a son) and worked in a factory within walking distance of his home in South Omaha. My mother told me the following story about him: One night, when she was about thirteen years old, there was a huge explosion at the plant where he worked, and he was killed. As a result of his sudden and violent death, my maternal grandmother did other families' washings in order to support herself and her children. When my mother told me about her father's tragic death, she also told me a related story. Her father was walking home from work one evening, about a week before he died, and he stopped to listen to a Salvation Army band because he loved music. As he stood there listening to the music, he found himself responding to the message as well, and when he arrived home he told my grandmother that he had experienced a religious conversion. In light of his death the very next week, my mother said to me that she viewed this as a sign of how the Lord works in our lives.

Although I never knew my maternal grandfather, this story about his conversion experience and his subsequent death in an explosion had a sobering effect on me as a boy. However, it was not until I read a brief autobiographical sketch by Harvard psychologist Henry A. Murray when I was in graduate school that I understood how these stories my mother told me about her father had shaped my religious understanding. These two sentences fairly leaped off the page:

> Of all these progenitors I was acquainted only with my daughter-venerated grandfather, aloof toward me, but a kindly gent whose white bearded visage resembled God's as painted, say, by Tintoretto. Remembering him I have been led to surmise that the image and concept of Yahweh must have come not from the all-too-familiar father figure, but from the more remote and lordly grandfather, the overruling patriarch of the clan. (1967, 296).

For Murray, his recollection of his maternal grandfather provided insight into the development of the Judeo-Christian religion. For me, however, the key phrase was "daughter-venerated grandfather." I realized that my own understanding of the divine Father was based on stories my mother had told me about my grandfather, a man whom I knew by hearsay only.

At about the same time, I encountered the following sentence in Erik H. Erikson's "Reflections on the American Identity" in *Childhood and Society*: "The boy's male ideal is rarely attached to his father, as lived with in daily life. It is usually an uncle or friend of the family, if not his grandfather, as presented to him (often unconsciously) by his mother" (1963, 271). A few sentences later, Erikson adds that a woman's identification with her father

> did not permit her to take a husband as strong as her powerful father. She married what seemed in comparison a weak but safe man and settled down. In many ways, however, she talks like the grandfather. She does not know how she persistently belittles the sedentary father and decries the family's lack of mobility, geographic and social. Thus she establishes in the boy a conflict between the sedentary habits which she insists on, and the reckless habits she dares him to develop. (271)

When I first read this passage about the maternal grandfather, I was aware that the picture fit but that certain modifications were needed. After immigrating to America, my maternal grandfather was as sedentary as my father was, but the very fact that he immigrated in the first place made him seem more courageous, especially in light of the fact that my father did not serve in World War II as my younger uncles did. Also, Erikson may overstate the case, though not by much, when he says that the daughter of this man "does not know how she persistently belittles the sedentary father and decries the family's lack of mobility, geographic and social." The part about how she establishes in her boy "a conflict between the sedentary habits which she insists upon, and the reckless habits she dares him to develop," may overstate the "reckless" side a bit, but behind the story of how my grandfather accepted the Lord the week before his violent death was an implicit assumption of some sort of heroism well beyond the safe and sedentary—indeed, of going out, perhaps, in a blaze of glory.

I read these passages from Murray and Erikson in the mid-1960s, at a time when theological schools were struggling over the death of God movement. Although I did not join the movement, neither was I a debunker of it, and the personal reason for this was almost certainly the fact that the human mortal on whom my perception of the divine Father was based was a man I never knew. It was not that I consciously identified God as my maternal grandfather, as though I could look at a photograph of him and say, "There's God." There was, however, an experiential link between my maternal grandfather and God, and this link was the sense of the heroic and the dramatic, of something in the works that was much more momentous than the routine life I lived day by day in our house on Spencer Street. My favorite Bible verse in my early adolescent years was John 14:6, where Jesus says, "I am the way, the truth, and the life. No one comes to the Father but by me." I wanted to be like Jesus, the loyal son of this powerful Father, and this meant pledging my very life to this Father and to whatever he wanted of me. This was to join, in a sense, the "Salvation Army," to enlist in the "band" of those who had given everything that they were—and possessed—for the sake of the heavenly kingdom and were now looking down upon boys like me from their places in glory, praying that we would make a similar solemn pledge—that we too would enlist, for the battle could not be won unless we too stepped forward.

It was no accident that my favorite hymn was "Onward Christian Soldiers." I adopted this hymn as my own before I learned that the words were written by a young vicar, Sabine Baring-Gould, and set to music by the church organist, Arthur S. Sullivan (who later teamed up with William Gilbert to write comic opera), to keep the church kids in line as they made their way to a picnic spot. Had I known that its original purpose was utterly lacking in some great heroic purpose, I may not have adopted the hymn as expressive of my personal faith. In any event, I especially loved the third stanza: "Like a mighty army / Moves the Church of God; / Brothers we are treading / Where the saints have trod. / We are not divided, / All one body we, / One in hope and doctrine, / One in charity" (Lutheran Church in America 1958, 560).

Of course, I lived another life as well: the routine life of going to school, playing games with friends after school, going to Saturday afternoon matinees, listening to comedians on the radio in the evening, and so forth. But this was not where the drama lay. The drama and the excitement were in my religious life, which was also the life of my imagination.

My Sunday School Teacher's Prophecy

When I was eleven, maybe twelve, a new element was introduced into my religious life and with it, the possibility of profound disillusionment. This year our Sunday school teacher was a man, and he and his wife were part of my parents' close circle of friends. Although he worked at the local post office and I had often seen him at church and at church picnics, I didn't know him very well. But he was a man about whom my father liked to tell this story: One Wednesday evening our pastor preached a sermon that so stirred his heart that when the collection plate was passed, he dropped a twenty-dollar bill into it. When he realized what he had done, he went to the ushers after the service and asked if he could have his twenty dollars back because his wife would wonder whatever happened to it and wouldn't believe his story. My father found it amusing that his friend had succumbed to the emotion of the moment, thereby getting himself in a jam from which he had to extricate himself. I found it funny too, though I felt a little guilty for thinking it so.

In the year he taught my Sunday school class he was very much into biblical prophesies, and he had done some computations on the basis of the book of Daniel that proved Jesus' second coming would occur that very year. I can no longer recall the exact date or even the year (1950? 1951?), but each Sunday he would tell us kids how many days were left—much as the newspaper told us how many shopping days were left before Christmas. He would tell us what a glorious event it would be when Jesus came in clouds of glory and, after a brief battle with Satan and his armed forces, the present world would end and a new world would replace it.

I recall having some anxiety about all this, but mostly it excited me because I wanted to see Jesus face-to-face. Meanwhile, of course, the usual routine of school, with lessons designed to prepare us for a productive adulthood, continued as though nothing was about to happen. I don't recall speaking to the other boys and girls in our Sunday school class about our teacher's prediction, nor do I remember any conversations with my parents or older brothers about it. If I talked with anyone about it, this would almost certainly have been my mother, and I doubt that she would have cast doubt on the teacher's prophecy. Had I talked with my father about it, he would probably have observed that this was the same fellow who retrieved his twenty-dollar bill from the collection plate and left me to draw my own conclusions.

The designated day came and, of course, nothing unusual happened. No

Jesus appeared in clouds of glory, no battle occurred between the armed forces of God and Satan, and no New World arose from the ashes and rubble of the old. The following Sunday our teacher explained that he had made a miscalculation. To the best of my recollection, I (and, I assume, the other kids) took his explanation at face value, perhaps because we knew how easy it is to make a careless mistake on an arithmetic test. He did not put forward a new revised date, and when Sunday school ended and summer vacation began, the prophecy was relegated to the past.

Many years later—again, when I was in graduate school—I read two books that helped me interpret the effects of this failed prophecy on my development into a reliably religious boy. One was *When Prophecy Fails* by L. Festinger, H. W. Riecken, and S. Schachter (1956), an account of their research involving a religious group in California whose leader had predicted a great cataclysmic event to occur on a given date. Several members of the group gathered in his living room that day to experience it together. It did not occur, of course, but what surprised Festinger and his colleagues was that the group did not break up, although those who had gathered with the others remained more faithful than those who waited elsewhere and alone. The group began contacting local newspapers, which they had not done before the predicted date, to report that the prophecy had *not* come true, which meant to them that there had been a reprieve. They appealed to others to join them in their vigil. Although the explanation—a last-minute postponement—and my Sunday school teacher's explanation of human error were different, neither the California group nor I became disillusioned. In fact, even as the Californians became more concerned than ever to publicize their group, I became more determined to lead a life that was pleasing to Jesus and the heavenly Father. Thus, the beneficiary of the failed prophecy was the religion of honor, its focus having expanded from working hard to win my mother's approval and admiration to proving myself worthy of Jesus and his Father in heaven.

The other book that helped me was Daniel J. Boorstin's *The Image: A Guide to Pseudo-Events in America* (1992). He pointed out that the earliest newspapers in America were printed and circulated when something noteworthy had happened. Because a newsworthy event could not be predicted in advance, newspapers would appear on a very random basis. But when they became dailies, editors needed to fill the space whether anything really newsworthy had happened or not, and the phenomenon of the "pseudo-event" was created. Events were not fabricated out of thin air, but "eventfulness" would be ascribed to happenings considered routine before the advent of the daily newspaper. An event would be blown out of all proportion to its importance. In time, "events" would, in fact, be manufactured or staged by the news media or by those who sought celebrity status.

As I reflected on my Sunday school teacher's prediction of the second coming, this too seemed to fit the category of the pseudo-event, and I began to think about how I had become emotional—both anxious and excited—about an event that never materialized. If the experience did not lead to disillusionment, it created wariness with regard to the religious imaginations of others. Also, although my own religious attitude remained solemn and serious, a light irony began to play about its edges, and this is where my very human father became significant.

My Father's Irreverence

I am uncertain how old I was when the following event occurred, but I was probably twelve. In fact, it could have happened the summer following the failed prophecy. I was mowing the lawn, and my father was cutting the hedges between ours and the neighbor's yards. In the path ahead of the lawnmower I saw the carcass of a dead robin. Should I pick it up or mow around it? I called to my father, and he came over. I expected him to solve my dilemma—which he eventually did—but not before he looked up in the sky and then down at the bird at our feet and said, "His eye is on the sparrow, but I see a dead robin." The comment implied, of course, that while God was watching over the sparrow, he had neglected the robin. His tone, though, was matter-of-fact, and not one of mockery or sarcasm. Still, although I wanted to laugh, I checked myself because I thought he was being a little too irreverent.

Later I learned about irony in courses in English and American literature. *Webster's New World College Dictionary* says it is "a cool, detached attitude of mind, characterized by recognition of the incongruities and complexities of experience" (Agnes 2001, 755). Although I did not know the word for it at the time, I began—cautiously at first—to incorporate the attitude itself into my religious view of life. In time, it became for me, as it had also been for my father, a means to avoid the "heavy grumbling and complaint" to which, according to James, religion is also hostile (James 1982, 38). My father's irony helped me to maintain the religion of hope by incorporating into my hopefulness an element of emotional detachment. My Sunday school teacher's failed prophecy could have led to disillusionment, a sense of having been duped, or to the belief that religion is fundamentally fraudulent. That this did not happen was due to the fact that my very human father did not take religion as seriously as others, such as my Sunday school teacher, did.

On the other hand, the very fact that my Sunday school teacher's prophecy did not come true led me to dissociate myself from the boy who had believed that Jesus was coming again in a matter of weeks. This deluded boy became something of an embarrassment to me, and whenever I recalled the experience,

I felt ashamed for having allowed myself to be taken in. My graduate school readings in Festinger and Boorstin helped me understand what had taken place, but it wasn't until I encountered the following poem by Stanley Kunitz a few years ago that I experienced a sense of being reunited with this boy who had so much wanted to believe that Jesus was coming that year. Kunitz's father committed suicide shortly before Stanley was born, and many of his poems explore what he calls "the theme of the lost father" (2000, 267). The poem is titled "Halley's Comet" (256–57):

Halley's Comet

Miss Murphy in first grade
wrote its name in chalk
across the board and told us
it was roaring down the storm tracks
of the Milky Way at frightful speed
and if it wandered off its course
and smashed into the earth
there'd be no school tomorrow.
A red-bearded preacher from the hills
with a wild look in his eyes
stood in the public square
at the playground's edge
proclaiming he was sent by God
to save every one of us,
even the little children.
"Repent, ye sinners!" he shouted,
waving his hand-lettered sign.
At supper I felt sad to think
that it was probably
the last meal I'd share
with my mother and my sisters;
but I felt excited too
and scarcely touched my plate.
So mother scolded me
and sent me early to my room.
The whole family's asleep
except for me. They never heard me steal
into the stairwell hall and climb
the ladder to the fresh night air.
Look for me, Father, on the roof
of the red brick building
at the foot of Green Street—
that's where we live, you know, on the top floor.
I'm the boy in the white flannel gown
sprawled on this coarse gravel bed
searching the starry sky,
waiting for the world to end.

Halley's Comet was last seen in 1986, so the appearance young Stanley antic-
ipated that night would have been in 1910, the very year that my father was
also a first-grader. Of course, there is a big difference between Jesus coming
on clouds of glory and Halley's Comet crashing into the earth. The poem,
though, brought me back in touch with the excitement I had felt as I antici-
pated the Lord's return and my first meeting with our heavenly Father. I too
was the boy searching the starry sky, waiting for the world to end, and I too
was bidding the Father to look for me even as I was looking out for him.

I have suggested that my maternal grandfather, whom I had never seen,
played a major role in the formation of my image of God as a Father who is
larger than life and of my own life as a participation in events that are highly dramatic and of heroic proportions. In *The Birth of the Living God* (1979), Ana-
Marie Rizzuto points out that our images of God may undergo significant
changes over the course of a lifetime and says that it is a good thing if these
images keep pace with our own growth and maturation. As an early adolescent,
I would not have thought of my *paternal* grandfather as a potential contributor
to my image of God. There was nothing very remote or larger than life about
him. Most of the time he lived in my family's home, but he and I did not have
very much to say to one another. I did not think of him in the same religious
terms in which I thought of my maternal grandfather. He was not an overtly religious man, and there were certainly no stories about him that were remotely
akin to the story of my maternal grandfather's conversion the week before his
violent death. He had a personal habit, though, that I too developed in my early
adolescent years. He would go into his room, close the door, and read.

As I have grown older, my visual image of this quiet, rather self-absorbed,
elderly man—sitting alone in his room reading and not bothering anyone but
happy to chat about this and that on the few occasions it occurred to me that
he might enjoy a little company—has become increasingly central to my image
of God. There may be an element here of what Rizzuto calls the "self-repre-
sentational" aspect of one's image of God, but when I imagine God as an older
man sitting in his room absorbed in a book, I think more of my seemingly reli-
gion-deficient paternal grandfather than I do of myself. So maybe both grand-
fathers shaped my image of God in my early adolescent years, one more
manifest, the other more latent. The main point, though, is that the boy who
became reliably religious in his early adolescent years has remained so despite
the fact that the drama and heroics have long since faded away.

THE SCOUT AND THE RELIGION OF HONOR

I have cited several books that I read during my graduate study days
that enabled me to understand the central religious experiences of my early

adolescent years. I was also an avid reader in these early adolescent years, however, and the books that I read at that time gave support to the religions of honor and hope. Two books were especially influential in this regard. One was the *Handbook for Boys* (1948) published by the Boy Scouts of America. The other book was John Bunyan's *The Pilgrim's Progress*, the first half of which was originally published in 1678. The *Handbook for Boys* reinforced the religion of honor. *The Pilgrim's Progress* supported the religion of hope. The "Scout" became for me an identity-theme relating to the religion of honor, while the "Pilgrim" became an identity-theme relating to the religion of hope.

For me, my older brothers, and my neighborhood friends, the *Handbook for Boys* was the Bible of the religion of honor. The second chapter sets forth the rules of scouting, and these rules include the Scout Oath and the Scout Law. The Scout Oath begins, "On my honor I will do my best," and specifies the three ways in which a Scout will do his best (Boy Scouts 1948, 20–25). First, he will do his duty to God and his country and obey the Scout Law. Second, he will help other people at all times. Third, he will keep himself physically strong, mentally awake, and morally straight. The paragraphs that explain what being "morally straight" is all about make a strong association between morality and religion. They note that "George Washington said that morality cannot be lasting without religion" and state that the "morally straight Scout knows how to love and serve God in the way He wants him to. We are created by God and we owe certain duties to this Heavenly Father of all of us" (25). This heavenly Father gave Moses the Ten Commandments and "laid down certain definite Laws for all. Not to steal, not to lie, not to abuse your body are some of these Laws. Keeping these Commandments is an important step towards being morally straight" (25). Thus: "A loving Scout son always asks his Heavenly Father's pardon before he goes to bed at night for any offense he may have committed in thought, word or deed during the day. This is a Scout's way of saying: 'I am sorry, dear God, and with your help I will not offend you again' " (25).

The Scout Law consists of twelve qualities of character: "trustworthy, loyal, helpful, friendly, courteous, kind, obedient, cheerful, thrifty, brave, clean, and reverent" (26–27). Several of the extended commentaries on these twelve qualities refer to a Boy Scout's obligations to his mother. The one on trustworthiness, for example, admonishes the Scout to do "exactly a given task" and provides the following illustration: "When your mother trusts you to look after the younger children in her absence, you stay with them instead of joining the ball game in the next lot" (28).

The one on helpfulness tells a story in which a troop of Boy Scouts helps a mother out when the father is incapacitated:

The father of a family of seven children had been injured and was in the hospital. The children were sure, however, that Santa Claus would fill their stockings while they slept. To the mother, the situation was desperate, because the family needed food and clothing, and there were long weeks ahead before her husband could leave the hospital. While the children chattered of roller skates, dolls and Christmas trees, she was trying to figure out how to scrape enough together to keep the home going. Then there came a knock at the door. "Santa Claus!" shouted the children. It was not Santa Claus, but a Boy Scout with a smile extending clear across his face. In his arms a bag overflowed with toys. Behind him stood another Scout, and another—a whole Troop of Boy Scouts, bringing toys and food and clothing, enough to carry the family through the weeks ahead. (31)

The extended commentary on obedience relates the story of an army officer asking George Washington's mother how she had managed to raise such a brilliant son. He expected her to mention his fame for telling the truth, his sense of honor, and his bravery: "But his mother's reply to the question touched none of these qualities. Instead, she answered, 'I taught him to obey!'" (34). To illustrate cheerfulness, the commentary offers the negative example of

the fellow who is all smiles as long as he gets what he wants but who grouses like a spoiled child, if he doesn't. He likes to cook the camp meal on a fine day, but not when the wind blows the smoke in his eyes. He's a good pal as long as you play the game he wants. He's a smiling son if his mother offers the gang a plate of cookies; but if she wants the eggs collected—he doesn't act like a Scout. (35)

The good Scout is a credit to his mother and would never do anything that would give his mother any cause for anger or grief.

Clearly, the *Handbook for Boys* reinforces the religion of honor. Discussing Scout spirit and citizenship, it observes, "People in every age and every race have had their codes of Honor" (118). Then, after quoting the Athenian Code in full, it states:

Your Scout code includes the ideals of the Athenian Code and of other splendid codes that have gone before you. It has in it some principles from the Mayflower Compact, an agreement drawn up by the Pilgrims after they landed in Plymouth. It includes some of the ideals in the Declaration of Independence. In many ways it resembles the Knight's code to which the Knights pledged their honor in the Middle Ages. (119)

An illustration bearing the caption "Men of all ages had their codes of honor" includes two medieval knights, a backwoodsman being handed a peace pipe by a Native American, and a Boy Scout (120). The visual image here is that the Boy Scout exemplifies a tradition rooted in medieval knighthood and elaborated in the figure of the frontiersman, one who lives at peace with his neighbors.

Considering that the twelfth quality in the Scout Code is reverence, it should come as no surprise that the *Handbook for Boys* emphasizes the importance of religion. The description of one's duty to God emphasizes faithfulness to "Almighty God's Commandments," being "proud of your religious faith," and remembering when "doing your duty to God, to be grateful to Him. Whenever you succeed in doing something well, thank Him for it. Sometimes when you look up into a starlit sky on a quiet night, and feel close to Him—thank Him as the Giver of all good things" (20–21). Also, "one way to express your duty and your thankfulness to God is to help others, and this too, is a part of your Scout promises" (21).

I am capable, as an adult, of distinguishing between the Christian faith and the honor code of the Boy Scouts. I doubt, though, that I would have made any such distinction in my early adolescent years. As far as I was concerned, a Christian boy was one who made a dedicated effort to be trustworthy, loyal, helpful, friendly, courteous, kind, obedient, cheerful, thrifty, brave, clean, and reverent. These were the very marks of Christian character. Although I have had no involvement with the Boy Scouts since the age of fourteen, I continue to look for these qualities in other men and try to exemplify them myself. The twelve qualities of the Scout are to me what the twelve steps are to an alcoholic in recovery.

Furthermore, the very notion of the "Scout" continues to have great metaphorical value for me because, as *Webster's New World College Dictionary* shows, it means that one is *observant*—taking in the world around him and interpreting what is going on—and is *sent out*, usually in advance of the others, to make an assessment of what lies ahead and to report back to the others (Agnes 2001, 1287). If the compass is to Scouting what the cross is to the church, the Scout is the boy—and the man—who can find his way about, who doesn't lose his way, who is not subject, at least for long, to mental or moral confusion. He keeps his wits about him whatever the pressures of life may be.

A few years ago, the Boy Scouts of America was in the news because a gay man was forced to resign from his role as a troop leader. Eventually, the federal courts supported the organization's action on the grounds that a voluntary organization may establish its own membership restrictions. In the 1948 *Handbook* there is no reference to homosexual behavior. I doubt that the phrase "morally straight" is a subtle allusion to heterosexuality, as the word *straight* as a synonym for *heterosexual* was coined a couple of decades later. On the other hand, the handbook's specific injunction against abusing one's body, and its rather dubious suggestion that this injunction may be found in the Ten Commandments, indicates that *masturbation* was of great concern to the organization at the time that I was in early adolescence. In a section on confiding any worries a boy might have to his family doctor, the *Handbook* says:

> Suppose you wet the bed once in a while. Don't be afraid to ask him how to stop it. Suppose you are worrying because you have "wet dreams" or have practiced masturbation once in a while. If it has happened, don't let it scare you. If it's a habit, break it! Sure, it takes courage, and the best way is to keep busy with lots of work and play. But talk it over with your parents, religious leader or doctor; just open up to them and let them set you right. (412)

In "From Masturbation to Homosexuality: A Case of Displaced Moral Disapproval" (2003), I contend that as the religious community has softened its stance against masturbation, it has increased its disapproval of homosexual behavior. Also, because masturbation was something "we" did whereas homosexual acts are something "they" do, there has been a shift over the last several decades from personal soul-searching to castigation of others. This shift is reflected in the writings of James Dobson, a psychologist who has had enormous influence on conservative parents in the rearing of their children. He advises boys not to "struggle with guilt" if they masturbate (Dobson 1992, 83–84) and advises parents not to wage battle against it (2001, 78–79). On the other hand, he condemns homosexuality in no uncertain terms, associating it with pedophilia, promiscuity, and effeminacy among boys and masculinity among girls (2001, 113–29).

Relevant to the argument presented in this chapter, Dobson endorses the view of Joseph Nicolosi that the major cause of male homosexuality is the mother's inclination "to hold onto her son in what becomes an unhealthy mutual dependency, especially if she does not have a satisfying, intimate relationship with the boy's father" (2001, 122). Therefore, if a father "wants his son to grow up straight, he has to break the mother-son connection that is proper to infancy but not in the boy's interest after the age of three" (2001, 122). In other words, a powerful rationale for the emotional separation of mother and son between the ages of three and five is to ensure that one's son will not become a homosexual. Neither Dobson nor Nicolosi discuss the painful effects of this "breaking" of the mother-son connection; nor, of course, do they consider the fact that this very break is a key to why boys become religious in the ways that I have identified here.

THE PILGRIM AND THE RELIGION OF HOPE

In my early adolescent years, John Bunyan's *The Pilgrim's Progress* had a special place on my bookshelf next to the King James Version of the Bible. I read a great deal about heroes and heroines in my early adolescent years, and the scrapbook I began to compile when I was ten years old had a lot of short biographical articles clipped from the *Weekly Reader* (a children's magazine distributed at school), *Reader's Digest*, and *Life* magazine. There were articles on Abraham Lincoln, Franklin Roosevelt, Irving Berlin, Jackie Robinson, Bob Feller, Raphael (the painter), Juan Ortiz (a Spanish explorer who assimilated into a Native American community in Florida), Nancy Hart (who captured five British soldiers single-handedly during the Revolutionary War), and Pocahontas ("America's First Great Lady"). Important as these heroes and heroines were to me, Bunyan's hero had special status in my imagination because his name was "Christian." As a Christian myself, I identified with him. What I learned from the book was that a Christian will meet many persons on the journey of life. Some will be good for him, helping him to remain on the path that leads to salvation. Others will not be good for him. At best, they will slow his progress. At worst, they will lead him astray. As he journeys along, Christian meets good persons such as Evangelist, Good-Will, Interpreter, Watchful, Discretion, and the three lovely virgins (Prudence, Piety, and Charity) who live in the home of Discretion, Faithful, and Hopeful. He also meets bad persons such as Pliable, Mister Worldly Wiseman, Formalist, Hypocrisy, Mistrust, Talkative, Envy, Ignorance, and Apollyon, which is the Greek name for Abaddon, the Hebrew name of the king, also the angel of the bottomless pit, mentioned in Revelation 9:11.

The Pilgrim's Progress gave me a powerful sense that life is a journey that culminates in the crossing of the River Jordan and entrance into the Celestial City. I do not recall whether particular passages stood out for me. Given that John 14:6 was my favorite Bible verse, it afforded a vivid impression of "the way" itself and of how vital it is to stay on course, straying neither to the right nor left and not looking backward but always straight ahead. Also, because Christian does not actually meet Jesus until he arrives safely in the Celestial City, it taught me that Jesus keeps Christian on "the way" by providing him with reliable companions, the most important being Faithful, whom he meets fairly early in his journey, and Hopeful, whom he meets later and in whose company he enters the Celestial City.

Because *The Pilgrim's Progress* is about a man who is continually looking toward the near and distant future—confirming, perhaps, the popular view that men are linear thinkers—it is a book about hope. When Christian and Hopeful realize that the only way they can reach the Celestial City is by swimming across the River Jordan, they ask the Shining Men who have come over to offer them encouragement how deep the waters are. The Men reply, "You shall find it deeper or shallower, as you believe in the King of the place" (Bunyan 1678/1957, 152). As he enters the river, Christian begins to sink and cries out to his good friend Hopeful, "I sink in deep waters; the billows go over my head, all his waves go over me!" Hopeful tells his friend to be of good cheer, and "had much ado to keep his brother's head above water; yea, sometimes he would be quite gone down, and then ere a while he would rise up again half dead" (152). All the while, Hopeful continues to comfort his friend, helping to hold his head above water, and assuring him that "Jesus Christ maketh thee whole" (152). At last, Christian breaks out with a loud voice, exclaiming, "Oh, I see him again, and he tells me, 'When thou passest through the waters, I will be with thee; and through the rivers, they shall not overflow thee'" (152). Presently, he finds solid ground to stand upon, and the rest of the river turns out to be shallow. So they make it to the other side of the river, where the Shining Men are there to welcome them.

Thus, the final test for Christian was whether he would be able to cross the River Jordan without drowning. I don't know if I made a connection at the time to this final test of courage—even heroism—and my father's confession to me that lifesaving was the only Boy Scout merit badge that had eluded his grasp. In any case, I must have been impressed with Christian's companion, Hopeful, because he was able to provide his friend the moral support he needed in order to make it safely across. Also, in contrast to my Sunday school teacher's version of the religion of hope, Bunyan's version was very this-worldly, as it centered on the journey of life and on the persons and places one encounters along the way.

For an early adolescent boy, *The Pilgrim's Progress* was a practical book, and it was even more practical, in a sense, than the *Handbook for Boys*, which emphasizes making one's way in the world of nature. Scouting began when Robert Baden-Powell, a young British army officer, was sent to South Africa to train new soldiers from England in the skills of tracking, trailing, and wilderness living. He found that his men were so accustomed to city life that they could not handle the vigorous life of the outdoors. So he developed a series of games and other activities to make his men physically strong, self-reliant, and able to live comfortably in the wilderness (Boy Scouts 1948, 7–8; see also Baden-Powell 1908/2004). Of course, he saw the value of wilderness training to his men's subsequent return to city life. Nonetheless, *The Pilgrim's Progress* has its locus in human society. It emphasizes choosing one's travel companions carefully and avoiding places like Vanity Fair. It advises one to listen to the men and women who are good, honest, and have one's best interests at heart.

Both texts, though, support a boy's need to make his way in the outside world, of nature and human society—a task and process that began with the emotional separation from his mother when he was three to five years of age. For me, they were the very crux of the religions of honor and hope.

JESUS AND A BOY'S NEED FOR TENDERNESS

I have discussed the *Handbook for Boys* and *The Pilgrim's Progress* as two books that reinforced the religions of honor and hope, thus helping me to become a reliably religious boy. Neither book, though, could hold a candle to the Bible, which I understood to have a unique status in the world of books. The scrapbook that I began to compile at age ten has a handwritten account of Alfred the Great that reads:

> Once there was in England a good king named Alfred. He was so brave and wise and did such fine things for his people that he is always called Alfred the Great. When Alfred was a little boy his mother had a copy of the Bible. She said: "I'll give this book to the one of you five princes who learns to read it first." The princes studied hard. They were anxious to win the Bible. Not long after one of the boys came to his mother and said, "I think I can read the book," and sure enough, he could. Now Alfred who won the prize got the Bible. He was the youngest of the five princes. He loved books all his life. He loved books so much he wanted the people to have them so he made schoolhouses and hired school-teachers. He liked books but the Bible was his favorite.

Since it was handwritten, I assume I copied it from a book or magazine. What is interesting in light of what I have said here about a boy's mother's role in his adoption of the religions of honor and hope is the connection between Alfred's mother and the Bible. The prince who learns to read the Bible gains his mother's favor. At some point in my early adolescent years I resolved to read the Bible from cover to cover. A notation on the title page of my Bible says that I completed this task on Easter Sunday 1953, which meant that I was fourteen years old and beginning the transition from early to late adolescence. In one sense, my faithful reading of the Bible was intended to win my mother's admiration (and, perhaps, as in the case of Alfred the Great, to secure her favoritism as well). But in another, deeper sense, the Bible was a symbolic compensation for the loss of my earlier sense of her unconditional love.

It was not until I read Erik H. Erikson's *Young Man Luther* as a graduate student that I became aware that the Bible had played such a compensatory role. Here is the key sentence: "I think that in the Bible Luther at last found a mother whom he could acknowledge; he could attribute to the Bible a generosity to which he could open himself, and which he could pass on to others, at last a mother's son" (Erikson 1958, 208). As an early adolescent boy, books were for me a compensation for my earlier loss of my sense of my mother's unconditional love, but the Bible was special in this regard, for the Bible was to a Protestant boy what Mother Church was to a Catholic boy. The Bible was a book that I could hold in my hands, turn its pages, and engage its words with all of my senses and not be concerned that I might cause "her" to be angry, upset, or hurt.

This brings me, finally, to another page in the same scrapbook, an article containing several paragraphs about "the golden age of painting." The last paragraph tells about the fifteenth-century Italian painter, Raphael:

> Raphael has sometimes been called "The Divine," for in his pictures he loved to express the tenderness and sweetness and joy of life. His picture, the Sistine Madonna, is one of the greatest pictures ever painted. It shows the Virgin Mary holding the beautiful Christ Child. He looks out over the world with *such tender joy that it seems as if he must still be hearing the song the angels sang on his birth night.* (Stephenson 1940, 15, emphasis added)

This article was published in the *Weekly Reader* in January 1940, exactly a year after my birth and some nine years before I began to compile my scrapbook. How I acquired a copy of an article published nine years earlier is anyone's guess. Why I saved it is the more interesting question. Was it because of another story my mother told me—the one about how she had heard a choir of angels as she lay in her hospital bed a day or two after she gave birth to me?[1]

In any event, the article emphasizes Raphael's portrayal of the Christ child who "looks out over the world with such tender joy." I recall how ardently I sang, "Softly and tenderly Jesus is calling, calling for you and for me. There by the ramparts he's waiting and watching. . . ." (Lutheran Church in America 1958, 578–79). In singing this hymn, I felt a tenderness exceeding anything a mother or father could offer or provide. I would have agreed then—as I do now—with William James when he added the word "tender" to his observation that the religious attitude must be "solemn" and "serious" (James 1902/1982, 40).

---

[1]In my skeptical college days, I attributed this heavenly choir to her having heard a nurse's chorus in the outside hallway while she was still under the effects of the anesthesia. Many years later, when I learned (via a letter she had saved that my father had written to her a day or so after my birth containing sixty-one boys' names, plus letters from her sisters and friends expressing surprise that I turned out to be a boy and offering reassurances that I would be as welcome as a girl would have been) that she had firmly believed that I was to be a girl, I adopted the view that the choir of angels provided her the reassurance that God had intended me to be a boy all along. In my early adolescence, however, I evidently took her story at face value. I have copies of poems I wrote at that time titled "He Will Take Us Home Above" and "Where the Angels Live—A Spiritual." The latter says that the gates to heaven are open wide, that heaven is a place where a car cannot go, and getting there does not cost a fare.

6

The Rebellious Spirit of the Early Adolescent Boy

In the preceding chapter, I noted that church was the place where I was introduced to negative connotations of the word *spirit*, while school was where I was introduced to its more positive connotations. In church, I learned that King Saul had an evil spirit, or that Jesus healed a man of a "dumb spirit," whereas in school I learned about the "spirit of '76," which enabled the American colonists to throw off British rule. These colonists were rebels, and because they were, I came to view rebellion—when it was justified—as an expression of a deep sense of spirit. In fact, this very spirit of rebellion comes immediately to my mind even now when I think of spirituality. Prayer? Meditation? Holiness? These may be other people's ideas of spirituality. They are not mine, and I no longer feel the need to apologize for the fact that they are not.

I am not alone. While rummaging around a local used bookstore, I stumbled upon *Eyes of Boyhood* edited by Clyde Brion Davis. It has twenty selections about early adolescent boys from works by Mark Twain, Ernest Hemingway, Stephen Crane, James Thurber, and others. It was published in 1953, when I was fourteen, the year I was transitioning from early to late adolescence. In his introduction, Davis says his goal is to represent "some of the most indestructible boys in American literature, both fiction and biography." Why indestructible? Davis explains:

> I am sure the normal pre-adolescent boy has a greater understanding of life around him than a great many adults suspect. I think a normal twelve-year-old boy is a pretty shrewd and crafty animal. But he usually is a congenital dissembler in the company of grownups. He likes to assume an air of sweet innocence because he knows on what side his

157

bread is buttered and that such adults as parents, school teachers and
Scout leaders expect him to be ignorant, boyishly gruff, persistently
inquisitive about matters he's not supposed to be old enough to understand, and to be at all times in dire danger of suffering psychological
trauma from undergoing unpleasant experiences or even reading
about them. (Davis 1953, xi)

Dissenting from the view that the early adolescent boy is vulnerable and in
need of adult protection from "unpleasant experiences" (xi), Davis instead
thinks they are tough little animals:

I believe the normally intelligent twelve-year-old, who has not been
too sheltered and pampered, is as elemental as a Cro-Magnon caveman, and probably able to adjust himself to rough going far better
than he will be six or eight years later as a more complex and sensitive
adolescent. . . .
    I have a conviction, drawn from memory and observation, that the
average American boy from the age of say nine to about fifteen is a
tough little tribesman, intensely loyal to his own group; cruel, amoral,
recklessly adventurous, a congenital showoff, noisy, brawling, boast-
ful, scornful of the outlanders on the other side of town, and at the
same time quite wistful with the sort of primitive mysticism common
to savages and which one may suppose was the rule with his caveman
progenitors. He instinctively believes in portents and fetishes, and,
although he may attend Sunday School or the church of his family
without pronounced rebellion, he frequently makes obeisance to
strange gods and supernatural forces. (xi–xii)

Whatever one may think of Davis's portrait of the early adolescent boy—
based on the notion that "any individual from conception to maturity passes
through all the stages of development the species has undergone" (xi–xii)—
there is something intriguing about his idea that the early adolescent boy's religion is a rather primitive affair yet he goes to church with his family "without
pronounced rebellion" (xii). Davis implies that church religion is a lot more
civilized than the boy's own religion, and he also implies that the spirit of
rebellion against civilized religion is present but remains unspoken. It may
even fail to attract the notice of the adults toward whom the rebellion is felt.
    On the other hand, Davis thinks that the boys of his generation were more
rebellious in spirit than the boys of my generation, and the reason for this is
that the adults have changed:

I do not believe the normal modern boy from about nine to fourteen
is quite as rebellious against the adult world as he used to be. It's possible, of course, that I am wrong in this, but I'm sure the average parent and school teacher is not as pompous and arbitrary and addicted

to "thrashing the meanness out of them" as they were when I was a boy, and it would seem, therefore, that there is less reason now than a generation or two ago for the "young bulls" to be in a state of revolt against their mortal enemies, the grownups. It could be that it is my perspective which has changed, but it does seem that adults try to be more tolerant of youngsters and to recognize that boys have some rights as human beings. I know that in my day we felt that most men took unfair advantage of their authority and physical strength. This was true not only of fathers and school principals and policemen but of men in general—or so it seemed. (xiii)

It is worth noting Davis's view that men—not women—were the offenders, the ones against whom boys of his generation would rebel. There isn't much point in debating Davis's view that times have changed and that there would have been less reason for boys my own age to have been "in a state of revolt against their mortal enemies" than there was for boys *his* age. The same goes for boys of my coauthors' generations and boys of today. Of greater interest to me is how he characterizes the ways in which early adolescent boys express their rebellious feelings against their mortal enemies. Continuing to invoke the idea that early adolescent boys are comparable to the primitives, Davis says that one of the things a boy will do is ask adults "silly questions just to see the grownups fumble around for an answer. Sometimes they apparently don't even know answers that he, despite his ostensible innocence, could explain readily. That also is a practice of cunning aborigines in dealing with the lordly white man" (xiii).

Davis illustrates the rebellious spirit of the early adolescent boy with a story he tells about himself and his pal, Sliver Elvin. Clyde and Sliver were going fishing one day, and they decided to drop in on the butcher to ask him for a piece of pork liver to use for bait. In those days even beef liver was considered almost worthless. It sold for five cents a pound or less. Butchers commonly gave away pork liver for cat food or fish bait. So Clyde and Sliver politely asked the butcher for a small piece of pork liver and he agreed, providing that they would turn his grindstone so that he could sharpen some of his knives. The two boys turned the huge grindstone as the butcher brought out knife after knife. Finally, as they were both dripping with sweat and nearly exhausted, the butcher felt the edge of the last knife and said, "All right, that's the last one. Now get out of here." Clyde asked, "How about our piece of pork liver?" The butcher replied, "Don't come whining around me for a free piece of liver." Sliver spoke up, "Look, mister, you made a bargain to give us a piece of liver if we turned your blamed old grindstone and we turned it, and now we want our liver." The butcher brandished one of his long, well-sharpened knives and snarled, "Don't talk back to me, you little stinkers! You get out of here before

I cut your throats." He lunged at the two boys. They grabbed their fishing poles and fled in terror (xiv).

Victims of a clear injustice, what were they to do? Noting that they "were in a constant state of guerilla warfare against pompous and tyrannical adults, being incapable, of course, of conducting a frontal attack and being compelled to resort to stealthy sorties, ambuscade and sabotage" (xiv), the two boys avenged the injustice by waiting until evening to inscribe the following words on the butcher shop windows with candle wax: "I sell rotten meat," "Tough and dirty beefsteaks," and "Ptomaine Charley is my name, stinking meat is my fame" (xiv–xv). The boys knew, of course, that candle wax cannot simply be washed off. It has to be scraped off. That the physical effort involved might be roughly comparable to the effort required to turn a heavy grindstone would rebalance, in a way, the scales of justice. Davis insists that boys reserve such guerilla warfare tactics for adults who are "asking for it":

> Boys are not and never were inclined to play malicious tricks on unas-suming, kindly men. But the pontificators of flapdoodle were asking for it—and they usually got it. Be cruel or unfair or ill-tempered with a boy of any era and, if he has a gang, they'll try to make your life a burden for you. Treat him with the respect and kindness and patience he deserves and he'll flatter you by opening his secret soul to you. (xvii)

When I first read this account it resonated with me, as I knew that if I had been Clyde or Sliver I would have done what they did—or something compa-rable. Unlike boys who might have retaliated by smashing the butcher's win-dows, but also unlike boys who would do nothing about the injustice committed against them, I too would have tried to find a third alternative, one that would let Charley know that it was *he*, not I, who had behaved like a "stinker." I would have taken special pride in the way his epithet—"little stinkers"—was used against him in the rhyme "Ptomaine Charley is my name, stinking meat is my fame." I would also, no doubt, have admitted to myself that what I had done was "bad"—especially in light of my knowledge of Jesus' injunction to "turn the other cheek"—but I would have justified this behavior on the grounds that an adult, who should know better, committed an injustice against a couple of kids. And didn't Jesus himself say that it is to kids that the kingdom of heaven belongs?

HUMOR AND VULNERABILITY

Although Davis doesn't come out and say that what he and Sliver did was funny, one senses that he now finds it so and expects that his readers will too.

The book's dust jacket states that "the keynote of the book is humor, which is always the humor of the boys themselves, not that of condescending adults." As the broad theme of the book is the "indestructibility" of early adolescent boys, we may reasonably conclude that humor is an important—maybe the most important—resource with which the boy arms himself in his battle against cruel, unfair, or ill-tempered adults. If the armor of the civilized religious boy is truth, righteousness, peace, faith, and salvation (Eph. 6:13–17), the armor of the primitive religious boy who lives inside of him—the boy possessed with the spirit of rebellion—is, first and foremost, humor. This is a humor that is neither malicious nor cruel, but neither is it innocuous or sweet tempered. Its purpose is to cut the "pontificators of flapdoodle" down to size and to make "life a burden" for adults who have treated the boy and his friends unfairly (Davis 1953, xvii).

If boys are "indestructible," this does not mean, as Davis claims, that they are not "in dire danger of suffering psychological trauma from undergoing unpleasant experiences" (xi). In fact, the very idea that they are "indestructible" would not come up if they were not also vulnerable. The early adolescent boy's resort to humor itself reflects the truth that he is, in fact, quite vulnerable, that he is in danger of suffering psychological trauma from undergoing unpleasant experiences. Davis's own story is a case in point. He and Sliver fought back with humor when the sun went down, but a few hours earlier they had "fled in terror" as the butcher lunged at them with one of his newly sharpened knives. If this was not an unpleasant experience capable of producing a physical trauma, I have to wonder what kind of experience *would* qualify as one? Davis's own story reveals that boys turn to humor precisely because they are vulnerable and not as indestructible as they may appear, or want others to think they are.

Billy Collins's poem about the ten-year-old boy expresses this sense of genuine vulnerability (Collins 2001, 63–64):

On Turning Ten
The whole idea of it makes me feel
like I'm coming down with something, something
worse than any stomach ache
or the headaches I get from reading in bad light—a
kind of measles of the spirit,
a mumps of the psyche,
a disfiguring chicken pox of the soul.
You tell me it is too early to be looking back,
but that is because you have forgotten the
perfect simplicity of being one
and the beautiful complexity introduced by two.
But I can lie on my bed and remember every digit.

At four I was an Arabian wizard,
I could make myself invisible
by drinking a glass of milk a certain way, at seven I
was a soldier, at nine a prince.
But now I am mostly at the window
watching the late afternoon light.
Back then it never fell so solemnly
against the side of my tree house,
and my bicycle never leaned against the garage
as it does today,
all the dark blue speed drained out of it.
This is the beginning of sadness, I say to myself,
as I walk through the universe in my sneakers.
It is time to say good-bye to my imaginary friends,
time to turn the first big number.
It seems only yesterday I used to believe
there was nothing under my skin but light.
If you cut me I would shine.
But now when I fall upon the sidewalks of life,
I skin my knees. I bleed.

The threats to which the early adolescent boy is subjected come from various sources. There are the other boys who are physically stronger, psychologically more resilient, or simply older. There are the boys who counter their own sense of vulnerability by adopting the role of the bully (see Coloroso 2003). There are the adults—parents, teachers, and others who no longer tolerate a boy's errors and mistakes and for whom his immaturity is no longer delightful and charming. His sense of vulnerability also comes from his growing understanding of how the social world works, and of how unfair and unjust it can be. Younger children go in for riddles, while boys and girls nine and older prefer jokes and funny stories (Wolfenstein 1954). This itself shows that early adolescents are becoming attuned to the social world and its capacity to hurt and injure them. Riddles, after all, are mind teasers, while jokes are stories about how human interactions are not what they are cracked up to be.

HUMOR AS A SOFT FORM OF REBELLION

There are many poses and personae that an early adolescent boy may adopt for fending off the world's attempts to hurt and injure him. He may develop a tough-guy demeanor and a physical swagger to match. His very bearing seems to say, "Don't mess with me if you don't want to get hurt." Or he may adopt a "holier-than-thou" attitude, one in which he dons the armor of moral superiority. This supermoral boy is not reluctant to tell teachers that one of his classmates has been guilty of wrongdoing; he knows that he is at least as safe from retaliation as an informant who has joined a witness protection program. Then there is the boy who becomes the class clown, who defends himself by intimating that he is not to be taken seriously.

Then there is the rebel, the boy who challenges the authority of the adults. Some boys do this in a hostile way, through direct attack. Others do it in a milder, perhaps cleverer way, through subversive acts. Clyde and Sliver were rebels in the second way. They didn't go back that evening and take a sledgehammer to the butcher's window. Had they done so, they could have been arrested for destruction of property. Instead, they came up with phony window signs and used candle wax to ensure that the butcher would have to expend as much physical energy in removing them as they had expended on the sharpening of his knives. Fair exchange. Could they have been arrested for defacing the butcher's property? Perhaps. But I suspect that the butcher would have realized that it would be a waste of his time to seek punitive damages, and that if he had gone to the police and told them that he knew who the boys were who did the deed, they would have asked him how he knew this, and the whole story—unfavorable to himself—would have come out.

For want of a better term, let's call the window-defacing boys "soft rebels" to distinguish them from the "hard rebels" who would have smashed the butcher's windows to smithereens and may well have wound up in the boy's reformatory. The "hard rebels" would have sneered in disdain at Clyde and Sliver's act of avenging the wrong that the butcher had done to them, accusing them of being chickens or lily-livered cowards. But Clyde and Sliver had the satisfaction of knowing that they had gotten the butcher's goat and that they had done no worse to him than he had done to them.

HUMOR AND THE POWER OF RESISTANCE

To most Christians, Sigmund Freud is Bunyan's Mr. Worldly Wiseman incarnate. But he wrote a book and an article on humor that shed a great deal of light on how humor serves the spirit of rebellion. In the article, titled "Humor" (1928/1963), he made a distinction between three Rs: resignation, revolution, and rebellion. Resignation is accepting things the way they are on the assumption that they cannot be changed. Revolution is the attempt to overthrow the existing social system by forceful means. Rebellion falls midway between resignation and revolution. It accepts the right of the existing social system to exist, but it does not assume that one simply has to accept it as it is. Even if the external situation is unchangeable, one can resist it in one's own heart and mind. To Freud, one means of such resistance is humor.

In his book *Jokes and Their Relation to the Unconscious* (1905/1960), Freud tells two stories about condemned men facing execution. The first criminal's execution was scheduled for Monday morning. As the guards led him to gallows, he remarked, "Well, this week's beginning nicely" (284). The second criminal's execution took place in winter. As he was being led to the gallows, he asked a guard to fetch him a scarf for his neck so that he wouldn't catch a cold (285). Freud repeated the first story in his article on humor and used it to explain the difference between resignation and rebellion. Supposing that the condemned had said, "What does it matter, after all, if a fellow like me is hanged? The world won't come to an end" (1928/1963, 265). We would have to admit that such a resigned statement was "wise and true," but there is not a "trace of humor" in it. In fact, "it is based on an appraisal of reality which runs directly counter to that of humor," because "humor is not resigned; it is rebellious" (265). The criminal's actual comment is rebellious because it signifies "the ego's victorious assertion of its own vulnerability," its refusal "to be hurt by the arrows of reality or to be compelled to suffer." It "insists that it is impervious to wounds dealt by the outside world, in fact, that these are only occasions for affording it pleasure" (265).

We could, of course, object that these criminals' witty comments don't change a thing. Whether resigned or rebellious, the end is the same. For Freud, though, there was a huge psychological difference between them. The rebellious attitude was liberating. It spared the onlookers and maybe even the guards the painful emotions they would have had if the two condemned men hadn't made these comments. Furthermore, the condemned men themselves achieved a certain emotional detachment from the fate that they were about to suffer at the hands of the authorities. In his book on humor, Freud concludes that humor saves the expenditure of painful emotions, costly inhibitions, and difficult thinking (1905/1960, 293). In the case of the two criminals, the savings involved painful emotions. This is not denial. The men knew full well that death was imminent. But they refused to suffer.

If the two condemned men were not resigned, neither were they revolutionaries. Neither tried to strangle the guards in a last-minute effort to break free or, at least, make someone pay for their impending execution. The second criminal expressed concern for his own throat. He had no designs on the throats of others. Naturally, neither was happy about the fact that the constituted authorities were about to execute him. But both knew that they hadn't the power or means to overthrow the system. What they could do, though, was to make a joke on their way to the execution platform. Whatever else they may have been before—and the fact that they were there at all suggests that they may well have been hardened criminals—they were now, in the face of death, what I would call "soft rebels." Maybe this is all one can be in the face of such a formidable opponent.

THE MAKING OF A SOFT REBEL

It is now time for me to tell the part of the story I didn't tell in the previous chapter. This is the story of how I acquired the spirit of rebellion. Two experiences, both in grade school, were responsible. One was a shaming experience. The other was an experience in which I felt I had been treated unjustly.

A Shaming Experience

The shaming experience happened when I was in sixth grade. Several boys in our school lived in an orphanage located a few blocks from the school. For the most part, I got along well with them, but there was the perception that the orphanage boys were rougher than the rest of us and the fear that they would defend one another if circumstances demanded such loyalty. One morning when we were out on the playground during recess, one of the orphanage boys hit me in the face. I don't recall the provocation for this, but whatever it was, I didn't hit him back. Instead, I laughed at him, which made him really angry, but he didn't hit me again. I have a vivid picture in my mind of his face registering a mixture of anger and helplessness, as if to say, "What's the point of hitting a kid who doesn't have the guts to hit back?" When recess was over, some of the kids told our teacher that "Charles hit Donald." The teacher asked me if this was true. I reluctantly admitted that it was, and my attacker was severely reprimanded. I recall that I had felt rather pleased with myself for not hitting him back but instead laughing in his face, as if to say, "If that was your best shot, I barely felt it." But when the teacher got involved and punished him, I felt pretty ashamed, as it implied that I couldn't take care of myself, that I needed adult intervention.

In that moment, the religion of honor had failed me. I felt as though I had behaved as a Christian boy *should* act—"If anyone strikes you on the right cheek, turn the other also"—but the fact that the other kids informed the teacher and she punished the other boy deprived me of my moral victory. Of course, I understood that she had to uphold school rules against fighting on the playground. On the other hand, her action implied that he had actually hurt me and that I was therefore, in some way, his victim. I recall thinking at the time that he became the hero of this whole sorry episode because he hit me and didn't get away with it but instead took his punishment "like a man," whereas my failure to hit him back now began to feel cowardly. Was I really afraid of him? Is this why I refused to fight him? Moreover, the teacher did not ask us what the conflict was all about, so my own innocence in the altercation was not considered. Perhaps she merely assumed what we boys did not, namely, that in any altercation the orphanage boys were automatically at fault.

As he probably would not have hit me without provocation, the fact that he was punished and I was not made me feel less than honorable, for an honorable boy accepts responsibility for his actions. In any event, I recall that Charles (who was "Chuck" to me) and I basically liked each other. This being the case, if the teacher had simply asked him to apologize to me and given me a chance to accept his apology and add that I, too, was sorry for provoking him to hit me, the matter would have been settled then and there (see Lazare 2004).

Against these feelings of shame, however, I experienced the spirit of rebellion. I had "turned the other cheek" as an honorable boy should. But it would have been much more satisfying if I had made some sort of witty comment, like "Did your mother teach you to hit like that?"

An Experience of Injustice

The experience in which I felt unjustly treated was this: As a serious devotee of the religion of honor, I took great pride in the fact that I was a member of the school safety patrol. Besides serving at the most strategically located school crossing (the most traffic and adjacent to the school itself), I was one of the boys assigned to raising and lowering the United States flag each morning and afternoon. This was a solemn ritual, and I took it very seriously. In sixth grade I was elected captain of the safety patrol by my fellow students, which meant that I was in line to become the lieutenant, the top position in the whole patrol, in seventh grade.

But things took a different and, in my view, a very unjust course. Another boy's mother went to the school principal and told him that she wanted her son, Larry, to be the lieutenant of the safety patrol. I have no idea why this was so important to her, but it was probably something Larry had told her he wanted, and she saw no reason why he shouldn't have it. She may not have known that it was normally a position to which one was elected by one's peers, and maybe the principal didn't know this either. He agreed to her request. In addition to not being promoted, I was also assigned to Larry's former post, which was several blocks away from school, a much less prestigious post, and without the flag raising and lowering responsibility. I was deeply hurt, and after a few weeks of enduring the humiliation of my demotion, I quit the safety patrol altogether. I couldn't endure the fact that he, as lieutenant, came around to check to see if I was at my post.

Whenever I encountered the story in Matthew 20:20–28 about the mother of the sons of Zebedee approaching Jesus to ask a favor of him—"Declare that these two sons of mine will sit, one at your right hand and one at your left, in your kingdom"—I thought about this incident, and I also thought about what a difference it would have made if the principal had responded as Jesus did.

The safety patrol had been one of the most important ways that I could exemplify the qualities of the Boy Scout, of being trustworthy, helpful, courteous, and kind. I also looked forward to the ritual of folding and unfolding the flag. After all, this was itself a solemn act of reverence.

When I resigned from the safety patrol, I remembered a story my oldest brother had told me about a friend of his that had occurred when he was about my age. One day his friend was performing his duties as a school crossing guard, and a girl on whom he had a crush began to cross the street. He experienced an embarrassing erection at that moment and in order to disguise it, he covered it with his safety patrol paddle. Another boy noticed what was happening and called out to him, "Hey, Billy, what's your paddle doing down there?" Just then a female teacher walked by and witnessed the scene. Billy, of course, was thoroughly humiliated and, according to my brother, turned his head away whenever he passed the girl in the hall. This story encouraged me to take a less serious view of the safety patrol and of the prestige I felt I had lost by not being promoted to lieutenant. After all, it was not the end of the world. Even so, the experience created a deep suspicion of how human organizations work and the feeling that the religion of honor is not always all that it is cracked up to be.

Finding an Ally

These two experiences were critically important for what happened next—the spirit of rebellion, fortunately of the softer type, got a firm grip on me. Like Clyde and his pal Sliver, it was assisted by a strong friendship I formed with a boy named Francis (whom I called "Boner," a nickname connoting a silly blunderer together with a sexual innuendo). He too had experienced frustrations at school, and judging from the way his mother yelled at him, at home as well. His father, a lawyer, seemed reluctant to come to his son's assistance. Later, when I was in graduate school, I read about Harry Stack Sullivan's "chumship" concept (1953/1997; also see Allan Cole's discussion in chapter 4), the idea that a couple of early adolescent boys will form a very strong attachment to one another. I realized that this was, in fact, what he and I had experienced. What added to our mutual frustration was the fact that a lot of kids from a neighboring kindergarten-through-sixth-grade school were transferred to our school for the seventh and eighth grades, and there were more of "them" than there were of "us." To us, they were like an invading army, and we were the ones who were forced to adjust.

Boner and I began cooking up what we considered harmless acts of mild rebellion. Both of us were having a difficult time in our industrial arts class. We had done well on the electricity unit, but we began to flounder when the class moved into the carpentry phase. The task was to make bookends. Our male teacher viewed this as a relatively simple task that, once completed, would lead to more difficult and more interesting projects. But neither of us was particularly adept with the planer, the tool used to make a perfectly level edge. When a boy felt that he had gotten one of the four edges level, he would take his block of wood up to the teacher, who would hold it up to the light. If he saw no light between the wood and his T-square, he approved it. Otherwise, the boy was sent back to his workbench to try again.

For several weeks Boner and I did our level best to get all four sides perfectly straight. Meanwhile, other boys forged ahead on far more interesting projects. One boy in particular, whose name was Frank, would make sarcastic comments about the fact that we were still working on our bookends. Eventually, we succeeded in producing a couple of blocks of wood that were perfectly level, though they were much smaller than the projected size, the victims of far too much planing. My brothers joked about my bookends when I brought them home, wondering where I was going to find miniature books to match.

During our several weeks of humiliation, the teacher left the room one day, and Boner and I seized the opportunity to avenge Frank's derisive comments. We picked him up bodily and carried him over to a coat closet, shoved him in, and locked the door. Frank banged on the door, but no one helped him. Apparently, we were not alone in feeling that he deserved it. When the teacher returned, he must have sensed that something was up. He looked around the room and asked, "Where's Frank?" "Frank jumped out the window," I said, adding, "Look, there he is, running across the playground!" Just as the teacher was heading for the window to check my story out, Frank let out a particularly loud howl from the closet, and the teacher went over and let him out. Then he asked who did this—as if he couldn't guess—and when the other boys fingered the two of us, he bawled us out and sent us to the principal's office.

We fared better after other misdemeanors. For reasons that I no longer remember, another teacher sent Boner and me out into the hall. Of course, this was a classic form of classroom punishment, but it had the effect of setting the miscreants loose. Our classroom happened to be adjacent to the boys' bathroom, so we made our way into the bathroom and began singing at the top of our voices, loud enough to be heard in our classroom. Sure enough, after a few minutes passed, the teacher opened the bathroom door, strode in, and growled at us, "Get back in the classroom, you two!" When we returned to the classroom, the other kids were fully aware that our time out in the hall was much briefer than usual. In effect, we had "beaten the system" through a second misdemeanor that nullified the punishment of the first.

Another act of soft rebellion stands out in my memory because, in this case, the teacher herself redeemed it. In music class, we had learned a German love song, "Lili Marlene." We were probably introduced to this song because our teacher wanted us to respect the German people after World War II. I loved this song, but that didn't stop me from writing a parody of it. Boner made copies of the parody on his father's typewriter and distributed them to several of the other boys. When our teacher announced that our next song would be "Lili Marlene," we were ready. I don't recall the parody in full, but it involved changing the first words of the first line—"*Standing by* the lamplight near the village gate to *"Leaning on* the lamppost . . . ," which suggested that the young lover was drunk.[1] As the rest of the class sang the original lyrics, we belted out the alternative lyrics, and our teacher (to our infinite relief) broke up in laughter. For me, this was an important affirmation of the softer form of rebellion. While our behavior was disruptive in a way, it was neither crude nor rude, and there was no attempt to embarrass the teacher or another student. To me, of course, it was witty and clever, though not in the same league as works by songwriters such as Cole Porter. Porter's biographer tells about the occasion when Porter's mother attended opening night of the stage production of *Kiss Me, Kate.* Mrs. Porter, a rather straitlaced woman still living in Porter's hometown of Peru, Indiana, whispered to Porter's physician, who escorted her to the theatre that evening, "Cole is a naughty boy" (McBrien 1998, 317). Like Mrs. Porter, our teacher had found our misdemeanor amusing, not grounds for punishment.

Enter the Mothers

Mention of Porter's mother brings me, however, to a more painful experience. Apparently our teachers began to feel that Boner and I were distracting one another from the serious pursuit of our studies. Or maybe we were subverting class decorum. Whatever it was, our mothers were separately summoned to the principal's office for a discussion of our behavior. I was unaware that this had happened. Either my mother chose not to tell me—which I doubt—or, more likely, the principal had called her that very morning after I had gone off to school and she dropped everything and went to see him. In any case, I remember the scene as if it were yesterday. My gym class was outside playing soccer as she made her way, on foot, around the playground and entered the school building. I immediately sensed that she had been summoned by the principal, and as I watched her slow, plodding walk, I suddenly felt very

---

[1]I recently acquired a Marlene Dietrich CD that includes her rendition of "Lili Marlene." I had hoped I could reconstruct my parody from the original. Unfortunately, the lyrics were very different, suggesting that we learned an Americanized version, possibly one in which an American soldier falls in love with a German girl and dreams of her after his return to the States.

ashamed. This was not the vigorous, determined, almost confrontational woman I had known her to be, the mother who would defend her boys to the hilt. Instead, she looked defeated and rather disconsolate, "weary," as she would later say, "of well-doing."

As I felt the emotional pain of having put her through an ordeal in which she would be deprived of her usual defenses and of her own sense of personal dignity, I decided then and there that it was time to amend my life and to become, in effect, an even more dedicated practitioner of the religion of honor. The school authorities reinforced this new dedication, for the next year Boner and I discovered that we did not share a single class together. As this required moving both of us out of the homeroom class that otherwise remained intact from seventh to eighth grade, we understood without having to be told that our rebellious days were over. Despite the fact that we would not be seeing each other very much at school, we vowed that our friendship would continue. In a way, it did. We would see each other, on occasion, after school. But this was our early adolescent version of the declaration that divorced couples make when they assure one another that they "will always be friends." Boner is, of course, missing from my homeroom class picture on the occasion of our eighth-grade graduation.

My rededication was perhaps best illustrated in the fact that, after another abysmal midterm grade in industrial arts, I asked the teacher if he would allow me to work on a special project. I had found a fairly thick tree limb in a nearby woods—after all, I *was* a Scout—and requested his permission to make a Christmas candle arrangement out of it.

In the preceding chapter, I pointed out that the main reason boys are expected to separate from their mothers at ages three to five is so that they will identify with their fathers and prepare to enter the world of productive men. It was probably no accident that my primary acts of rebellion occurred in industrial arts class, that the teacher was a man, and that the class consisted of boys only. According to my report cards at the time, the grade in industrial arts was based on the following criteria: (1) shows skill in the use of common tools and equipment, (2) recognizes good design and workmanship, and (3) is interested in industry and its products. Girls were assigned to homemaking education and were graded according to the following criteria: (1) understands significance of home and family, (2) shows an understanding of good grooming and appropriateness in dress, and (3) is proficient in homemaking skills. Although one could raise all sorts of questions about the gender assumptions operating here, I find it interesting that the criteria in the two cases are reversed, with skills having top priority in the case of boys, and interest in industry—the world of productive males—placed last. (Interestingly enough, industry versus inferiority is the developmental issue that Erikson ascribes to the school age, roughly ages 5–12, in his life cycle model [Erikson 1963, 226–27). For girls, understanding home and family receives first priority, and proficiency in basic homemaking skills comes last. Of course, these priorities may not have been reflected in the way the homemaking education class was actually taught, but this was, in fact, the case with the industrial arts class. In fact, the third criterion—interest in industry and its products—was never discussed, much less assessed.

Like most boys of my generation, I was very interested in the world of industry and its products, and in good design and workmanship. The production and design of automobiles especially interested me, but so did radios and phonograph machines. Perhaps the greatest irony, though, was that my career as a craftsman came to early grief around bookends. I was a great lover of books. When I had exhausted our local branch library, I would take the streetcar downtown after school to check out books from the main branch of the public library. Books were becoming a major industry in the United States as new methods of mass production were being developed. The paperback would revolutionize the publishing industry, enabling boys like me to afford to buy their own books. After checking out a few books from the library, I would walk over to the shop where saddles and other leather goods were still being produced by hand and rummage through the barrels of leather scraps in order to find pieces to make billfolds and purses for family Christmas gifts. Then I would head over to the Union Pacific Railroad Company headquarters, where my father worked in the accounting department, and hitch a ride home with him.

It seems clear to me now that I was very interested in industry and that I would have had a very different experience in industrial arts if these interests had been considered. But carpentry skills were to this class what knot tying was to Scouting—another skill that eluded me—and there wasn't much that I could do to rectify the situation. Or so it seems to me in retrospect.

The industrial arts teacher agreed to my request to make a Christmas candle arrangement, my grade improved slightly, and there was no industrial arts class the second half of the year. Also, despite the fact that the music teacher was not offended by the "Lili Marlene" parody, I felt a need to atone for it. So I wrote new words in tribute to Monroe Grade School, to be sung to the tune of the Notre Dame "Victory March." Unlike my "Lili Marlene" parody, the words were very respectful, and, compared to the rousing lyrics of the original "Victory March" (Melrose Music Corp. 1945, 2–3), mine were serious and solemn. These are the original lyrics:

> Cheer, Cheer for old Notre Dame,
> Wake up the echoes cheering her name,
> Send the volley cheer on high,

Shake down the thunder from the sky.
What though the odds be great or small
Old Notre Dame will win over all,
While her loyal sons are marching
Onward to victory.

Here are mine:

Monroe, we hail you, Monroe,
To you we rise and sing of our praise.
You have helped us learn and grow,
And on high goals have set our gaze.
Monroe, your colors maroon and gold,
We'll carry with us your high ideals.
When we leave you we will hold
To this love for you we feel.

This time, the teacher herself made copies, enough for all of my classmates to sing at our graduation ceremony. I had redeemed myself. The Christmas candle, symbolic of the religion of hope, and the paean of praise to Monroe Grade School, expressive of the religion of honor, meant that I was back on the right track. But I was also lonely. I had lost a good friend, a bosom buddy. The loneliness Allan Cole describes in his chapters now applied to me.

In addition, my rebellious spirit continued to trouble me. After all, I could no longer view myself as being the reliably good citizen that I had been before the altercation with the kid from the orphanage and the safety patrol fiasco. In retrospect, however, I can see more clearly than I could see then that my rebellion was primarily based on an awareness of the injustices that were occurring in the social world to which I was deeply committed. All of us— Chuck, Donald, Larry, Francis, and Frank—were vulnerable, and we did what we could to protect ourselves. It would be a great mistake to suggest that we were the victims of an oppressive system. In fact, it was probably my experience of grade school as an essentially caring and nurturing environment that made me sensitive—perhaps supersensitive—to the occasional injustice toward me and others. In the end, through my acquisition of a spirit of rebellion, I gained a new sense of self-sufficiency. This was because I learned how easily a boy—even a fundamentally good boy—could get himself on the wrong side of the adults who were in a position to bestow upon him the awards of affirmation and approval on which he had come to depend. To discover that one can survive without these awards is perhaps the greatest gift that the spirit of rebellion afforded me. And this boy, I freely admit, is a very large part of who I am today.

CRACKING (UP) THE HONOR CODE

As spirituality is often contrasted with religion, so the spirit of rebellion described above seems to be at fundamental odds with religion as normally understood or defined. As an early adolescent boy, I certainly did not consider the behaviors that were reflective of this spirit of rebellion to have any association with religion. This is probably because it never occurred to me that religion had anything to do with challenging injustice (now, of course, I know differently). On the other hand, to say that my spirit of rebellion was primarily motivated by some sort of altruistic desire to right human wrongs would be to ascribe to it an intention that would only occur to an adult who, in retrospect, needed to rationalize his early adolescent behavior. It would also detract from the primary lesson my spirit of rebellion taught me, which was that I could be more self-sufficient—especially as far as adult affirmation and approval are concerned—than I had ever imagined. This, though, is itself an insight that we rarely associate with religion, for religion teaches us to expect rewards for good and faithful service (if not in this world, then certainly in the next).

So perhaps the best that I can do here is to make the case that the spirit of rebellion is an essential feature of the religion of humor and admit that humor's relationship to religion is itself rather tenuous. I think, though, that the foregoing account of my experiences of soft rebellion explain why this is so. Like Clyde and Sliver's retaliation against the butcher who cheated them out of their pork liver, Boner and I thought that our misdemeanors were pretty funny. Stuffing Frank in the closet, singing in the boy's bathroom, parodying the German love song: maybe these were not exactly sidesplitting, but to us they were funny, all the more so because we made them up out of the situations that the classroom afforded us. Also, unlike the class clowns who were show-offs, our brand of humor was more subtly subversive, less an attempt to gain attention and more an expression of our frustration and disappointment in the manner in which adults exercised authority. On the larger scale, however, our antics attacked the pretensions and false assurances of the religion of honor. In fact, the very reason that humor is not considered religious is probably because the religion of honor is so central to what most of us consider religion to be.

In the previous chapter, I mentioned that the Boy Scouts of America's *Handbook for Boys* was the book that taught me the essentials of the religion of honor even as John Bunyan's *The Pilgrim's Progress* portrayed the religion of hope. There was no corresponding book to teach me the fundamentals of the religion of humor. Joke books existed, but they were printed in clothbound covers, and boys like me could not afford them. But even if we could, they would never have had the sacred aura of the *Handbook for Boys* or *The Pilgrim's Progress*, much less the Bible, to which these other books appealed in support of their own authority.

On the other hand, *Reader's Digest* was an important source of jokes and other forms of humor. The scrapbook to which I alluded in the previous chapter has as much humor as it does articles about heroes and heroines, suggesting that the religions of honor and humor coexisted in my life and mind at the time.[2]

To make up for this boyhood deprivation, I now make regular visits to the humor section in local bookstores. Having the means to do so, I purchase a lot of joke books. (I have discovered that early adolescent boys and girls are by far the most likely groups to be hanging around the humor section.) I want now to show how the religion of humor challenges the false assurances and empty pretensions of the religion of honor. This is not for the purpose of calling the essential legitimacy of the religion of honor into question. In fact, the jokes that I will share suggest the very opposite. If one was unaware of the fundamental assumptions of the religion of honor, one would not be in a position to find these jokes funny.

To show that the religion of honor is no less influential on today's preadolescent boys than it was in my own early adolescent era, I will mostly use contemporary joke books, but to demonstrate that jokes haven't changed very much from the time I was an early adolescent, I will also include a few jokes from Martha Lupton's *The Treasury of Modern Humor* (1938), which contains 2,500 "funny stories." If the primary congregants around the humor section of local bookstores are early adolescent boys (and girls), this is itself evidence that early adolescent boys do in fact embrace the traditional values of the religion of honor but that they also turn to humor as one way of coping with their own experiences of unfairness and injustice—those times when the honor code or system fails them and their friends—as well as their experiences of vulnerability, loneliness, and despair.

Some of these jokes may be offensive to some readers of this book

---

[2]In *A Time to Laugh: The Religion of Humor* (2005), I mention in a footnote on page 175 that I pasted into this scrapbook an excerpt from *Reader's Digest* of an article on Burma-Shave jingles. Scattered throughout *A Time to Laugh* are some of my own Burma-Shave jingles based on biblical stories. I view these as an expression of solidarity with the boy—my younger self—who appreciated this type of humor. This may reflect the truth of William Wordsworth's observation in "My Heart Leaps Up" that "the Child is father of the Man" (Stuart 1996, 415). My personal favorite, an expression of my tendency, shared by many other men, to need to turn a tender moment into an occasion for joking, is the one based on the account in John 20:15–16 of Mary Magdalene's failure to recognize Jesus in the garden on Easter morning. I titled it "Mary, It's Me": "Mary, O Mary, / What's the trouble? / Could it be / My three-day stubble?" / Burma-Shave. All 600 official Burma-Shave jingles (from 1927 to 1963) are presented in Frank Rowsome Jr., *The Verse by the Side of the Road: The Story of the Burma-Shave Signs and Jingles* (1965).

because they employ ethnic and sexual stereotypes and make allusions to physical disabilities and characteristics. I have discussed the issue of offensiveness in several publications (Capps 2005, 2006; see also Cohen 1999). I will not attempt to summarize these discussions here. I note, however, that this issue is itself illustrative of my basic argument that the religion of humor, with its spirit of rebellion, relativizes *and thereby preserves* the religion of honor.

As the Boy Scout Law with its twelve qualities of moral character served as the basis for my discussion of the religion of honor, I use it here as the basis for my selection of jokes that call the religion of honor into question. Where possible, I use jokes that feature the early adolescent boy, especially the boy who fits Davis's description of the "normal twelve-year-old" who is "a pretty shrewd and crafty animal" and "a congenital dissembler in the company of grownups" (Davis 1953, xi).

An Honorable Boy Is Trustworthy

The Boy Scout Law states that a boy may be required to turn in his badge if he violates his honor by telling a lie, cheating, or failing to carry out a task exactly as directed. Here's a joke that plays on the issue of lying:

> **Voice on phone:** "Johnny has a cold and can't come to school today."
>
> **School secretary:** "Who is this?"
>
> **Voice:** "This is my dad."

As for cheating:

A boy was having some difficulty with his homework and finally, out of desperation, asked his father,

> **Boy:** "Could you help me with this?"
>
> **Father:** "I could, but it wouldn't be right, would it?"
>
> **Boy:** "I don't suppose it would, but have a shot at it anyway."

Another cheating joke:

> **Teacher:** "Billy, I hope I didn't see you looking at Sally's paper."
>
> **Billy:** "I hope you didn't either."

One more:

> **Teacher:** "Well, at least there's one positive thing I can say about your son."
>
> **Father:** "Please tell me."
>
> **Teacher:** "With grades like these, he couldn't be cheating."

We can imagine the three men in the following joke as once having been early adolescent boys, and think of one—the judge—as an honest boy, the pickpocket as a dishonest boy, and the lawyer as a boy pulled in both directions but leaning toward empathy for the dishonest boy:

> A pickpocket was in court for a series of petty crimes. The judge delivered his sentence: "Mr. Jones, you are hereby fined $100." His lawyer stood up and said, "Thank you, your honor. Unfortunately my client only has $75 on him at this time, but if you'd allow him a few minutes in the crowd . . ."

An Honorable Boy Is Loyal

The *Handbook for Boys* emphasizes that loyalty begins in the home, and it also points out that the success of one's patrol and troop depends on the loyalty of each member (Boy Scouts 1948, 30). Here's a joke about a Boy Scout who didn't get the message:

> Two Boy Scouts were walking together through the woods when they spotted a vicious looking bear. The first boy reached into his backpack, pulled out a pair of sneakers, and began putting them on. The other boy said, "You're crazy, you'll never be able to outrun the bear!" The first boy replied, "I don't need to. I only need to outrun you."

Then there's the story of an old codger who learned loyalty in his Boy Scout days but didn't learn the corresponding lesson from *The Pilgrim's Progress* that one should choose one's friends carefully:

> Having spent a couple of hours at the local pub, an old man wandered into a church by accident on his way home. He entered just as the preacher was requesting everyone who wanted the Church of the Almighty God to prosper to raise their hands. The whole congregation stood. After they were seated again, the preacher continued, "Now, if there is a single person here who wants Satan and his kingdom to prosper, stand up." The old fellow slowly rose to his feet and said, "If the vote had been less than unanimous, I would have kept my seat, but I make it a point of honor never to abandon a friend under adverse circumstances."

An Honorable Boy Is Helpful

A Scout is expected to be prepared to save lives, help injured persons, and share home responsibilities (Boy Scouts 1948, 26). He is also expected to do at least one "good turn" to somebody every day (30–32). Here's a story in which a fellow who had learned the importance of helpfulness when he was a boy failed to take account of all the contextual clues when he tried to help a man he virtually stumbled upon in another local bar:

> Sam was throwing back a few beers at a busy local bar when he glanced over and noticed a drunk passed out at a nearby table. The bartender told him the drunk was Mr. Murphy, and asked Sam if he could drive him home. Being a good-hearted sort, Sam immediately agreed. The bartender wrote down Mr. Murphy's address for Sam and went back to his other customers. Sam went over to Mr. Murphy and tried to rouse him, but he was very groggy. Sam helped him to his feet, but he fell to the floor in a heap. So Sam had to drag him to the car. He propped Mr. Murphy up against the side of the car while he fumbled for his keys, but the hapless fellow slid to the ground. Sam found his keys and managed to stuff Mr. Murphy into the car. When they arrived at the address the bartender had given him, Sam opened the passenger door and helped Mr. Murphy out of the car. Again he fell to the ground in a heap. Sam dragged him to the front door and propped him against the doorway. Just then, Mrs. Murphy appeared at the door. "You must be Mrs. Murphy," Sam said. "Your husband had a little too much to drink tonight, so I gave him a ride home." "Oh, that was so nice of you," she replied, looking around. "But where's his wheelchair?"

Here's an adult male whose understanding of the meaning of helpfulness is somewhat askew:

> **Judge:** "Mr. Johnson, I have reviewed this case carefully and I've decided to give your wife $800 a week alimony."
>
> **Mr. Johnson:** "That's very generous, your honor. And believe me, I'll try to help out a little myself now and then."

Early adolescence is a period when many—perhaps most—boys begin thinking about what they will be when they grow up. Boys with a keen sense of honor often think of going into professions in which they can be helpful to others. Here's a joke in which one of these boys, now a grown man, is trying to be helpful to another grown man:

> A guy had been feeling down for so long that he finally decided to seek the aid of a psychiatrist. He went there, lay on the couch, spilled his

guts, then waited for the profound wisdom of the psychiatrist to make him feel better. The psychiatrist asked him a few questions, took some notes, then sat thinking in silence for a few minutes with a puzzled look on his face. Suddenly he looked up with an expression of delight and said, "I think your problem is low self-esteem. It is very common among losers."

An Honorable Boy Is Friendly

The *Handbook for Boys* points out, "The best way to have a friend is to be one," and, "A smile helps you to feel friendly. Try it and see" (33). Here's the story of a fellow who hasn't learned that, in the Boy Scout Law, friendliness and trustworthiness go together:

> A fellow struck up a conversation with the woman he was sitting next to on the airplane.
> "Hi, I couldn't help noticing the book you are reading."
> "Yes, it's about finding sexual satisfaction. It's really interesting. Did you know that studies have proven that Native American and Polish men are the best lovers? By the way, my name is Jill. What's yours?"
> "Flying Cloud Kowalski. Nice to make your acquaintance."

An Honorable Boy Is Courteous

The *Handbook for Boys* emphasizes being polite to everyone, especially to women, children, old people, and the weak and helpless (26). Reflecting the kind of thinking that led Clyde Davis to suggest that the early adolescent boy may be compared to the Cro-Magnon man, the *Handbook* observes:

> The caveman was all right in his day. He squatted beside the fire, snatched his lump of meat, pulled it apart with his hands and teeth. If he saw anything he wanted he grabbed it. If someone was in the way, he knocked him down. But who wants a caveman around today? Along with houses, tables, knives and forks, we have developed standards of friendship and courtesy which make life a lot more enjoyable. (33)

One of the quintessential forms of courtesy is for an able-bodied boy or man to give up his seat on a bus or train so that a woman or an older person will not have to stand. Here's a vintage illustration:

> The streetcar was very crowded, so a boy was sitting on his father's knee. A lovely young woman boarded the car and looked around in vain for an empty seat. Noticing her predicament, the boy leaped to his feet and said, "Here, lady, you can have my seat!"

Here's another:

> A very heavy-set woman boarded a crowded streetcar and as she stood and swayed with the movement of the car, she said, "If there were a gentleman on this car, he wouldn't allow a lady to stand." Her comment prompted a boy to get to his feet. But as he looked at her very large frame, he said as he offered her his seat, "At least this will be good for starters."

An Honorable Boy Is Kind

The *Handbook for Boys* emphasizes kindness to animals. The Scout "is a friend to animals. He will not kill or hurt any living creature needlessly, but will strive to save and protect all harmless life" (26). Here's a joke that challenges the handbook on this point:

> A blind man was walking along the street with his guide dog when it suddenly stopped, cocked its leg, and urinated all over the man's pant leg. Immediately, the blind man reached in his pocket, produced a dog biscuit, and fed it to his dog. A passerby was impressed by what she had just witnessed. "In view of what the dog just did to you," she said to the blind man, "that was an incredible act of kindness." The blind man replied, "Not at all. I only did it to find out which end of the dog to kick!"

Then there's this story about:

> A guy met a beautiful girl at work and asked her for a date. When he arrived at her place, he discovered she lived on the tenth floor of a high-rise apartment building. While she was in her bedroom making last-minute preparations, he amused himself by tossing a ball to her pet terrier. After a few tosses toward the wall, he tossed the ball toward the patio door, which happened to be open. The dog chased after it, only to go skidding across the terrace and over the railing, falling ten stories below. When his date came out to the living room, he asked, "Has your dog been kinda depressed lately?"

An Honorable Boy Is Obedient

The *Handbook for Boys* emphasizes obeying parents, teachers, and all other duly constituted authorities and, following the established rules, complying with them without questioning, whining, or grumbling (35). The boy in the following anecdote is off to a rocky beginning:

> It was the first day of class, and the kindergarten teacher was explaining the classroom rules: "If anyone has to go to the bathroom, hold

up two fingers." A boy in the back of the room asked, "How will that help?"

Then there's the man whose obedience to a duly constituted authority—a judge—was not exactly what it purported to be:

> Mr. Smith was sued by Mrs. Johnson for defamation of character. She charged that he had called her a hog because she piled her plate high with mashed potatoes at the local buffet. He was found guilty and fined $100. After the trial, he approached the bench and asked the judge, "Does this mean that I cannot call Mrs. Johnson a hog?" The judge said that this was true. "Then does this also mean that I cannot call a hog Mrs. Johnson?" The judge replied, "No, you are free to call a hog 'Mrs. Johnson' without fear of legal action." So the man looked directly at Mrs. Johnson and said, "Good afternoon, Mrs. Johnson."

Finally, here's a man who, having been ordered by his superior to perform more professionally, tried his best to comply:

> The army sergeant called for his morning formation and lined up all the troops. "Listen up, men," said the sergeant. "Johnson, report to the mess hall for KP. Smith, report to personnel to sign some papers. The rest of you men report to the motor pool for maintenance. Oh, by the way, Rudkin, your mother died. Report to the commander." Later that day, the captain called the sergeant into his office. "Hey, Sarge, that was a pretty cold way to inform Rudkin that his mother died. Please be more tactful next time." "Yes, sir," answered the sergeant. A few months later, the captain called the sergeant in again, saying, "Sarge, I just got a telegram that Private Fogle's mother died. You'd better go tell him, and send him in to see me. And this time, be more tactful." So the sergeant called for his morning formation. "Okay, men, fall in and listen up. Everybody with a mother, take two steps forward. *Not so fast, Fogle!*"

An Honorable Boy Is Cheerful

The *Handbook for Boys* says that a good Scout smiles whenever he can, his obedience to orders is prompt and cheery, and he never shirks or grumbles at hardships. To "work for the satisfaction of accomplishment, and self-respect, is the measure of the greatness of a person or a nation. . . . We hear a lot of talk these days about opportunities for leisure, but very little about the glory of work" (122). Here's a guy who didn't get the message:

> Ever since he graduated from high school, Brian spent most of his waking hours lounging on the couch, watching sports programs, and drinking beer. One day, as he reached for another can, he tumbled off

the sofa onto his head and had to be rushed to the hospital. After x-rays were taken, the doctor went immediately to Brian's bedside: "I'm sorry, young man, but I have some bad news for you. Your x-rays show that you've broken a vertebra in your neck. I'm afraid you'll never work again." "Thanks, Doc," replied Brian. "Now what's the bad news?"

We can imagine that Brian had a brother with a similar attitude toward work:

As a gesture to welcome him into the family, a successful businessman gave his new son-in-law a half share of the firm. "From now on," said the businessman, "we're equal partners. All you have to do is go down to the factory each day and learn the ropes." "I couldn't do that," said the son-in-law. "I hate factories. They're such noisy places." "That's no problem," said the businessman. "We'll put you in the office. You can oversee the clerical staff." "No way," said the son-in-law. "I'm not going to be stuck behind a desk all day." Not surprisingly, the businessman was becoming irritated by this display of ingratitude. "I've just made you half-owner of this thriving company. First, I offer you a management position in the factory, but you don't want it. Then I offer you a management post in the office, and you don't want that either. What am I going to do with you?" "Well," said the son-in-law, "you could always buy me out!"

Then there's this vintage story about the perils of cheerfulness:

The hospital chaplain stopped at the bedside of a pale young man covered from head to foot with bandages. "Cheer up, young man," the chaplain said. "Keep smiling—it's the very best medicine!" "Oh no, I'll never smile again," replied the young man. "Nonsense," the chaplain exclaimed. "You may feel awfully down now, but you will smile again. Just wait and see!" The young man responded, "I appreciate your confidence, Chaplain, but it's true, I'll never smile again—at least, not at another fellow's girl!"

An Honorable Boy Is Thrifty

The *Handbook for Boys* explains that genuine thriftiness is not just about saving money:

It is saving with a purpose and spending wisely the money you save. Thrift actually consists of four things: earning, saving, spending wisely, and sharing. It takes hard work to earn money. When you work for it, you appreciate it. If you save it toward your education or toward a future ambition, you are saving with a purpose. When you spend it, spend it carefully and wisely. Remember always to share what you have with those less fortunate than you. (36–37)

The following two jokes about thriftiness are strictly vintage ones:

> A boy rushed into his father's study and asked him if he would be glad
> to hear that his son had saved him a dollar. The father expressed
> delight at this evidence of juvenile economy and handed his son a
> quarter to encourage such thrifty habits. "But how did you save me a
> dollar?" "Well, remember that you said you'd give me a dollar if I
> brought home a good report card? Fact is, I didn't."

We can imagine that this boy grew up to become the college student in the
following joke:

> "Be more thrifty," wrote the father of a very extravagant son. "While
> you are reading this letter Henry Ford is saving eleven dollars." The
> college sophomore responded, "That's great, Dad, but while you are
> reading this letter I am cashing your check for fifty."

We can also imagine this boy as an older man who recalls his boyhood discovery that thriftiness may conflict with the desire to be popular with the other
guys:

> A guy goes into a bar and shouts, "When I drink, everybody drinks!"
> He gets a cheer from everybody in the bar. A few moments later, feel-
> ing pretty happy about the response to his earlier proclamation, he
> shouts out, "When I drinks again, everybody drinks again!" Again, he
> gets a cheer, but this one is louder. Upon finishing his drink, he pulls
> out his wallet and shouts, "When I pays, everybody pays!"

An Honorable Boy Is Brave

The *Handbook for Boys* says that a good Scout has the courage to face danger
and to stand up for the right against pressure from friends and the jeers or
threats of enemies (27). Here's a story about a guy who did just that and almost
certainly regretted it:

> Eddie waited patiently at the Pearly Gates while St. Peter leafed
> through his ledger book to see if he was worthy of admission. Finally,
> Peter looked up: "Young man, I can't see that you did anything really
> bad in your life, but you never did anything really good, either. If you
> can point to just one really good deed, I'll let you in." Eddie replied,
> "Well, there was this time when I was driving down the highway and
> I saw a motorcycle gang tormenting a terrified young woman. Infuri-
> ated, I got out of my car, grabbed a tire iron out of the trunk, and went
> up to the gang leader, a huge guy with a studded leather jacket and a
> chain running from his nose to his ear. I ripped his chain off his face
> and smashed him over the head with the tire iron. He collapsed to the

ground in a heap. Then I turned to the rest of them and snarled, "Leave this poor innocent girl alone! You're all a bunch of sick, deranged animals! Get out of here before I teach you all a lesson in pain!" Impressed, St. Peter inquired, "Eddie, my lad, when did this happen?" Eddie replied, "Oh, about five minutes ago."

Here's a vintage story about a boy's misplaced spirit of bravery:

The schoolteacher was coaching her class of boys on what to do in the case of air raids. She said to them, "Now let's make believe that we hear sirens warning us that planes are coming." As she imitated a siren all the boys dived under their desks for protection except one. The teacher all but shrieked at him, "Marvin! Why are you sitting there with your chin cupped in your hands as if nothing is happening? Don't you understand? Don't you realize that this is war?" Marvin replied, "And don't *you* know, Miss Smith, that in every war there are heroes?"

We can imagine that this boy grows up and, in a similar gesture of bravery, decides to enlist in the army:

After enlisting in the army, Marvin had second thoughts about serving. Thus, when he was told to bring a urine sample to the selective service medical officer, he filled a bottle with specimens from his father, sister, dog, and then a bit of his own. Striding confidently into the lab, he waited a full hour while the sample was analyzed. Finally the technician returned. "It took some doing," she said, "but according to our analysis, your father has herpes, your sister is pregnant, your dog is in heat, and you're in the army."

One more bravery joke. This one takes place in a hospital, another setting where bravery is often required:

A man dressed in a sterile gown and mask was pacing up and down the hallway when the nurse came out of the delivery room and approached him. "The delivery is going very well," the nurse said. "Wouldn't you like to come in now?" "No!" replied the man. "I can't stand all that blood and screaming. Leave me alone!" A few minutes later the nurse came out again and said, "It's almost over. Wouldn't you like to come in now?" "No. Leave me alone!" exclaimed the man. "I told you I can't stand all that blood and screaming!" "But you must," the nurse insisted. "The delivery is almost over and you're the obstetrician."

An Honorable Boy Is Clean

The *Handbook for Boys* emphasizes that a good Scout keeps his body clean, but physical cleanliness is merely one part of a more general commitment to cleanliness in thought, speech, and personal habits: "A little soap and water and rubbing will remove the dirt from outside of your body. But no soap will remove the dirt that gets inside your mind." It advises living an active, worthwhile life, because "fellows who hang around street corners or waste their time in other ways are the ones generally who have time for dirty stories and thoughts" (38). The distinction between "clean" and "dirty" jokes is reflected in contemporary joke books, with some titles announcing that they are clean, others insisting that they are dirty. Some readers may feel that some of the jokes I have chosen to illustrate cleanliness are themselves unclean. In self-defense, I would note that they illustrate the very struggles of an early adolescent boy in deciding whether or not to use profanity, obscene language, and so forth, a struggle that has much to do with his desire to belong versus his desire to maintain high standards of decency.

When I was an early adolescent boy, I made a very conscious effort to avoid using swear words. I agreed with the view of James V. O'Connor in his book *Cuss Control: The Complete Book on How to Curb Your Cursing* (2000), that "swearing is lazy language": "When we get mentally and verbally lazy, these words are always on call, sparing us the task of scanning our brains and downloading even the most simple noun or adjective. There seems to be no need to make the effort when talking intelligently is rarely a social requirement, and curse words are as common as bad grammar" (18). I continue to believe this.

On the other hand, I find the following personal testimony of Penny Currier, a 45-year-old professional harpist and former Miss America contestant, rather sanctimonious: "I didn't have much exposure to swearing in my upbringing, so when I hear it on the streets and buses in Chicago, I'm appalled. . . . I was raised in a suburb of Denver, Colorado. My father was both an attorney and an engineer, and my mother was a legal secretary and homemaker. They never swore, and it was not allowed in our home. If any of us seven kids used a bad word, they would correct it on the spot, so swear words never passed through my lips" (88). Then, after describing the Miss America contestants whom she, Miss Colorado, met at the Miss America Pageant in 1975 as "mature, polite, gracious women" who did not utter a curse word upon learning that they hadn't won, she writes, "Since then I have been enjoying my career as a professional solo harpist performing at parties, corporate events, and weddings. I wear a long flowing gown and project an angelic image" (89).

In contrast, the following anonymous account of a boyhood experience of swearing at the most inopportune moment is funny, and, to me, inoffensive despite the storyteller's use of profanity: "When I was 17, a company hired me to dress like Barney the dinosaur for a promotion in a shopping mall. The costume was really clumsy. I could hardly walk. As soon as the mall opened, some moms with preschoolers came in, and the kids were all over me. I kind of panicked and tried to run away, but all I could do was waddle. The kids chased me like we were playing a game. I fell, and a kid jumped right on my big Barney head, knocking it off. I screamed, 'Goddam it! Get the fuck off me!' I laugh about it now, but I felt terrible. It was such a simple job, and I blew it after five minutes" (53).

Jokes that concern themselves with clean speech often center on the talk-ing parrot and its penchant for bad language. Here's an example:

> Bob received a parrot for his birthday. The parrot was fully grown, with a bad attitude and worse vocabulary. Every other word was an expletive. Those that were not expletives were, to say the least, rude. Bob tried hard to change the bird's behavior by constantly saying polite words, hoping to teach him by example. But it didn't work. So Bob began yelling at the bird, and this only made matters worse. He shook the bird, and the bird got ruder, his speech more crude and vul-gar than ever. Finally, in a moment of desperation, Bob put the parrot in the freezer. For a few moments he heard the bird squawking and cursing—and then suddenly there was quiet. Bob was afraid he had actually hurt the bird and quickly opened the freezer door. The par-rot calmly stepped out onto Bob's extended arm and said, "I'm sorry that I might have offended you with my language, and I ask you for your forgiveness. I will endeavor to correct my behavior." Bob was astonished at the bird's change in attitude and his new polite manner and was about to ask what had made such a drastic change when the parrot said, "Sir, may I ask what the chicken did?"

This joke also illustrates the quality of obedience, though the parrot's rather obsequious language after he comes out of the freezer raises some doubts whether he has genuinely reformed.

An important cleanliness theme in the handbook concerns the boy's treat-ment of his own body, and it specifically emphasizes avoidance of "self-abuse" by keeping busy with lots of work and play (412). Here's a joke bearing on this theme:

> A father enters the bathroom to brush his teeth and finds that his son, Billy, is already there. The father says in a stern and exasperated voice, "Billy, how many times do I have to tell you not to play with that thing? If you keep doing that, you could go blind." Billy responds, "Hey, Dad, I'm over here."

Here's a joke in which another one of an honorable boy's qualities—helpful-ness—is used to excuse the absence of cleanliness:

> A girl brought her new boyfriend home to meet her parents, and they were horrified by his greasy hair, tattoos, dirty language, and air of hostility. After he left, her mother said, "Dear, he doesn't seem like a

very nice person." The daughter replied, "Mother, if he wasn't a nice
person, why would he be doing 500 hours of community service?"

Finally, here's a joke in which a well-intentioned lawyer's defense of an early
adolescent boy jeopardizes his case that the boy is incapable of the sexual act
of which he has been accused:

> In court to answer a paternity suit, 11-year-old Ray stood at his
> lawyer's request. To emphasize the spuriousness of the charge, the
> attorney unzipped the boy's pants and held his flaccid member.
> "Ladies and gentlemen of the jury," the lawyer said, rattling the organ,
> "I ask you to study this undeveloped penis. Examine this limp, pread-
> olescent genital and ask yourselves, 'Is it possible that the defendant
> could have fathered a baby with *this?*'" Suddenly, from the corner of
> his mouth, Ray whispered, "Hey, Mr. Bigshot! If you don't let go real
> soon, we're gonna lose this case!"

An Honorable Boy Is Reverent

The *Handbook for Boys* emphasizes that a good and faithful Scout is reverent
toward God and is constant in his religious duties (27). Reverence is also
reflected in the respect and courtesy one shows for churches and religious
leaders (39). A joke that plays on the issue of reverence is this one:

> Bored and restless during the Sunday morning service, Billy began to
> take out his frustration on the worshipers through continual chatter
> and whistling. Finally, his father lost patience and dragged Billy out of
> church. On the way out, Billy called loudly to the congregation, "Pray
> for me!"

Here's a story that suggests that there's a more acceptable way than constant
chatter and whistling to gain attention in church:

> Johnny told his mother after church one Sunday morning that he had
> decided to become a minister when he grew up, whereupon she looked
> toward heaven in gratitude, then asked him, "What made you decide
> to become a minister?" "Well," he replied, "I have to go to church any-
> way, so I figured it would be a lot more fun to stand up and yell!"

We can imagine Jesus telling both jokes and then saying to his audience, "Now
I ask you, which of these boys, if either, won the approval of the Father-Who-
Art-in-Heaven-Hallowed-Be-His-Name?"

Then there's the story about a young penitent that suggests there are other
than spiritual benefits that might accrue from confessing one's sins:

Tommy O'Connor went to confession and said, "Forgive me, Father, for I have sinned."

"What have you done, Tommy O'Connor?"

"I had sex with a girl."

"Who was it, Tommy?"

"I cannot tell you, Father. Please forgive me for my sin, but I cannot tell you who it was."

"Was it Mary Margaret Sullivan?"

"No, Father. Please forgive me for my sin, but I cannot tell you who it was."

"Was it Catherine Mary McKenzie?"

"No, Father. Please forgive me for my sin."

"Well, then, it must have been her sister, Sarah Martha McKenzie."

"No, Father. Please, Father, please forgive me; I cannot tell you who it was."

"Okay, Tommy, go say five Hail Marys and four Our Fathers and you will be absolved of your sin."

Tommy walked out to the pews, where his friend Joey was waiting. "What did ya get?" asked Joey. "Well, I got five Hail Marys, four Our Fathers, and three good leads."

Finally, there's this story that combines the quality of reverence with the quality of helpfulness:

A drag queen walks into a Catholic church as the priest is coming down the aisle swinging the incense pot. As the priest approaches his pew, the drag queen says, "Oh, honey, I just love your dress, but did you know your handbag's on fire?"

In the preceding chapter, I told a story about my father's irreverence. His irreverence, though, was, I think, his way of relativizing *and thereby preserving* the religion of honor. Several years before my early adolescence, he himself was a Boy Scout leader, and during my early adolescent years, he served faithfully as an usher at Sunday morning services. I knew only stories from my older brothers about his career as a Boy Scout leader, but I also knew that he wanted his boys to be involved in Scouting. As for his ushering role, I wondered if this was his way of serving the church without having to become involved in the usual doctrinal disputes that exercised the minds of other members. Once when I had to go to the bathroom during the worship service, I went to the church basement and found my father and his fellow ushers chatting together. The audio system would alert them to the conclusion of the sermon and for their need to rush upstairs to pass the collection plates. Trustworthy, loyal, helpful, friendly, courteous, kind: these are qualities that make one an outstanding church usher. Reverence, no doubt, is exhibited when the ushers proceed to the altar with the collection plates. But hymn singing, praying, listening to the sermon, and other expressions of reverence—and more central to the religion of hope—are somewhat optional.

THE HOLES IN THE SKY, THE SHIP IN THE SEA, AND THE EPIPHANY AT THE STATE FAIR

If boys and men were not deeply devoted to the religion of honor, they would not have developed a joking tradition that subjects it to gentle ridicule. By focusing on the Boy Scout Law, with its delineation of the twelve qualities of a boy—and man—of honor, I have provided a few examples of how humor pokes fun, and pokes holes in, the religion of honor. And this brings me, finally, to the following thoughts from Robert Baden-Powell, the founder of Scouting:

> I often think that when the sun goes down the world is hidden by a big blanket from the light of heaven, but the stars are little holes pierced in that [blanket] by those who have done good deeds in this world. The stars are not all the same size; some are big, some are little, and some men have done small deeds, but they have made their hole in the blanket by doing good before they went to heaven. (Boy Scouts 1948, 23)

The story of the poor fellow who stopped to help the young woman being tormented by the motorcycle gang—his one dramatic "good turn"—suggests that *his* heavenly reward was a lot nearer at hand than he could ever have imagined when he got out of bed that morning. This makes the guy who spent most of his waking hours lounging on the sofa, watching sports programs and drinking beer, seem the wiser of the two. If it's a choice between tumbling off the sofa as one reaches for another can of beer and suffering a broken vertebra, or being beaten to death by a motorcycle gang, who in his right mind would choose the latter course?

But maybe these two stories make the point that, when all is said and done, the differences between the religions of honor and of humor are mainly differences in the priorities they place on the qualities that make up the religion of honor. The religion of honor gives *bravery* a very high priority in the hierarchy of the qualities of the good and faithful Scout, whereas the religion of humor gives special place to *cheerfulness*. Here is a biblical text that meant a great deal to me as an early adolescent boy:

> But the ship was now in the midst of the sea, tossed with waves: for the wind was contrary. And in the fourth watch of the night Jesus went

unto them, walking on the sea. And when the disciples saw him walking on the sea, they were troubled, saying, It is a spirit; and they cried
out for fear. But straightway Jesus spake unto them, saying, *Be of good
cheer*; it is I; be not afraid. (Matt. 14:24–27 KJV)

We honor the early adolescent boy who lives within us by being brave when
we are up to the challenge and being of good cheer when we are feeling vulnerable. As the chaplain said to the fellow who made the mistake of smiling at
another fellow's girl, "Keep smiling—it's the very best medicine." Oh, and
about fighting: only do it if you really have to.

This chapter began with a story about boys being threatened by a knife-
wielding butcher. They fled in terror. In "Adults Only," William Stafford
(1998, 94) relates a very different experience—an epiphany of sorts—that
could not have happened if he and his buddies had been slaves to obedience:

Adults Only

Animals own a fur world;
people own worlds that are variously, pleasingly, bare.
And the way these worlds *are* once arrived for us kids with a jolt,
that night when the wild woman danced
in the giant cage we found we were all in
at the state fair.

Better women exist, no doubt, than that one,
and occasions more edifying, too, I suppose.
But we have to witness for ourselves what comes for us,
nor be distracted by barkers of irrelevant ware;
and a pretty good world, I say, arrived that night
when that woman came farming right out of her clothes,
by God,

At the state fair.

References

Agnes, Michael, ed. 2001. *Webster's New World College Dictionary*. Foster City, CA: IDG Books Worldwide.

Baden-Powell, Robert. 1908/2004. *Scouting for Boys: A Handbook for Instruction in Good Citizenship*. Edited by Elleke Boehmer. Repr. Oxford: Oxford University Press.

Biermann, Karen L. 2004. *Peer Rejection: Developmental Processes and Intervention Strategies*. New York: Guilford Press.

Body Image for Boys. 2002. Videocassette. Cambridge Educational.

Bollas, Christopher. 1987. *The Shadow of the Object: Psychoanalysis of the Unthought Known*. New York: Columbia University Press.

———. 1992. *Being a Character: Psychoanalysis and Self Experience*. New York: Hill & Wang.

Boorstin, Daniel. 1961/1992. *The Image: A Guide to Pseudo-Events in America*. Repr. New York: Vintage Books.

Boy Scouts of America (BSA). 1948. *Handbook for Boys*. New Brunswick, NJ: National Council of the Boy Scouts of America.

Bunyan, John. 1678/1957. *The Pilgrim's Progress*. Repr. New York: Washington Square Press.

Capps, Donald. 1983. *Life Cycle Theory and Pastoral Care*. Minneapolis: Fortress Press.

———. 1995a. *Agents of Hope: A Pastoral Psychology*. Minneapolis: Fortress Press.

———. 1995b. *The Child's Song: The Religious Abuse of Children*. Louisville, KY: Westminster John Knox Press.

———. 2001. Male melancholia: Guilt, separation, and repressed rage. In *Religion and Psychology: Mapping the Terrain*, ed. Diane Jonte-Pace and William B. Parsons, 147–59. New York: Routledge.

———. 2002. *Men and Their Religion: Honor, Hope, and Humor*. Harrisburg, PA: Trinity Press International.

———. 2003. From masturbation to homosexuality: A case of displaced moral disapproval. *Pastoral Psychology* 51:249–72.

———. 2005. *A Time to Laugh: The Religion of Humor*. New York: Continuum Press.

———. 2006. Religion and humor: Estranged bedfellows. *Pastoral Psychology* 54:413–38.

Cohen, Ted. 1999. *Jokes: Philosophical Thoughts on Joking Matters*. Chicago: University of Chicago Press.

Collins, Billy. 2001. *Sailing Alone around the Room: New and Selected Poems*. New York: Random House.

Coloroso, Barbara. 2003. *The Bully, the Bullied, and the Bystander*. New York: Harper Resource.

Culbertson, Philip L., ed. 2002. *The Spirituality of Men: Sixteen Christians Write about Their Faith*. Minneapolis: Fortress Press.

Dabbs, James McBride, with Mary Godwin Dabbs. 2000. *Heroes, Rogues, and Lovers: Testosterone and Behavior*. New York: McGraw-Hill.

Davis, Clyde Brion, ed. 1953. *Eyes of Boyhood*. Philadelphia: J. B. Lippincott.

Day, Dorothy. 1952. *The Long Loneliness: An Autobiography*. San Francisco: Harper & Row.

Diamond, Jonathan. 2006. *Fatherless Sons: Healing the Legacy of Loss*. Hoboken, NJ: Jay Wiley & Sons.

Dittes, James E. 1996. *Driven by Hope: Men and Meaning*. Louisville, KY: Westminster John Knox Press.

Dobson, James C. 1992. *Preparing for Adolescence*. Wheaton, IL: Tyndale House Publishers.

———. 2001. *Bringing Up Boys*. Wheaton, IL: Tyndale House Publishers.

Dykstra, Robert. 2001. *Discovering a Sermon*. St. Louis: Chalice Press.

———. 2003a. Out of one's depth: Seeking soul in solitude. *The Princeton Lectures on Youth, Church, and Culture*, 1–13. Princeton, NJ: Princeton Theological Seminary.

———. 2003b. Out of one's depth: Finding faith on the fringe. *The Princeton Lectures on Youth, Church, and Culture*, 14–28. Princeton, NJ: Princeton Theological Seminary.

Erikson, Erik H. 1958. *Young Man Luther*. New York: W. W. Norton & Company.

———. 1959/1980. *Identity and the Life Cycle*. Repr. New York: W. W. Norton & Co.

———. 1963. *Childhood and Society*. Rev. ed. New York: W. W. Norton & Co.

———. 1968/1994. *Identity: Youth and Crisis*. Repr. New York: W. W. Norton & Co.

———. 1995. The human life cycle. In *A Way of Looking at Things*, ed. Stephen Schlein, 595–610. New York: W. W. Norton & Co.

Festinger, Leon, H. W. Riecken, and Stanley Schachter. 1956. *When Prophecy Fails: A Social and Psychological Study of a Modern Group That Predicted the Destruction of the World*. New York: Harper & Row.

Freud, Sigmund. 1905/1960. *Jokes and Their Relation to the Unconscious*. Translated by James Strachey. Repr. New York: W. W. Norton & Co.

———. 1916/1957/1971. Some character-types met with in psycho-analytic work, part 2, those wrecked by success. In *The Complete Psychological Works of Sigmund Freud*, ed. James Strachey, vol. 14. London: Hogarth Press.

———. 1928/1963. Humor. In *Character and Culture*, by Sigmund Freud, ed. Philip Rieff, 263–69. Repr. New York: Collier Books.

HarperCollins Study Bible. 1993. New York: HarperCollins.

James, William. 1902/1982. *The Varieties of Religious Experience*. Repr. New York: Penguin Books.

———. 1902/1987. *The Varieties of Religious Experience*. 4th ed. Repr. New York: Literary Classics of the United States.

Jeremias, Joachim. 1971. *New Testament Theology: The Proclamation of Jesus*. New York: Charles Scribner's Sons.

Kahn, Michael. 2002. *Basic Freud: Psychoanalytic Thought for the Twenty-First Century*. New York: Basic Books.

Kaufman, Gershen. 1992. *Shame: The Power of Caring*. Rochester, VT: Schenken.

Kindlon, Dan, and Michael Thompson with Teresa Barker. 2000. *Raising Cain: Protecting the Emotional Life of Boys*. New York: Ballantine.

Kierkegaard, Søren. 1844/1980. *The Concept of Anxiety*. Repr. Princeton, NJ: Princeton University Press.

Kunitz, Stanley. 2000. *The Collected Poems*. New York: W. W. Norton & Co.

Lazare, Aaron. 2004. *On Apology*. Oxford: Oxford University Press.

Lewis, Michael. 1992. *Shame: The Exposed Self*. New York: Free Press.

Lupton, Martha. 1938. *The Treasury of Modern Humor*. Indianapolis: Maxwell Droke.

Lutheran Church in America. 1958. *Service Book and Hymnal*. Philadelphia: Board of Publication, Lutheran Church in America.

McBrien, William. 1998. *Cole Porter*. New York: Vintage Books.

Meissner, W. W. 1984. *Psychoanalysis and Religious Experience*. New Haven, CT: Yale University Press.

Melrose Music Corp. 1945. *The All-American College Football Songs*. New York: Melrose Music Corp.

Mill, John Stuart. 1873/1989. *Autobiography*. Edited by John Robson. Repr. Harmondsworth: Penguin Books.

Moltmann, Jürgen. 1992/2001. *The Spirit of Life: A Universal Affirmation*. Translated by Margaret Kohl. Repr. Minneapolis: Fortress Press.

Murray, Henry A. 1967. *Henry A. Murray* (autobiography). In *A History of Psychology in Autobiography*, vol. 5, ed. Ernest G. Boring and Gardner Lindzey, 283–310. New York: Appleton Century-Crofts.

Muuss, Rolf E. 1988. *Theories of Adolescence*. 5th ed. New York: McGraw-Hill.

O'Connor, James V. 2000. *Cuss Control: The Complete Book on How to Curb Your Cursing*. New York: Three Rivers Press.

O'Hanlon, Bill. 2003. *A Lazy Man's Guide to Success*. Web book from http://www.brieftherapy.com. Santa Fe: Possibilit-E Press.

Phillips, Adam. 1993. *On Kissing, Tickling, and Being Bored: Psychoanalytic Essays on the Unexamined Life*. Cambridge, MA: Harvard University Press.

———. 1994. *On Flirtation: Psychoanalytic Essays on the Uncommitted Life*. Cambridge, MA: Harvard University Press.

———. 2002a. *Equals*. New York: Basic Books.

———. 2002b. Futures. In *The Vitality of Objects: Exploring the Work of Christopher Bollas*, ed. Joseph Scalia, 53–57. Middletown, CT: Wesleyan University Press.

———. 2005. *Going Sane: Maps of Happiness*. New York: HarperCollins.

Pollack, William. 1998. *Real Boys: Rescuing Our Sons from the Myths of Boyhood*. New York: Random House.

Pollack, William, with Todd Shuster. 2001. *Real Boys' Voices*. New York: Penguin Books.

Rank, Otto. 1964. *The Myth of the Birth of the Hero and Other Writings*. Edited by Philip Freund. New York: Random House.

Rapaport, Ernest A. 1958. The grandparent syndrome. *Psychoanalytic Quarterly* 27:518–38.

Riesman, David. 1954. *Individualism Reconsidered, and Other Essays*. Glencoe, IL: Free Press.

Rizzuto, Ana-Marie. 1979. *The Birth of the Living God*. Chicago: University of Chicago Press.

Rogers, Carl R. 1961. *On Becoming a Person: A Therapist's View of Psychotherapy*. Boston: Houghton Mifflin.

Rowsome, Frank, Jr. 1965. *The Verse by the Side of the Road: The Story of the Burma-Shave Signs and Jingles*. Brattleboro, VT: Stephen Greene Press.

Sandage, Scott A. 2005. *Born Losers: A History of Failure in America*. Cambridge, MA: Harvard University Press.

Siegel, Daniel J. 1999. *The Developing Mind: How Relationships and the Brain Interact to Shape Who We Are*. New York: Guilford Press.

Stafford, William. 1998. *The Way It Is: New and Selected Poems*. St. Paul: Graywolf Press.

Stephenson, Mark. 1940. Facts from here and there. *Weekly Reader*, January.

St. Clair, Michael. 1994. *Human Relationships and the Experiences of God: Object Relations and Religion*. Mahwah, NJ: Paulist Press.

Storr, Anthony. 1988. *Solitude: A Return to the Self*. New York: Ballantine Books.

Stuart, Sarah Anne. 1996. *A Treasury of Poems: A Collection of the World's Most Famous and Familiar Verse*. New York: Galahad Books.

Sullivan, Harry Stack. 1953/1997. *The Interpersonal Theory of Psychiatry*. Repr. New York: W. W. Norton & Co.

Tillich, Paul. 1957. *Systematic Theology*, vol. 2: *Existence and the Christ*. Chicago: University of Chicago Press.

———. 1963. *The Eternal Now*. 7th ed. New York: Charles Scribner's Sons.

Winnicott, D. W. 1965. The maturational process and the facilitating environment. In *Studies in the Theory of Emotional Development*, 28–36. New York: International Universities.

———. 1971/1989. *Playing and Reality*. Repr. New York: Routledge.

———. 1994. *Psycho-Analytic Explorations*. 4th ed. Cambridge, MA: Harvard University Press.

Wolfenstein, Martha. 1954. *Children's Humor: A Psychological Analysis*. Glencoe, IL: Free Press.

Index